Human Awareness

Psychology Editor Brian Foss
Professor of Psychology, Royal Holloway and
Bedford New College

For Pavel and Ivana

Human Awareness
Its social development

Ivana Marková

Hutchinson
London   Melbourne   Sydney   Auckland   Johannesburg

Hutchinson Education

An imprint of Century Hutchinson Ltd

62–65 Chandos Place, London WC2N 4NW

Century Hutchinson Australia Pty Ltd
PO Box 496, 16–22 Church Street, Hawthorn,
Victoria 3122, Australia

Century Hutchinson New Zealand Ltd
PO Box 40–086, Glenfield, Auckland 10,
New Zealand

Century Hutchinson South Africa (Pty) Ltd
PO Box 337, Berglvei 2012, South Africa

First published 1987

© Ivana Marková 1987

Set in 11/12pt Bembo by
Input Typesetting Ltd, London

Printed and bound in Great Britain by
Anchor Brendon Ltd, Tiptree, Essex

British Library Cataloguing in Publication Data
Markova, Irana
    Human awareness: its social development.
    1. Interpersonal relations
    I. Title
    158'.2   HM132

ISBN 0 09 164671 5

Contents

Acknowledgements   7

Introduction   9

1 The biological and cultural nature of human   14
awareness
Human awareness as a developmental and cultural
phenomenon – The socio-biological nature of
human awareness – Animal awareness – The cultural-
historical nature of human awareness – Summary

2 Awareness of the feelings of other people   44
Empathy in early childhood – Research evidence of
early empathy – Methodological issues in the study
of child empathy – The nature of empathy: cognition
and affect – Empathy and related phenomena –
Modifiers of empathy – Summary

3 Awareness of human agency   67
People as perceivers and as perceived – Awareness of
actions and intentions – Development of awareness
of action – The different perspectives of the perceiver
and of the perceived in their awareness of action –
Language and awareness of action – Summary

4 Self-awareness   95
The I – the experiencer and agent – The Me – the
experienced – The I and the Me as relational
concepts – Mead's and Freud's theories of the self –
Self-awareness and related notions – The growth of
self-awareness – The I and the Me in self-awareness
research – Can the I be studied empirically? –
Summary

5 Communicative awareness   134
Communication as co-operation and the mutual
adjustment of participants – Synchrony and turn-
taking in communication – Regulation of a dialogue

Contents

through turn-taking – Modification of speech due to
the speaker's other-awareness – Contextualization
and decontextualization – Summary

6 **The manipulative and aggressive self**   175
The search for social recognition – The Me-strategies
for recognition – The I-strategies for recognition –
The machiavellian self – Summary

7 **Human awareness in its societal context**   205
The effect of the collective other upon the self – The
effect of the self on the collective other

References   232

Name Index   263

Subject Index   269

Acknowledgements

This book is based on lectures I have given on social and developmental psychology to Part I and Part II undergraduate students at the University of Stirling. I am grateful to all of my students who listened, expressed their interest and questioned my ideas, and thus helped me to clarify my thinking. I would like to thank my colleagues, Mrs Patricia Wilkie, Bill McGrew, Karel Gijsbers and Robin Campbell, for drawing my attention to empirical and theoretical research which I would otherwise have overlooked; also Simon Naji who read the manuscript and made helpful comments.

I would like to express my particular thanks to Professor Rob Farr who read the whole manuscript, provided detailed and invaluable suggestions and directed my attention to numerous sources and important references. His insights undoubtedly considerably improved the text. Mr Colin Wright gave me most generous help at every stage of writing this book. He read and re-read my numerous drafts and questioned my wording, thus enabling me to express myself more clearly. He has also prepared the index.

Finally, I wish to express my gratitude to Mrs Anne Goldie who patiently typed and altered the manuscript as I was developing my ideas.

The author and publishers would like to thank the copyright holders below for their permission to reproduce the following material:

Academic Press and R. Selman for the extracts on pages 120, 121, 122 and 124–5, from R. Selman, *The Growth of Interpersonal Understanding*, Academic Press, 1980.
American Psychological Association and F. Heider for the figure on p. 73, from F. Heider, 'On social cognition', *American Psychologist*, **22**, 1967, p. 27, copyright (1967) by the American

Psychological Association. Reprinted by permission of the author.

Penguin Books Ltd and Farrar Strauss and Giroux Inc for the extracts on pages 211 and 212–13, from Susan Sontag, *Illness as Metaphor*, Allen Lane, 1979, copyright Susan Sontag, 1977, 1979.

Wildwood House for the extract on page 226, from H. E. Gruber, *Darwin on Man*, Wildwood House, 1974.

John Wiley & Sons Inc and M. Lewis and L. Rosenblum for the figure on p. 144, from T. B. Brazelton, B. Koslowski and M. Main, 'The origin of reciprocity: the early mother-infant interaction', in M. Lewis and R. Rosenblum (eds.), *The Effect of the Infant on its Caregiver*, Wiley, 1974.

Introduction

Human beings characteristically respond to the emotions, thoughts and actions of others. For example, on hearing that a friend's daughter is in hospital with a serious illness, one may react by oneself feeling sad and distressed. Or, to the news that one's sister has just given birth to a long wanted child, one may oneself respond with feelings of joy and of happiness. Similarly, one expects sympathy or an expression of pleasure from others when one communicates to them one's sorrow or happiness. People also react emotionally to the suffering of human beings they do not know personally. The sight on television of the homeless, of victims of earthquake and famine, may also provoke feelings of distress in oneself.

One's awareness both of one's own and of other people's responses to emotions, thoughts, and actions is also important in various kinds of *social interaction*. If one wants to convince a local government that more funds should be spent on child nurseries and play groups, one plans one's approach to the negotiations bearing in mind the possible objections by the opponents and constructs one's own arguments accordingly.

Young children learn to assess the thoughts of others very early in life, as Hoffman (1976)* observed in reporting an incident with a 20 months old girl, Marcy. Marcy's sister Sara was playing with a toy which Marcy wanted herself but Sara refused to give to her:

Marcy then paused, as if reflecting on what to do and then began rocking Sara's favourite rocking horse (which Sara never allowed anyone to touch), yelling 'Nice horsey! Nice horsey!' and keeping her eye on Sara all the time. Sara came running angrily, whereupon Marcy immediately ran around Sara directly to the toy and grabbed it. Without analyzing the full complexity of Marcy's behaviour, one can infer from her action that she had deliberately lured her sister away from the toy. Though not yet 2 years of age, Marcy

*Full references quoted in the text are contained in the references beginning on p. 232

9

was capable of being aware of another person's inner states that were different from her own (Hoffman, 1976, p. 129).

People's capacity for self– and other-awareness is perhaps the most fascinating phenomenon in the evolution of species and of cultures, and in the development of individuals. It not only makes human interaction highly efficient but, more importantly, highly flexible. The form it takes depends on the individuals and situations involved. Their capacity for self – and other-awareness enables people to co-ordinate their actions and to make decisions, to reinterpret their past actions and decisions, to understand the intentions of others, and to plan for their own and others' futures. Indeed, all human activities and psychological processes involve a capacity for awareness in one way or another.

The aim of this book is to introduce students to the subject of human awareness and to bring them to a realization of its role in social and developmental psychology. For this purpose, we shall define human awareness rather broadly, including the following:

1   people's ability to recognize their own existence and experience, and the existence and experience of others;
2   people's knowledge of their own agency and of that of others; and people's ability to monitor events in their own lives, and to make decisions about their own future on the basis of that knowledge;
3   people's ability to communicate their awareness of themselves and others to other human beings.

This definition makes it quite clear that human awareness involves both *awareness of the self* and *awareness of other people*. Indeed, it will be argued in the book that self-awareness and other-awareness come into existence together, both in the process of biological evolution and in the social development of human beings. One can become aware of oneself only in so far as one becomes aware of other people. We perceive, interpret and act on the basis of our understanding of each others' thoughts, abilities, emotions, intentions and actions, and at the same time we are aware that others can perceive, interpret and act on the basis of their understanding of our activities. This mutuality of awareness between our own and other selves leads to more complex forms of interaction involving *the self, the other person, social groups*, and *social establishments*.

Although the capacity for awareness of oneself and of others appears to be a universal characteristic of human beings, the *kind* and the *developmental level of self- and of other-awareness* differs from one person to another. With respect to *the kind*, one's awareness of oneself and of others results from the inter- action of *individual factors* such as differences among people, the inborn capacity for social sensitivity, and so on, and of *environmental* factors such as child-rearing practices, parental influence, the experience of particular life events, and culture in general. For example, training in counselling, psycho- therapy, and social skills is based on the assumption that people can learn to become better at imagining and at understanding the mental processes of other people, and at offering help in times of personal crisis and illness. Or, experiencing for oneself what the other person experiences, at least in one's imagination, is believed to be a particularly effective means of improving the quality of one's awareness both of self and of others. Thus, Humphrey (1983) refers to curative rituals common among the Ndembu of Zambia where the treatment of patients is carried out by 'doctors' whose chief qualification consists in their having themselves suffered and been cured from illness. In one ritual the 'doctor' would even take the same medicine as the patient and both enter a state of paroxysms of quivering (Turner, 1967), so that the patient gets better.

With respect to the *developmental* level both of self- and of other-awareness, as children grow older their capacity for self- and for other-awareness undergoes transformations. Such transformations are related to the child's cognitive, emotional and social abilities interacting with interpersonal and societal experience and constraints upon the child. For example, it will be shown that while 3–5 year olds are only partly aware of the differences between things that are real and things that only appear to be real, older children not only make clear distinctions between reality and appearance but they themselves are aware of their own ability to put on expressions that do not match their true feelings.

Human awareness is both a *developmental* and a *social process*. In the past, developmental and social psychology have been conceived most often, and rather artificially, as two separate disciplines. Only recently have *developmental psychologists* real- ized the importance of a *social perspective* in their theories and empirical research. *Social psychologists*, on their part, have come to realize that since human beings are agents who continuously develop and change in the process of acting and experiencing, a *developmental perspective* is essential in the study of social phenomena. It is thus important that psychologists conceptualize and explore human awareness from the socio-developmental point of view, and the chapters that follow will adopt such a perspective.

Human awareness as a subject attracts the attention of psychologists not only because it is academically and theoretically stimulating, but also, and more importantly, because human awareness is an essential aspect of individuals' monitoring of their own actions, and of their understanding of the consequences of their actions with respect to future decision-making. For example, only if people become truly aware of the importance of preserving energy and minimizing pollution can they take responsible collective action and save the earth's resources for generations to come. A proper understanding of the underlying processes of human awareness has implications in all psychological disciplines involving interpersonal interaction, such as educational, clinical, organizational and management psychology. It is thus implied that human awareness is not just another aspect of the whole of the psychological process, but rather that all *psychological processes must be conceptualized in terms of human awareness.*

This book has seven chapters which, without imposing a rigid structure, follow a certain kind of logic. The first chapter introduces the subject of awareness, discussing it as a developmental and socio-cultural phenomenon. The following three chapters focus on one's awareness of the feelings, thoughts, intentions, and actions of others, and on one's own self-awareness. Chapter 5 is concerned with human awareness in interpersonal communication, while Chapter 6 discusses one's search for social recognition. The last chapter focuses on human awareness as a relationship between the self and the collective other, with particular attention to social stability and change. The book makes use of a variety of psychological and other sources, both classic and more recent. In this sense it cannot be pigeon-holed into one of the existing categories of texts presenting reviews of the recent literature on specialized subjects. Human awareness, however, is a complex psychological phenomenon that cannot be dealt with adequately from the point of view of a single psychological discipline, whether developmental, social, or other clearly defined category. Instead, to deepen our understanding of human awareness a variety of psychological disciplines must integrate their findings in a coherent manner. For these reasons this book will find the sympathy of those students who are prepared to read more broadly and to consider the contributions to the study of human awareness from the perspectives of both social and developmental psychology.

1 The biological and cultural nature of human awareness

Human awareness as a developmental and cultural phenomenon

Psychologists and other scientists have long been intrigued by the following issues. First, whether, and to what extent, animals can imagine, understand and experience other animals' or even people's mental processes. This issue involves such questions as whether awareness of the self and of others is specific to human beings or whether it also exists in some animal species; or at what evolutionary level awareness emerges. Second, whether awareness of the self and of others exists in all human societies, cultures, and historical epochs. Satisfactory answers to the questions raised by these two issues are not easy. They very much depend on how such phenomena as self- and other-awareness are defined.

For a better understanding of the first issue, that of the developmental level at which awareness begins to emerge, consider, as an example, the totally different question: 'What is an apple?' The *Oxford English Dictionary* defines an apple as 'the round fleshy fruit of a rosaceous tree; found wild as the crab-apple, in Europe, etc., and cultivated in innumerable varieties all over the two temperate zones'. The definition is clear and there should be no problem. Imagine an apple tree: its blossom is just over, and little green 'apples' have appeared instead. But are these really apples? Yes and no. One knows that the little green things will grow and eventually turn into real apples. At what point is it appropriate to call these developing things 'apples'? One can make a firm decision and say: 'let us call them apples when they reach stage x'; but another person might disagree, pointing to particular features that demonstrate their appleness much earlier; or, on the other hand, much later.

Just like a growing apple, both self- and other-awareness are phenomena that change and develop. They may, therefore, encompass a variety of activities, such as certain kinds of mental processes in animals, the manipulative activities of the 20 months old Marcy mentioned in the Introduction, one's awareness of the feelings of a rape victim, and so on. These activities involve awareness of the self and of the other, but the levels of awareness differ with respect to the depth and complexity. The task for the psychologists is to identify different levels of awareness, to explore the transitions between such levels, and to discover the similarities and differences between them. Since the nature of self- and other-awareness is developmental, both self- and other-awareness must be *conceptualized* and *studied* as *processes*, rather than as *static* phenomena. In the process of development, not only does the *phenomenon* change, but so also does its *environment*. For an 'apple' to become an apple, interaction between its *internal*, e.g. genetic factors, and its relevant *external* environmental factors, e.g. water, sun, temperature, is required. As the internal factors of an apple and the external factors of the environment interact, the apple grows and ripens while the environmental factors are consumed, and change their chemical composition and physical properties. Similarly, for 'other-awareness' to become other-awareness, the interaction between the individual's internal characteristics, e.g. personality, and his or her environment, e.g. parental child-rearing practices, is required. It is through interaction of these two kinds of factors, internal and external, that more complex levels of other-awareness, and modification of the environment, takes place.

Let us consider the definition of an apple once again. The definition in the *Oxford English Dictionary* states that an apple is cultivated in innumerable varieties. Consequently, there are apples that are more or less tart, sweet, juicy; those that look more like a pear; big and small; apples of different colour. There might even be 'apples' produced by cross-pollination with other kinds of fruit, and the question might even be raised as to whether it is intelligible to call such fruit 'apples' at all. Biological science has demonstrated that the enormous range of 'cultural' varieties among apples came into being through the interaction of the internal, constitutional, and external, environmental factors. Analogically, historical and anthropological research has demonstrated that phenomena such as self- and other-awareness are culturally determined and manifest themselves differently in various socio-economic and cultural environments.

It is to be hoped that it has now become obvious that in order to understand human awareness as defined in the Introduction, it is essential to conceptualize and study it as interactional in nature, in both the developmental and cultural sense. Therefore, in this chapter we shall discuss the phenomena of self- and of other-awareness in their biological and historical-cultural contexts.

The socio-biological nature of human awareness

In his *The Descent of Man*, Darwin (1871) suggested that the moral sense of human beings has developed in the process of evolution from the social instincts and advanced intellectual powers of animals. Of the social instincts, the feeling of sympathy, i.e. of harmony, between members of the same community, was particularly important. This compelled them to take notice of each other's approval and disapproval, such attitudes serving as a crude rule of right and wrong. Through natural selection the moral sense became more and more refined, it extended to people of all races, and standards of morality grew higher and higher. According to this view, human beings are biologically predisposed to act co-operatively and altruistically towards each other. Moreover, there is a direct connection between the biological social instincts of lower animals and the highly developed human moral standards.

In recent years, the relationship between the biological and the social evolution of co-operation and altruiism has become a subject of vigorous theoretical and empirical exploration, among scientists with a variety of professional backgrounds (see for example Campbell, 1975; Rushton and Sorrentino, 1981; Boorman and Levitt, 1980; Trivers, 1985). From our point of view it is of particular importance that the evolution of awareness is associated with the evolution of altruism and co-operation. Several researchers, such as Humphrey (1979), Crook (1980), and Griffin (1984), have forcibly argued that awareness has developed in the process of the socio-biological evolution of altruism and co-operation because it has adaptive and survival value. To be aware of the other means to respond to the other *as* an individual and to respond to his or her idiosyncratic characteristics. Responding to the other *as* an individual makes communication flexible and efficient. Flexibility and efficiency is particularly important for the co-operation and complex interaction that occurs in mutually interdependent individuals functioning in social groups (MacLean, 1967, 1973; Humphrey, 1983).

In his attempt to understand the development of complex co-operative behaviour, MacLean (1973) postulated the hypothesis of the *triune brain*. According to this hypothesis the human brain consists of three hierarchically organized and evolutionary different parts: the reptilian brain or subcortex, the limbic brain or paleomammalian brain, and the neocortex or neomammalian brain (Figure 1). The subcortex, which humans share with reptiles, seems from the behavioural point of view to be involved with activities assuring survival and establishing territory. The limbic brain, the evolutionary older part of the mammalian cortex, is connected with the hypothalamus, a part of the brain that is essential in integrating emotional expression and for functions related to self-preservation, and to the preservation of species. The limbic brain is connected by several pathways with the brain stem. The most important, from the point of view of self- and species-preservation is the pathway connected with the neocortex. This pathway does not really exist in reptiles, and it develops more and more in the higher mammals and reaches its greatest size in humans. MacLean maintains that this pathway reflects a shift from olfactory to visual guidance in socio-sexual behaviour. He points out that the limbic brain is crucial to the emotional behaviour of the higher primates and human beings and that vision is the dominant guiding sense in socio-sexual behaviour, altruism and empathy:

Altruism depends not only on feeling one's way into another person in the sense of empathy. It also involves the capacity to *see with feeling* into another person's situation. To accomplish this with vision – our oldest, most objective, and analytic of senses – nature has had to accomplish a neurological *tour de force* (MacLean,1973, pp. 42–3).

In order to find support for his hypothesis that, from the evolutionary point of view, there is a close relationship between the structure of the brain and socio-emotional behaviour, MacLean explored clinical data from both animals and neur-

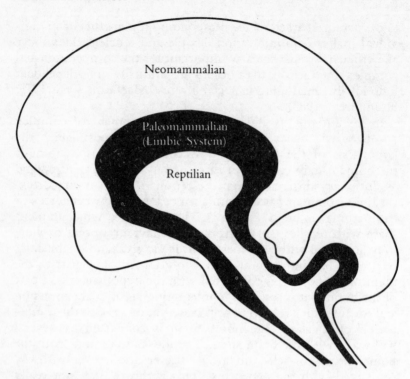

Figure 1 Diagram of hierarchic organization of three basic brain types
Source: MacLean, P. D. (1973), *A Triune Concept of the Brain and Behavior.*

ologically impaired people. With respect to animals, it was found that electric stimulation of the relevant parts of the limbic brain produces particular emotional and sexual reactions. With respect to human beings, observations have shown that patients with limbic epilepsy experience feelings important in the struggle for physical survival, such as hunger, thirst, nausea, suffocation, increased heart beat, and that these may be associated with a variety of intense feelings such as terror, fear, anger, sadness or paranoia. Clinical evidence also suggests that people with injuries to the frontal lobes find it difficult to plan for themselves and for others, and have problems with understanding the feelings of others. MacLean's conception of a triune brain thus suggests that there is a direct neurological connection between the structure of the brain and the organism's awareness of others.

The hypothesis of the triune brain has found both supporters and critics. The critics maintain that while the structure and function of the brain in the evolution of different species has remained similar, all parts of the brain, nevertheless, have undergone essential qualitative changes in the process of evolution, and therefore what was originally a reptilian brain in prehistoric reptiles is very different when it becomes a part of the human brain (Harth, 1982). For these reasons, Harth argues, one cannot make direct connections between the structure of the brain and socio-emotional behaviour, as MacLean does. However, it is sufficient for my purpose that MacLean's hypothesis of the triune brain has drawn attention to the evolutionary connection between the biological and socio-emotional functions. Although the hypothesis may not be correct in all its detail – this has still to be explored – it provides a basis for the joint investigation by biologists and psychologists into the relationship between biological structures and the capacity for awareness.

Another thought-provoking case of the relationship between biological processes and human awareness is discussed by Farr (1980a) in his important paper 'On reading Darwin and discovering social psychology'. Farr draws attention to Darwin's book on *The Expression of the Emotions in Man and Animals* (1872), and in particular to Darwin's account of human blushing. Although blushing is an autonomic response that cannot be restrained by voluntary actions, it is socially determined. Darwin points out that the essential characteristic, common to all mental states that induce blushing, such as shyness, shame, and modesty, is self-attention:

It is not the simple act of reflecting on our own appearance, but the thinking what others think of us, which excites a blush. In absolute solitude the most sensitive person would be quite indifferent about his appearance (Darwin, 1872, p. 325).

It is usually a human face that attracts the attention of others, and therefore blushes more than other parts of the body. Darwin argues that it was through frequent attention to the same part of the body over many generations that blushing developed. He hypothesized that close attention directed to a particular part of the body tends to interfere with the contraction and dilatation of blood vessels and affects the circulation of blood. Relaxed blood vessels are filled with blood which manifests itself in blushing (for more about blushing see pp. 188–9). Darwin goes on to point out that attention or consciousness focused on almost any part of the body produces some physical effect in that region. He lists voluntary and involuntary movement of muscles, secretion of the glands, activity of the senses, sensations, and so on. Farr emphasizes that the contemporary social psychologist has still much to discover from the reading of Darwin, whose insight into the relationship between the biological and social nature of human awareness was so profound.

Animal awareness

Although the question of the relationship between the neurological structures of the brain and the behavioural manifestations of self- and of other-awareness still awaits future research, various issues of animal awareness have been explored independently at their differing behavioural levels. These issues can be divided into two areas: first, awareness of the self as a unique individual and different from others; and second, awareness of the physical and mental processes of others.

Animal self-awareness

In any discussion concerning animal self-awareness it is important to make a distinction between the assumption that an animal has some mental experience, and that an animal is *aware* of having some mental experience (Mason, 1976; Crook, 1980). While many ethologists and psychologists accept that animals have mental experiences such as fear and pleasure, and interpret certain aspects of animal behaviour as expressions of such experiences, it is much more difficult to make any inferences about animals being aware of having mental experiences. While our understanding of, and inferences about the awareness of the mental processes of people are based on communication, it is our limitation in understanding animal 'language' that makes it difficult to find evidence for animal self-awareness. As Crook (1980, p. 5) maintains, the essential feature of human beings is that they are aware of having experiences, are able to communicate their experiences to other human beings, and can distinguish between themselves as experiencing agents, and between others.

Although there is abundant evidence that animals communicate with each other, whether or not animal communication is accompanied by an awareness of thinking and/or by an experiencing of the self is a different matter (Griffin, 1984). Most of the evidence for animal self-awareness comes from research exploring whether chimpanzees can learn to recognize themselves in a mirror, and from attempts to teach them sign language.

Concerning the former, Gallup (1970) carried out ingenious experiments in which chimpanzees were first given the experience of observing themselves in a mirror for about a week. Then they were anaesthetized, and when completely unconscious a part of one eyebrow and a part of the opposite ear were painted with an odourless, non-irritative and alcohol soluble, bright red paint. Following the animal's recovery of consciousness, Gallup recorded the number of times the animal touched the painted parts of its face in the presence of a mirror, and in the absence of a mirror, interpreting the difference as an indication of self-recognition. It was found that those chimpanzees who had had previous experience with mirrors, in contrast to those who did not, attempted to touch the painted areas of their face while watching their images in the mirror. Similar results were obtained with orangutans who also learned to recognize themselves in the mirror, while gorillas failed the self-recognition test (Ledbetter and Basen, 1982; Suarez and Gallup, 1981), and so did other primates and monkeys. Gallup argues that animals incapable of recognizing themselves in a mirror cannot possibly have a sense of self.

Evidence for animal self-awareness as distinct from awareness of other objects comes from Premack's (1976) sign language studies. When one of the chimpanzees involved in the exploration, Elizabeth, became proficient at describing, in sign language, the trainer's actions such as cutting a piece of fruit or inserting an object into a container, attempts were made to induce Elizabeth to describe her own actions. Following some trials Elizabeth, *after* having carried out an act such as cutting an apple, inserting an apple in the container, and washing an apple, actually produced sentences in sign language, e.g. 'Elizabeth apple cut', 'Elizabeth apple insert' and 'Elizabeth apple wash'. On other occasions she produced such sentences *before* carrying out the act in question. Premack suggests that producing sentences before an act is carried out by an animal may be an indication of intentionality although, as he points out, there is no way of proving it. The author also claims that the films of Washoe, the chimpanzee, studied intensively by the Gardners (Gardner and Gardner, 1969), seem to show considerable evidence of spontaneous self-description such as signing 'in' or 'head in' before and after Washoe put her head into a hat while tumbling.

Other kinds of animal behaviour implying the possibility of a sort of self-awareness are discussed by Griffin (1984, p. 74f.). For example, he points to various predator-prey interactions in which a potential prey animal develops a number of ways of reducing the likelihood of being caught and killed. Griffin refers, in this context, to his correspondence with Olsen, for whom some kinds of animal self-concealment imply awareness of the self. Olsen was particularly intrigued by the tactics of grizzly bears in seeking places from which they can watch human intruders without being seen themselves and without leaving tracks behind them. Animal 'self-awareness' has also been explored by Beninger *et al.* (1974) in the laboratory. These researchers trained rats to make discriminations among four kinds of their own behaviour such as face-washing, walking, rearing and immobility by pressing appropriate levers. The authors argue that such 'self-reports' of own behaviour suggest that there may be some level of self-awareness in rats. These studies and observations clearly are in no way conclusive evidence concerning animal self-awareness. Instead, they are temporary stepping stones in the development of knowledge. They provide hypotheses to be further tested, raise questions, and stimulate curiosity.

Animal other-awareness

Studies of animal self-awareness go together with studies of animal other-awareness, for which evidence has been sought both in laboratory and field investigations.

With respect to laboratory studies, Church (1959) observed the emotional reactions of rats to the distress of other rats. Church trained a group of rats to press a lever in a box in order to obtain food pellets. After training, the rats were deprived of food for twenty-two hours, transferred into an exploratory box, and then witnessed another rat in a duplicate compartment receiving an electric shock. The electric shock elicited motor activity and squeaks in this rat. As a result, the observing rats stopped pressing the lever to obtain food, although this lack of activity lasted only a short time and the lever pressing quickly restarted. However, since Church did not control for the rats' reactions to other kinds of noises it could be argued that they were responding to noise in general rather than to a distress noise in another rat.

In a series of studies Miller and his collaborators (Miller *et al.*, 1963; Miller, 1967; Miller *et al.*, 1966) explored non-verbal communication of affect in rhesus monkeys. The authors created experimental situations in which two monkeys were paired together in co-operative conditioning situations. In preliminary sessions both monkeys were trained to expect an electric shock when a violet light went on, and to avoid the shock by pressing a bar. In the experimental sessions both monkeys were paired together in such a way that the first monkey saw the light coming on but had no access to the response bar, while the second monkey did not see the violet light coming on but had access to the response bar. However, the second monkey saw the change in the expression on the face of the first monkey. It therefore knew that they were both about to receive a shock and made the appropriate response on behalf of them both.

Premack and Woodruff (1978) have carried out a series of studies in which they demonstrated chimpanzees' ability to infer mental states, such as wants, purposes and affective attitudes, in human beings. In these experiments chimpanzees were shown films of human actors trying, unsuccessfully, to achieve a particular goal, e.g. to escape from a locked cage or to wash a dirty floor using a hose that was not properly attached to the tap. When then presented with two photographs, one of which depicted a correct solution for the human actor while the other did not, the chimpanzees chose the photographs with the correct solutions although the researchers had no evidence of the chimpanzees having any past experience with the problem in question. Obviously the chimpanzees' observations of the daily activities of human beings were sufficient for them to make correct inferences.

If we now turn our attention to field studies, Teleki (1973) observed the reactions of a group of Gombe chimpanzees to the accidental death of another chimpanzee. The author points out that natural death among wild living primates is not often observed by people, and is therefore poorly documented. In this particular case an adult male member of a group of seventeen Gombe chimpanzees fell from a tree and broke his neck. The other sixteen chimpanzees reacted vigorously to the death of this familiar member of their group for about four hours. Various activities were performed at a high level of arousal: among these, group vocalization was persistent and intense, and group interaction such as interest in feeding, grooming and mating was temporarily heightened.

Dolphins, more than other animals, have been the subject of anecdotal evidence and careful observation concerning their awareness of others, creative problem-solving and general level of inventiveness. As Griffin (1984) points out, most impressive has been the provision of help to other dolphins by pushing or lifting them to the surface when they are injured, ill, or even when they died. Moreover, when they help their companions, they lift them in a sensibly co-ordinated fashion. They are also more likely to help females and young animals than adult males.

Animal awareness of intentions in others

A further step in the exploration of mental states in animals is the study of intentional communication. In his observations of problem-solving in chimpanzees, Köhler (1927) often refers to chimpanzees' expressions of their intentions, desires and urges. For example, a chimpanzee uses the 'language of eyes' to indicate his sexual desires to a female chimpanzee; if he wants to be accompanied he pulls the other's hand, and so on. Goodall (1968), in her observation of wild chimpanzees, found that chimpanzee mothers often tried to distract their children by tickling or grooming them rather than punishing them when they persistently attempted to attain an objective that the mother considered undesirable. For example, when the young persisted in playing with objects of which, for some reason, the mother did not approve, she forced the attention of the young on to something else. Another example of intentional behaviour that Goodall describes concerns the chimpanzee mother distracting the playmate of her own infant when the play became rather rough. When her infant screamed or expressed distress during play, the mother sometimes attacked the playmate's mother rather than the playmate itself.

Field studies of wild chimpanzees indicate that animals who know where food is hidden can inform other chimpanzees about its direction, its approximate distance, and its relative desirability or undesirability. Moreover, it was found (Menzel, 1975) that older chimpanzees can actively inhibit signs of their emotions if they wish to do so, and withhold information from each other, if not lie. For example, if an animal knows where food is hidden it may choose not to disclose the place in front of a stranger but wait until the stranger has gone. Brilliant observations and experiments on the same issues, but with honey bees, were carried out by Frisch (e.g. 1967, 1974), in his life-long studies. Frisch was the first to decode the messages conveyed by various kinds of honey-bee dances. Thus he found that bees employ lively and lengthy dances to indicate to others the availability of desirable food, e.g. of highly concentrated syrup. On the other hand, if food is scarce or if it is available in weaker concentrations, the dancing becomes slower and finally ceases. While round dances signify that food is to be found in the vicinity of the hive, wagg-tailing dances indicate the distance and direction of food that is further away, some-times as far off as several kilometers. Frisch and his followers have insisted that the nature of such communications is symbolic. Other researchers, however, criticize such a view-point, arguing that whether or not honey bees have a symbolic language cannot be answered with any certainty (e.g. Wells and Wenner, 1975; for a detailed discussion of arguments on this issue, see Griffin, 1981, p. 49ff.).

Woodruff and Premack (1979) argue that although the field studies with wild chimpanzees provide provocative ideas about animal intentionality, they are, at best, only suggestive and other factors could be responsible for what appears to be inten-tional communication. Thus, not all instances of an animal's misleading behaviour qualify as actual deceit. For example, a signal cannot be assumed to be intentional if the behaviour is *always* triggered off by a particular situation; rather, it is instinc-tive. Or, a signal cannot be called intentional if the sender makes occasional 'errors': 'A claim for intentionality requires demonstration that an individual can reliably use his communi-cative behaviour to convey either accurate or misleading infor-mation, as the situation demands' (Woodruff and Premack, 1979, p. 335). In their carefully designed studies the authors found evidence that chimpanzees can deliberately deceive human beings by selectively withholding information or providing wrong information in order to mislead them. More-over, their studies have demonstrated that chimpanzees take into consideration the individual characteristics of the recipient of the information, e.g. whether it is in a competing or in a co-operating role. It is, indeed, responding to others as individuals, rather than responding, non-selectively, to situations, that points to intentionality and other-awareness, and we shall look at this issue in the next section.

Animal awareness and the recognition of individuals

One of the essential characteristics of *human* awareness is the recognition of individuality. In other words, people react to each other *individually*, i.e. with an understanding of this or that person's needs, personality, social roles and social status, and according to the social context in which the social interaction takes place. For example, people generally recognize that what one person may take as a joke another may consider offensive. If the speaker is unable to judge what to say to whom, how to say it and under what circumstances, it is likely that a breakdown of communication will follow. Recognition of individuality and treating people as individuals contributes to the effectiveness of social interactions.

With respect to animal awareness the question arises as to whether animals, too (or, at least some of them), recognize and treat others as individuals. It is well known that the amount and kind of interaction among members of a particular animal social group differs from that directed towards outsiders. Interactions that are beneficial to participants, such as grooming, playing and feeding, are prevalent among group members but occur much less among strangers. Outsiders to a group are often attacked or prevented from joining in. For example, when a strange hen is placed in a flock, it becomes a target of aggression (Schjelderup-Ebbe, 1935). Zajonc *et al.* (1975) carried out a study with 1 day old domestic chicks to find out whether very young birds discriminate between individual strangers and familiar companions. In order to explore this issue the authors observed the pecking behaviour among chicks under different conditions. Pecking behaviour is assumed to be a form of social exploration (Evans, 1967), and consequently it would be expected that its amount would be higher among strange chicks. Indeed, Zajonc *el al.* found that the amount of pecking behaviour was consistently increased when a new element was introduced into a social encounter. For example, more pecking behaviour was present among strangers than among companions; pecking was more frequent among strangers of unfamiliar, rather than of familiar, colour; and so on. The experiment thus showed that domestic chicks learn to discriminate among members of in-groups and out-groups very early in their lives. It has been observed that some mammals, and primates in particular, treat members of their own group differentially, according to their status. Griffin (1984, p. 187) points out that such recognition may facilitate empathy, assessment of other's moods and response to threats and other's signals and requests. In fact, evidence for the recognition of others as individuals comes from observation of vervet monkeys (Griffin, 1984, p. 165f.). African vervet monkeys live in open areas and so their observation by ethologists is relatively easy. They live in groups consisting of several generations of parents, children, cousins and other relatives while young males sometimes emigrate to neighbouring groups which reduces inbreeding. Griffin points out that, among vervet monkeys and also in many other primate societies, dominance depends largely on who your parents are. For example, a young monkey cannot, successfully, threaten stronger animals, but it may be given access to food by others if it is the offspring of a dominant mother, who might help her child should any problem arise.

It has already been pointed out that awareness of others appears to have important survival value. It has emerged, in the process of evolution, as an adaptive phenomenon in non-human primates, who are highly interdependent and whose preservation requires a considerable degree of co-operation. However, even more interdependence is to be found among social insects such as ants, honey bees and wasps. Some insects are so highly specialized that they must be fed by others. In spite of their close social interdependence it seems unlikely that these insects would recognize themselves as individuals since their colonies contain too many members and the life of each member is too short to make recognition of individuals biologically adaptive (Wilson, 1971). Griffin (1984), nevertheless, argues that it cannot be taken as established that social insects function just like physical atoms that are totally indistinguishable from one another. There has been very little research into insects' differentiation in subgroupings, and into the specializations of subgroupings. However, Lindauer (1971) reviewed studies on honey bees showing that workers specialize in the tasks they perform. Thus, in honey bees each worker passes through successive occupational stages during its lifetime, the youngest cleaning cells in the honeycomb, at about 3 to 10 days they build the comb, including capping cells already built, and only at about 18 days do they begin to spend much time gathering food outside the hive. Although there is no evidence that these workers recognize themselves as individuals, it is still necessary for them to distinguish themselves as belonging to one category of worker rather than to another in order to communicate efficiently. It is not known, of course, whether such interaction is based on anything similar to other-awareness (Griffin, 1984, p. 191). The possibility that co-ordinating behaviour in colonies of insects are due to bio-chemical and physiological processes, rather than to symbolic ones, was discussed by Mead (1934, pp. 227–37). For further elaboration of this issue see also the discussion in Griffin already mentioned (1981, p. 49f.).

There are still tremendous gaps in our knowledge concerning animal awareness and one must be prepared to consider different kinds and different types of awareness in their own rights. Moreover, more imagination and other-awareness on the part of the investigators is needed in their studies of animal awareness. Most often the investigators, although quite under-standably, try to find out whether animals have the capacity of being aware of *precisely* those things that people are aware of. In other words, it is *human awareness* that is used by psychol-ogists as a criterion for *animal awareness*, and *human meanings* are taken as criteria of *animal meanings*. Such an approach on the part of researchers, however, is unjustified. Griffin presents an instructive example in his discussion of the chimpanzee Washoe's learning of American Sign Language. This example indicates that imputing human meanings to animal behaviour may be quite misleading:

The Gardners taught Washoe to use a sign that meant flower to them. But Washoe used it not only for flowers but for pipe tobacco and kitchen fumes. To her it apparently meant smells. Washoe may have been thinking about smells when she used the sign, rather than about the visual properties of colored flowers, but she was certainly thinking about something that overlapped with the properties conveyed by the word flower as we use it (Griffin, 1984, p. 201–2).

This case clearly demonstrates a general problem that can arise from taking it for granted that one's own point of view, one's own concepts and meanings, should be the criteria for evaluating the significance of the actions of others. Piaget (1926) attributed this inability to consider points of view other than one's own to young children, and he called it *egocentrism* (cf. Chapter 2). One can see, however, from the above example, that a form of egocentrism can also become an obstacle in the research of an experienced scientist.

The cultural-historical nature of human awareness

People's awareness of themselves and of others undergoes remarkable changes in the context of historical and cultural development. The vicissitudes of human awareness are closely related to personal and societal values, to moral beliefs and ethical needs, to the structure of the family, to the level of education of particular social groups, and to social organizations. The purpose of this section is not to present a review of the varied expressions of human awareness in different cultural and historical contexts but, by providing examples, to help the student to come to a better understanding of two main issues. First, the role that the social environment plays in the development of human awareness and, second, the reasons for the diversity of forms in which human awareness manifests itself.

Analysing the origin of consciousness – or awareness, to be consistent in the use of terminology – in human beings, Jaynes (1976) goes so far as to argue that the people of the ancient Mycean culture in Greece had no awareness of subjective mental states either of their own or of those of other people:

Iliadic man did not have subjectivity as do we; he had no awareness of his awareness of the world, no internal mind-space to introspect upon. In distinction to our own subjective conscious minds, we can call the mentality of the Myceans *a bicameral mind* (Jaynes, 1976, p. 75).

According to Jaynes, the bicameral mind was split into two components. First, a component called 'gods' who gave people orders for the conduct of their lives. Second, a component that obeyed the gods' orders, called 'man'. Neither of these components had consciousness (or awareness) as we know it today. The gods, who were 'organizations of the central nervous system', supposedly pushed humans around like

robots, indeed Jaynes likens the gods' voices to the hallucinations of people with schizophrenia or epilepsy. Analysing
some passages in the *Iliad* referring to the Trojan War, Jaynes
maintains that the participants were guided by hallucinations:
they were 'noble automatons who knew not what they did'.
Reading such accounts of the Iliadic heroes one wonders what
Jaynes means by such claims, and what evidence he has for his
views. Jaynes bases his claims on the following observations:
The great epic poem, the *Iliad*, supposedly written about 900
or 850 years BC, does not contain any words that refer to
subjectivity, mental states or what we would now call *subjective
consciousness* (or self-awareness). The poem describes the actions
of gods and heroes but not their mental processes. Although
such words as *psyche* or *thumos* occur in the *Iliad*, their meanings
are different from those which these words have in later Greek.
Thus, in the *Iliad psyche* means life substances such as blood or
breath, and *thumos* is motion or agitation. It is only in later
Greek that 'psyche' changed its reference to mean conscious
mind, and 'thumos' became emotional soul. The fact that the
Iliad contains no words referring to mental states is, for Jaynes,
sufficient proof that the Mycean people had no consciousness,
since words are not *just* words but refer to concepts: 'Word
changes are concept changes and concept changes are behavioural changes' (Jaynes, 1976, p. 292). Jaynes is, of course, right
in arguing that changes in the meaning of words are
accompanied by changes in concepts, in social attitudes and in
the activities of people. The problem, however, is that Jaynes
makes judgements about the existence or non-existence of
human self-awareness and about the meanings of words from
the point of view of the kind of self-awareness existing in
twentieth-century culture rather than on the basis of the culture
that existed 3000 years ago. While one must certainly assume
that the self-awareness of the Iliadic people was different from
that of present western culture, simply because the social and
cultural context of ancient Greece was different from that of
today, there is no evidence, whatsoever, to justify the claim
that the Iliadic people had no self-awareness and were just
walking automata. Once again, part of the problem concerns
one's definition of self-awareness. If one takes as the criterion
of self-awareness its twentieth-century form in western culture,
which means the ability to give verbal evidence of one's ability
to evaluate one's own and others' mental processes, then neither
chimpanzees' self-recognition in a mirror nor the form of self-

awareness in Mycean culture would count. If, on the other hand, one adopts a developmental definition of self-awareness, as discussed at the beginning of this chapter, then chimpanzees' self-recognition in the mirror, just like the form of self-awareness in the Mycean culture, represent different stages of the self-awareness process. Moreover, if one accepts the argument of a number of philosophers, linguists, and psychologists that verbal language, itself, is a manifestation of self-awareness (e.g. Herder, 1771; Humboldt, 1836; Mead, 1934; Farr, 1981; Markova, 1982, 1983), then Jaynes's claim does not stand up at all. The task for the researcher is not so much to make judgements about the existence of self-awareness using the present criteria of western culture, as to consider the various possible forms in which self-awareness may manifest itself. Thus, one of Jaynes's examples mentioned earlier was the word *psyche*, which, in the *Iliad*, meant life substances such as blood or breath rather than a mental state or process. The question one might ask is whether the words 'blood' or 'breath' had the same meaning in Mycean culture as they have in present western languages. Even today the word 'blood' does not mean just a bodily liquid with certain biological and chemical properties but it also has a number of symbolic meanings, some of them based on religious and mystical sources. Bearing in mind the lack of any scientific knowledge concerning blood in the Mycean culture and the important role that myth and magic played in all primitive cultures, why should one assume that 'blood', then, meant just life substance in today's sense? It is a great mistake to take one word after another from ancient languages, translate them, *literally*, into today's languages, and then claim the non-existence of various meanings in ancient cultures. Instead, one must consider an ancient language as a whole, its words as organic parts of the whole, all having different meanings from those of today's languages, although in various respects overlapping with today's meanings. Consequently, concepts in Mycean culture had different contents from our own because they referred to a different body of knowledge, to different values and beliefs, and to different kinds of social relationships. For example, the fact that there was slavery in ancient Greece made the definition of humanity different from that of today: biological similarity for the Greeks was certainly not a criterion for treating all human beings *as* human beings. Moreover, even in our present culture, changes in the treatment of the physically and mentally handicapped, the mentally ill, and animals, to take just a few examples, indicate fundamental changes in the process of self– and of other-awareness. In the later Greek one can notice an increase of psychological terms with meanings more similar to those of today's, and a growing emphasis on subjective consciousness. For example, the *Dialogues* of Plato were very much concerned with the discovery of the individual's inner experience and with the nature of one's self-awareness.

With the decline of classical culture, however, feudal Europe broke off, for several hundred years, from the search for the individual's inner experience and a renewed search for it is assumed to have occurred some time during the eleventh and twelfth centuries (Morris, 1972). Christianity contributed greatly to this renewed interest, focusing on the possibility of strengthening the individual's personality by spiritual means and ascetic discipline. The medieval individual was thought of in terms of moral virtues rather than in terms of the awareness of the self as a unique individual with idiosyncratic psychological characteristics (Lyons, 1978). In the Renaissance, and the Humanism that followed, the interest in the self continued to develop, with increasing emphasis being placed on the individual as an active and creative being. This progressive stress on human action and efficiency, going hand in hand with the development of free enterprise, the appearance of a mercantile elite, and the decline of feudalism, had important consequences for the conception of the self.

Societal change and human awareness

Ideally, any discussion of the development of the concept of human awareness, up to its present form in western society, should be based on clearly documented psychological evidence. In its absence, I shall draw attention to the work of an historian. In his study of the history of the family in England from the sixteenth to the nineteenth centuries, Stone (1977) provides an excellent analysis of the forces leading to the rise of individualism and to modern notions of self– and of other-awareness. These forces included the following: economic pressures, the growth and mobility of the population, religious forces, and the growth of public education, leading to *societal changes* on the one hand, and to changes in *personal relationships* on the other.

Hand in hand with economic pressures and the decline of

traditional communities, the growth of self- and of other-awareness in the sixteenth and seventeenth centuries, according to Stone (1977), was mainly due to two sources: first, to the Calvinist theology and morality that encouraged soul searching and introspection; and second, to the growth of public literacy. Writing and reading is largely an individual activity and with increased literacy the leisure time of the middle and upper classes was filled more and more in this way. New literary genres, diaries and autobiographies, emerged on a large scale. Stone maintains that over 360 English diaries and over 200 autobiographies have survived of those that were written before the eighteenth century, although the majority of these are still reports of deep religious, rather than daily life, experiences. During the eighteenth century diaries and autobiographies became less religious and more personal in their contents. Many of these were written by middle- and upper-class women whose educational 'accomplishments' were promises of successful marriages. Letter writing was filled with self-expression and observation of one's feelings, as is well documented in the English eighteenth-century novel. As paper became cheaper, novels achieved higher sales and subscription libraries were established in towns, and the interest in emotional life and inner experiences became widespread. Similar developments occurred all over Europe and later, too, in the United States. The importance of literacy in the shift from a tradition-driven to an inner-driven society was discussed by the sociologists Thomas and Znaniecki (1918–20) in their work *The Polish Peasant in Europe and America*. The authors pointed out that the rural press contributed significantly to the change of values and attitudes among the peasants in the last century. A tradition-driven society not only leads to a traditional style of living but determines standards of work, in this case of farming, and standards of life in general. The press destroyed such standards (Riesman, 1950) and introduced values based on orientation towards the building of people's characters, personal standards, and inner drives.

The effect of the printing revolution, with the subsequent growth of literacy, on societal and psychological change is also explored by Eisenstein (1979, 1983). In the two volumes of her *The Printing Press as an Agent of Change*, Eisenstein (1979) emphasizes the role of printing in the transition from medieval to modern European society. Sociologists of knowledge and historians have usually focused their attention on the political and economic change in society that took place in that transition, and have overlooked the importance of printing and literacy. Eisenstein, also a historian, points out that printing meant not just the existence of libraries and the increase of reading as such. It also meant the growth of new cultural, economic and intellectual activities. The availability of books, manuals, and graphic illustrations made it possible for the public to become self-educated on a large scale. In this sense such self-education rivalled the learning acquired at the traditional type of university. Eisenstein refers to the 'avalanche' of material that was published to explain

by a variety of 'easy steps' (often supplemented by sharp-edged diagrams) just 'how to' draw a picture, compose a madrigal, mix paints, bake clay, keep accounts, survey a field, handle all manner of tools and instruments, work mines, assay metals, move armies or obelisks, design buildings, bridges and machines (Eisenstein, 1979, I, p. 243).

In addition to the effect of printing on public self-learning, Eisenstein also refers to the growth of individual achievement. Those who took leading roles in various intellectual and industrial activities, started to be advertised *as* individuals and their private affairs became public property. Idiosyncratic characteristics and uniquely personal features of successful individuals became part of their published biographies. Moreover, Eisenstein points out, since such artistic products as pictures and books were duplicated on a mass scale, the original product from the hand of the artist was assigned a value that had not existed before. Winchester (1985) maintains that the impacts of literacy on the individual were of three major kinds. First, literacy frees the mind from dwelling on global aspects of knowledge and enables it to focus on details. Such details can then be catalogued, classified and organized. The second impact of literacy is that the mind can attend to several things at the same time since it does not need to rely upon memory to the same degree as when the written record is not available. Finally, literacy makes it possible to extend arguments endlessly, to consider and reconsider them from a variety of points of view.

It is thus clear that the effect of literacy in contributing to change in society and the growth of new kinds of self-awareness took a variety of forms. These ranged from the rise of new intellectual activities to a focus on mental capacities that had barely been employed before. Olson (1985) maintains that the fundamental consequence of literacy is reflexion, and, so, intellectual and social change. A written text makes it possible to look back, to interpret and reinterpret the text, as well as one's own understanding of that text. It is in this sense that printing has contributed to the change in human awareness.

Evidence for suggestions that literacy may be closely related to the modern form of self-awareness is supported by Luria's exploration of self- and of other-awareness in the remote villages and mountain pastureland of Uzbekistan and Kirgizia, where people had lived for centuries in a state of economic stagnation and illiteracy, and with the religion of Islam (Luria, 1976). Luria carried out his study in 1931–2 during the Soviet Union's radical elimination of illiteracy and the transition to a collectivist agriculture. His hypotheses were that people's ability to be aware of themselves and of others as individuals having psychological characteristics, and their ability to make judgements about the capacities of others, are functions of socio-cultural development. The method of his research was based on discussion in the course of which people were asked to evaluate their own character, point to perceived differences between themselves and others, and to express their positive personality traits and shortcomings. Participants of the study were illiterate peasants, active members of collective farms with experience in discussing work issues collectively, and students in technical schools or people with at least some formal education.

The results of this study showed that illiterate people totally failed the task. For example, when the illiterate villagers were asked to describe their personal shortcomings, 'shortcomings' were understood only as material things they were lacking, such as clothing, food, external conditions of life; and as general situations, for example: 'yes . . . well, for instance, my clothing's poor . . . after all, I'm no longer young' (Luria, 1976, p. 151), or 'I don't have enough wheat' (ibid., p. 153). When the researcher prompted the person to describe his good and bad traits, the answers were, once again, in terms of material things: 'I have a big shortcoming: I borrowed 125 rubles and I can't pay them back' (ibid, p. 152). Even probing with a request as to whether there was nothing in the person to be changed for the better, the answer was:

I am a good person, everyone knows me, I'm not rude to anyone, and I always lend a hand. I feel good about myself, there's nothing to change (ibid, p. 152).

When the illiterate villager was asked to describe his comrades and say what sort of people his comrades were, the answer was as follows:

There's one comrade who grew up under the same blanket with me; he gave me fifty rubles when I was sick, so I think he's a good fellow and don't see any bad qualities in him. Generally I don't talk to bad people or become friendly with them; I'm a good buddy and have good buddies. I don't talk to people who play cards for money (ibid., p. 152).

These examples show that the illiterate villagers in Luria's research were unable to describe themselves and others in terms of psychological characteristics. Instead, they dealt with such questions by pointing to material property, to situations, or to external forms of behaviour. Only people with formal education were able to characterize themselves and others in psychological terms. In this sense, Luria's findings corroborate Stone's historical analysis, showing that literacy is closely related to the modern notion of human awareness.

Changes in personal relationships and in human-awareness

In his historical analysis Stone (1977) describes some essential changes that occurred in the English family between 1500 and 1800. In the sixteenth century the high mortality rate made members of the family replaceable. In the majority of families most of the children died but belief in the immortality of the soul contributed to a weakening of grief. Marriages were prearranged and the relationships between husband and wife were usually without much affection. Personal privacy was virtually non-existent. Parental discipline in child-rearing practices was based on parental authority and total obedience:

The result was a family type whose characteristics of psychological distance, deference and publicity were congruent with the basic values and organization of the hierarchical, authoritarian and inquisitorially collectivist society of Early Modern England (Stone, 1977, p. 653).

The decline of kinship and control of the community, the changing attitudes to death, and the growth of personal privacy that took place in the course of the seventeenth and eighteenth centuries led to considerable developments in personal relationships within the family. People were no longer perceived in replaceable terms and the death of a family member was now felt as a tragedy. Stone points out that the change in attitude towards death was also reflected in the treatment of churchyards. While in the past these served a number of purposes – such as places where the dead were buried, where children played, adults gossiped, bargained and made love, and cattle grazed – they now became places restricted to the peaceful rest of the dead and the mourning of the survivors. The rich of the seventeenth and the eighteenth centuries started to emphasize personal privacy, i.e. to have spaces either for their own individual use or private spaces for making love, sleeping or for various kinds of interpersonal interaction.

As a result of the above changes in societal and family relationships the idea of the uniqueness of individual human beings gradually became commonly accepted. Stone suggests that due to the fundamental changes in child rearing practices that took place between the sixteenth and the eighteenth centuries, basic personality changes occurred during this period. In the sixteenth century people's capacity for affectionate relationships was limited and personal relationships were rather distant and diffused among various members of kin, the greater family, and neighbours. In the eighteenth century, however, the capacity for intimate relationships became much greater, and at least among the middle and upper classes it became concentrated between husband and wife, and parents and their children. Hand in hand with such changes, domestic affection became one of the most important aims in human life. The child's socialization in the family and regulation in interpersonal relationships were now important forces in the development of self- and of other-awareness. However, while on the one hand family relationships grew closer, on the other hand the child, more than ever before, in a period of increasing literacy, became able to free him- or herself from his or her family. Reading on his or her own under the light of a lamp or candle allowed the child self-education and independent development of ideas. Books in general and biographies in particular provided the child with the models of heroes who had succeeded in life's battles, if they disciplined themselves and worked hard (Riesman, 1950). The growth of literacy and a self-directed outlook on life has also contributed to the growth of our modern notion of human self-awareness.

Modern self-awareness born in Romanticism

Mead (1936) argued convincingly that the notion of self-consciousness (or self-awareness, in our terminology) as used today is the product of the Romanticism of the nineteenth century. Romanticism became an important artistic and philosophical movement in Central Europe after the failure of the French Revolution and the subsequent disillusionment. There were two particular aspects of Romanticism that contributed greatly to the development of the present notion of self-awareness or self-consciousness.

First, the Romantics were profoundly aware of the relativity of the values and norms of individual cultures, historical epochs, and societies. They argued that each stage in history was important for the progress it brought about, and that it was wrong to despise previous cultures just because they were not as advanced as the existing one. Their tremendous interest in history led to the realization that past events should not be judged by contemporary criteria, values and moral standards. In order to understand history and to grasp its meaning, one must immerse oneself in that history and reconstruct that meaning for oneself. In other words, one must feel oneself into the past, put oneself into the shoes of those who lived in the past, and attempt to see the world through their eyes. In general, this ability to look at the world through the eyes of others also enables one to look at *oneself* through the eyes of others: the self becomes self-conscious (or self-aware), i.e. becomes an object of its own observation.

Second, hand in hand with the emphasis on the practical activity important in economic growth, the idea that people become aware of themselves through their active experience of, and interference with the world was supported by Romanticism. Hegel (1807) maintained that it is through their own action upon the world, that is, through practical involvement, that people not only transform things but also change themselves and gain self-knowledge. The idea of 'odyssea', i.e. picturing human beings as pilgrims who, on their journey in the world, and through their own active transformation of the world, eventually recognize themselves, was quite common in nineteenth-century German literature, philosophy and social science. It was also a fundamental idea in Goethe's *Faust*. The essence of this motif can be conceived as based on a three step development. First, pilgrims who return from their journey through the world are different from what they were at the beginning of the journey because of their activities during that journey. Second, the world itself is different because the pilgrims' activities affect it. Third, the world as it appears to the pilgrims after completion of their journey is different, not only because their activities have had an effect on the world but also because their activities have had a profound effect upon themselves: their experience and perception, both of the world and of themselves, is now different.

In conclusion, it was through Romanticism that a person learned to look at him- or herself as an *object*, which resulted from his or her ability to take the role or the attitude of others. Moreover, a person also became aware of him- or herself as a *subject*, as a doer with the ability to influence the world. These two aspects of self-awareness, i.e. *the self as object* and *the self as subject*, seem to have first appeared in the work of philosophers such as Kant and Hegel. In psychology, it is to James (1890), and then to Mead, that we owe the distinction between the *I*, the self as a subject, and the *Me*, the self as an object, in its present form (for details see Chapter 4).

Awareness of the self and of others in non-western cultures

While the concern with the self and its various attributes is a matter of relatively recent interest in western culture, inquiries into the nature of the self in various Asian cultures have had a very long history. The purpose of this brief section is not just to point to this fact, but rather to emphasize that the western concept of self- and of other-awareness is only one of many possible approaches to human awareness, determined by particular historical and cultural circumstances.

In all Hindu systems of thought analysis of the self appears to be the central theme of interest. The Hindu Real Self – *ātman* – is immaterial, non-experiential, impersonal and eternal. The striving of the Hindu is for total union with this Real Self which is immutable and absolute (Bharati, 1985). In western terms, the Hindu search for the Real Self takes the individual away from society (DeVos, 1985). In contrast to the Real Self that is the concern of Hindu philosophy and religion, the empirical self, which is associated with individual human beings, is of a low status and involves cognition, sensation and action. In other words, it is material and experiential, and as such is totally ignored in Hindu philosophical writings. If it ever does occur in writing it is not for the purpose of analysis but as a subject of contempt (Bharati, 1985). Moreover, the empirical self is not simply comparable to the western concept of the self. While the western concept of the self is bound up with the uniqueness of the individual, the Hindu self is conceived as a 'dividual', i.e. as divisible (Marriott, 1976). Thus people expose themselves to experiences that might be considered inconsistent in the west but are totally acceptable in Hindu. For example, one and the same person may hold Christian, Marxist and Nazi views without any internal conflict, simply because such situational activities are only expressions of the empirical self and have nothing to do with the Real Self (Bharati, 1985). However, Paranjpe (1987) points out that some Hindu thought systems such as Yoga and Vedanta attempt to develop practical programmes to achieve unity between the impersonal Real Self and the personal and experiential self.

The traditional Chinese conception of self- and of other-awareness is based on Confucian thought. In this tradition, the self is defined as a focus of social relationships and as a dynamic process of spiritual development (Wei-ming, 1985). According to this conception the self is not defined in terms of the individual's idiosyncratic characteristics but of the roles the individual is expected to fulfil. For example, in traditional Chinese society a person would be defined as a father, a brother, a husband, a son but not as *himself* (Chu, 1985). Self- and other-awareness, as defined in terms of these social roles, can be seen both as a strength and a weakness for the individual. On the one hand, definition in terms of significant others provides security and a feeling of belongingness; at the same time it is a source of constraints since a person's behaviour is governed by what is expected by tradition and custom. Moreover, the self as a dynamic process of spiritual development is realized in fulfilling the above social roles. Thus, it is through one's experience in significant social relationships that one cultivates one's sense of brotherhood, loyalty, discipline, and so on. Through such experience one becomes a whole person. One of Confucius's maxims states: 'Wishing to establish oneself, one establishes others; wishing to enlarge oneself, one enlarges others' (Wei-ming, 1985, p. 232); self-cultivation through one's fulfilment of social roles is not only altruistic but is essential for one's own spiritual development. Although the traditional Chinese conception of self- and other-awareness is undergoing essential changes both through westernization and through cultural and ideological changes in their communist society, the self is still defined in terms of relationships to others. The Communist Party ideology cultivates the self-concept defined by the individual's dedication to the spirit of collectivism as laid down by Chairman Mao (Chu, 1985).

The Japanese conception of self- and of other-awareness is, in some ways, similar to the Chinese and has also been influenced by the Confucian tradition. The idea of harmony in social relationships and of avoidance of conflict and disorganization seems to be the major principle guiding the individual's self- and other-awareness. From early childhood, children in traditional Japanese society are taught to conform to social expectations and customs rather than to express their individual goals and self-assertiveness (DeVos, 1985). Just as in the Chinese conception, the self is defined in terms of the role the individual is expected to fulfil. Group identity nurtures the sense of duty and obligation toward others. Within the group one cultivates one's sense of responsibility and co-operation and subdues one's own personal desires. As one would expect, however, a tension between the individual's hidden inclinations and group expectations with respect to fulfilment of outward tasks often arises, particularly as the traditional values undergo change. In spite of such changes, outward self-presentation and self-control still prevail in Japanese society, whatever the inner desires or feelings of the individual may be (Wagatsuma and DeVos, 1978). In his book *Why Has Japan 'Succeeded'?* Mori-shima (1982) compares and contrasts Chinese and Japanese forms of Confucianism, and their effect on the present economic standing of these two countries. Thus he points out that throughout history Chinese Confucianism relied on different kinds of values than did Japanese Confucianism. In China, *benevolence* has been a central virtue, the assumption being that human nature is fundamentally good. Therefore, the aim of Chinese Confucianism has been to reach perfection in the individual and in the social order at large. *Loyalty* for the Chinese means being true to one's own conscience. In contrast, Japanese Confucianism, is nationalistic. Japanese nationalism, Morishima explains, is a reflection of historical circumstances, such as the long-term economic and cultural isolation of Japan as against the trade and cultural superiority of the Chinese. The nationalistic tendencies in Japan have led to the interest in weaponry, science and technology. On the social and human side, obedience to the ruler and the sacrifice of the individual to the public interest have, consequently, been more important than the individual's own conscience. As Morishima maintains, individualism and liberalism have been virtually non-existent in Japan, and even China, in contrast to Japan, has been less collectivist. Thus, although Japan has acquired western technology, it has not, so far, acquired western individualism.

Summary

Self- and other-awareness are socio-developmental processes and must be defined in developmental terms. These processes emerge and grow in mutual interaction between the organism and its environment, both in the biological and the historical-cultural contexts.

Most evidence for animal self-awareness is based on research with chimpanzees. This research has suggested that chimpanzees can be taught to recognize themselves in a mirror and to describe their own actions in sign language. Animal other-awareness has been explored both in laboratory and field studies. These studies have demonstrated that some mammals, and chimpanzees in particular, have the ability to infer various mental states and intentions in others.

Self- and other-awareness have undergone essential changes in European history. Societal changes have facilitated the growth of individualism and changes in interpersonal relationships, and have contributed to the emergence, in Romanticism, of self- and of other-awareness in their present forms. The Romanticism of the nineteenth century defined self-consciousness or self-awareness on the basis of the individual's ability to take the role of the other person and of the individual's practical involvement in the world. Consequently, two aspects of self-awareness, i.e. the self as object and the self as subject, have been discerned. In psychology, they are known as the I and the Me.

The present western conception of self- and of other-awareness is only one of the many that are possible, and a product of the particular socio-historical conditions in Europe.

The biological and cultural nature of human awareness

Different systems of thought, such as Hinduism and Confucianism, based on different socio-historical conditions, have led to other conceptions of self- and other-awareness.

2 Awareness of the feelings of other people

The notion of *empathy* as the feeling of another's emotion was probably introduced into social psychology by Herder, a German scholar of the eighteenth century. Discussing the problem of understanding the historical development of different nations, Herder pointed out that, in order to empathize with others, one must attempt to feel oneself into the situation of the other person or nation. The German word *Einfühlung*, translated literally, means 'feeling into another' and it was adopted by the German psychologists of the early twentieth century. Both Lipps (1926, 1935) and Köhler (1927) defined empathic response as sharing an affect with another person. However, in spite of these early beginnings, there has not, until recently, been much research in the subject of empathy. In his article on 'Some neglected problems in social psychology', Cottrell (1950) identified the study of empathy, along with the study of the self, as areas that social psychologists have successfully ignored almost completely. He saw the main reasons for such neglect in the difficulty of developing appropriate techniques to study empathy empirically. However, in spite of his call for more research, it took another two decades before empathy became a field of a vigorous study.

Even now, the subject of empathy poses serious conceptual problems. Thus, there has been little agreement among psychologists about how to define empathy. For example, psychologists cannot agree what biological and socio-cognitive capacities are required for empathy to occur; whether empathy is a response to another's affect or to a situation provoking affect; at what age empathy emerges; how to distinguish it from identification, projection and role-taking; and whether empathy is a cognitive or an affective process, or indeed both a cognitive and an affective process.

In this chapter we shall first discuss the emergence of empathy in early childhood and the methods used to explore it. Second, we shall attempt to clarify the conceptual issues with respect to the role of emotion and cognition in the study of empathy and the effect of these issues upon the choice of research method in the study of empathy. Finally, some of the factors modifying empathic reaction will be considered.

Empathy in early childhood

Anecdotal observations of infant cries as responses to the sounds of other infants' cries have been reported for some time. While Arlitt (1930) and Humphrey (1922) described infant cry in response to distress cry in other infants at 4 months of age, Bühler and Hetzer (1928) observed such response cries in newborns 1–14 days old. In his carefully designed study, Simner (1971) confirmed that 3 day olds responded to the sound of another newborn's cry much more than they responded to an intermittent noise of the same intensity produced by a noise generator. Sagi and Hoffman (1976) replicated Simner's study with even younger infants. The infants in their study were only 34 hours old on average, and the researchers used either natural or synthetic cries as stimuli. The pattern of infants' crying, as a response to such stimuli, confirmed Simner's findings that it is to the vocal properties of the human voice that newborn infants respond rather than just to sound in general. Hoffman (1978b) suggests that the newborn's distress cry as a response to distress in another infant is a possible early precursor of empathic arousal.

It is difficult to decide whether these early responses of infants to distress in others are innate or whether they are a result of very fast learning in early childhood. Both hypotheses are equally feasible. On the one hand, as we have seen in Chapter 1, there is ample evidence for animal other-awareness, and, therefore, an innate capacity for empathy in human beings is a likely hypothesis. On the other hand, it may be that babies cry when they hear other babies crying simply because of association between their own past crying and distress experiences (Hoffman, 1978a). It is well known that associative learning with respect to pain occurs also in older children. For example, one child sees another's arm bleeding after a fall and the victim crying. On another occasion the sight of blood either on his or her own body or on someone else's may be enough to set the child crying him- or herself. Another kind of response to distress in others has been observed with respect to physical contact between infants and their caretakers. Escalona (1945) reported her observation of feeding disturbances among young babies whose mothers were prisoners in the Massachusetts Reformatory. In several instances babies less than 4 weeks old refused their mothers' breasts for no obvious physical cause. The author points out, however, that the mothers were highly anxious: they held their babies tightly, or trembled, or moved restlessly while holding them. Particular problems with respect to feeding were faced by all the mothers on days with special significance such as Christmas or 'parole days'. The latter were days on which some women were released on parole and everyone was anxious, either expecting a decision on their own cases or expecting others to leave while they had to stay. Escalona also refers to other reports in the literature indicating the transmission of emotional states from caretakers to babies. Hoffman (1978b), referring to Escalona's observations, points out that the mother's distress may produce bodily tension: the mother's body may stiffen, this stiffness may be experienced unpleasantly by the infant, to whom the bodily tension of the caretaker is transferred through bodily contact. Moreover, the mother's stiffened holding of her infant may be accompanied by distinct facial expressions and a changed tone of voice.

Infant reactions to distress stimuli in general, and to distress in others in particular, appear, initially, to be undifferentiated and global, involving movements of the body as a whole, crying, not eating (Bridges, 1931; Sroufe, 1979). As the child grows older, this global reaction to unpleasant stimulation gradually becomes differentiated and directed, and co-ordinated responses appear which are specific to particular events. The original, global, distress reaction to hunger, physical discomfort, changed tension in the body of the caretaker or the distress cries of others appears to be the *precursor* of the emergence of proper emotion, and a more complex empathic response.

Hoffman (1978b) distinguishes four stages in child empathic development. The first stage covers most of the child's first year and is characteristic of a period in which there is no evidence of the child having acquired the concept of 'person permanence'. At this stage the diffuse global reaction serves as a response to any stimulus whatsoever. Infants do not seem to be able to distinguish whether something is happening to them or to someone else. Hoffman gives the example of the 11-month-old daughter of a colleague who saw another child fall and cry. First, she simply stared at the child, then put her thumb in her mouth and finally buried her head in her mother's lap. Thus, 'the first stage of empathic distress may be described as a primitive, involuntary response based mainly on the "pull" of surface cues and minimally on higher cognitive processes' (Hoffman, 1978b, p. 182).

The second stage is characterized by the emergence of a differentiation between the 'self' and the 'other'. According to Bridges (1931) and Sroufe (1979) this differentiation also signifies the emergence of emotion proper. At first, the distinction between the children's own inner states and those of others is only transient and momentary. Since children do not appreciate the difference between their own inner states and those of others, they react to the others' states in the same way that they react to their own. Thus, they *extend* or *project* their own states on to others. Hoffman gives several examples of such responses. One boy typically responded to his own distress by sucking his thumb with one hand and pulling his ear with the other. At 12 months, on seeing a sad expression on the face of his father, the boy himself put on a sad look, sucked his thumb and pulled *his father's* ear. One girl, on seeing distress on the face of an adult, responded by looking distressed herself and then offered her beloved doll to the adult. Another boy fetched his own mother to comfort a crying friend although the friend's mother was equally available. We can see from these examples that children respond to other people's distress as they would respond to their own. These first stages in children's empathic development appear to be characterized by their projection of their own inner states on to those of others rather than by their responding to feelings in others in their own right.

The third stage, according to Hoffman, is characterized by children's awareness that *other people's feelings and thoughts may differ from those of their own;* that one and the same event may be interpreted differently by different people. Children show signs of such a distinction by the age of 2 or 3 years. This does not mean, though, that once children are aware of their own inner states and processes as being distinct from those of other people, they always make precise distinctions between themselves and the other person in all areas of mental and behavioural activity.

Finally, according to Hoffman, children reach the fourth stage in the acquisition of the ability to empathize when they realize that the other person feels emotions not only in particular situations but also as a result of the broad context of life experience. For example, children may become aware of the chronically distressed conditions of disadvantaged groups in society, of the oppressed, the poor, the physically and mentally handicapped, and so on.

What do Hoffman's four developmental stages demonstrate? They certainly do not define exact criteria according to which the child can be said to be at one, rather than at another, stage. Rather, they provide a description of the development of the capacities that a child must acquire in order to proceed to higher stages, though this does not mean that once the child has acquired these capacities, he or she will never regress to a lower stage. Most importantly, Hoffman's stages show that while the child's responses to distress in others are, originally, primarily global and purely emotional, during the process of ontogenetic development they gradually become more specific and cognitive–emotional.

Research evidence of early empathy

The evidence for the first two of Hoffman's stages is based on anecdotal observation rather than on systematic research. In contrast, the third stage, characterized by the child's awareness of other people's feelings, has been researched extensively. Most of the research evidence comes from the study of children older than 3 years. However, evidence that a child younger than 2 years could be aware of an inner state of another child was given by Borke (1971) and Hoffman (1975, 1976).

The study of empathy in pre-school children was undertaken partly in order to challenge the Piagetian concept of child *egocentrism*. According to Piaget (1926) young children are individualistic, imprisoned in their own points of view, unaware of other people's perspectives. Egocentric thinking is characteristic of children of 2 to 7 years of age and children decentre only with the emergence of operational thought. Most of the evidence for egocentrism was derived by Piaget and his students from studies involving cognitive tasks and moral judgements. In such tasks it was found that children find it difficult to inform another person about something they know but the other does not know (Krauss and Glucksberg, 1969); that children are unable to make distinctions in judgements of events that were caused either by bad intentions or by bad luck (Piaget, 1932); that they find it difficult to predict what a doll could see from a position different from that of their own (Piaget and Inhelder, 1956; Flavell *et al.*, 1968), and so on.

In contrast to this research, a number of psychologists have been trying to demonstrate that egocentrism may be an artefact produced by the experimenter's demands of children that they perform tasks that are far beyond their cognitive abilities. If the task is simple enough it can be shown that even very young children are aware of the perspective of the other person.

Among the researchers who challenge Piaget's views on child egocentrism is Borke (1971, 1973, 1975). In her 1971 study, children of 3 to 8 years of age were presented with a series of short stories. The stories depicted situations which were supposed to elicit in the child one of four emotional states: happiness, sadness, fear or anger. Before presenting the stories the children's ability to identify these emotions was checked by showing them drawings of faces expressing these emotional states. Each story was accompanied by a picture of a blank face and the child was asked to complete the picture by selecting the face that best expressed the emotion of the child in the story. The second part of the experiment involved stories depicting peer interactions that made the story-child either happy, angry, afraid or sad. The study demonstrated that, by the age of 3 to 4 years, a child is capable of identifying, in others, various emotional states, in particular the *happy* ones, and so is aware of the perspective of another person. A variation of Borke's study was used by Light (1979) in his exploration of role-taking abilities in 4 year olds. The majority of the children were able to match *happy* faces to stories although some confusion occurred in their matching of sad, scared and cross faces to stories.

In the above studies, inspired by the cognitive developmental approach of Piaget, empathy is defined as *understanding* how the other person feels. In contrast, Feshbach and Roe (1968) in their study distinguished between social comprehension or *understanding* how the other person feels, and empathy or *feeling* how the other person feels. Forty-six children, aged 6–7 years, participated in Feshbach and Roe's (1968) study. The children were shown a series of three slide sequences projected on to a screen, each sequence being accompanied by a narrative describing what was going on in these slides. Immediately after viewing each sequence the child was asked 'How do you feel?' Twenty-seven of these children were then presented with the same series of slides again. This time, having viewed each sequence, the child was asked 'How does this child feel?', referring to the central actor in each slide story sequence. In asking the question 'How do you feel?' the authors intended to explore whether the child was affected by the feelings presumably experienced by the actor in the story. In other words, it was assumed that such a question tapped the child's empathy, i.e. his or her feeling as to how the story child feels. On the other hand, the question 'How does this child feel?' was intended to explore whether the child understood the kind of feeling experienced by the story child. In other words, it was intended to tap his or her social comprehension.

The actual material presented in the slide series was supposed to represent four affects: happiness, sadness, fear and anger. The narratives accompanying each slide sequence were short, matched for number of words over all affects. The use of affective words was avoided in order not to bias the child's response. An example of a sad story was the following:

Slide 1:   Here is a boy and his dog. This boy goes everywhere with his dog, but sometimes the dog tries to run away.
Slide 2   Here the dog is running away again.
Slide 3   This time the boy cannot find him, and he may be gone and lost forever.

Two different scorings, *specific* and *broad*, were used for both empathy and social comprehension. In order for a response to score as a specific empathic response, it had to have an appropriate verbal expression to match with the affective situation. For example, if the child was asked 'How do you feel?', having viewed the anger sequence, and answered 'not so good' his or her response was not scored as empathic, while the answer 'I feel mad' was considered empathic. In *broad* scoring, on the other hand, it was enough if the affective category and verbal response were of the same, either positive or negative, value. For example, if a child replied 'not so good' to an anger provoking sequence, his or her reply would score as empathic under the broad criterion, although under the former specific scoring criterion it was not acceptable.

These two different kinds of scoring were sensible for at least two reasons: first, children with low communicative competence (cf. Chapter 5) might, under specific scoring, fail to score simply because of their low ability to express themselves verbally rather than because of their inability to empathize.

Second, those children who appeared to be giving less discriminating specific empathic responses – and as the authors point out these were mainly the boys – might, in fact, have been unwilling to admit that they were experiencing fear and thus used a less 'unmanly' description such as 'not so good'.

Two important results have emerged from this study. First, the responses of the children to the slide sequences depicting actors of their own sex were much more empathic than those depicting the opposite sex. Second, the score for social comprehension was considerably higher than that for empathy with respect to all affects. Indeed, when the broader scoring was applied, 100 per cent accuracy in the social comprehension judgement was obtained. The authors concluded that 'social comprehension may be a necessary prerequisite for empathy' (Feshbach and Roe, 1968, p. 141). The studies of empathy, by Borke on the one hand, and by Feshbach and Roe on the other, have become the classic models in the study of the emergence of empathy in childhood (e.g. Shantz, 1975; Deutsch and Madle, 1975; Hoffman, 1978b).

Methodological issues in the study of child empathy

The main contribution of studies using either the Borke or the Feshbach and Roe methods is the demonstration that even a very young child has the ability both to recognize and to understand the feelings of other people and, in some instances, to report themselves as having feelings similar to those of a child in a story.

From the methodological point of view, however, the above studies have a number of shortcomings that should be considered before any further claims about empathy are accepted.

First, Feshbach and Roe's study of empathy is based on the unjustified assumption that human beings can change their emotions in step with rapid changes of stimulus. Thus, children are presented with a series of stories with happy, sad, fearful or anger-provoking contents. They are required to respond to each of these stories independently of each other. Moreover, consider the way Feshbach and Roe distinguished between empathy and social comprehension. The child was asked first: 'How do *you* feel?' and then 'How does the *child in the story* feel?' It is assumed that a child responds to these questions as if they were independent of each other. There is thus an underlying presupposition in Feshbach and Roe's approach that one's experiences of different emotional stimuli are independent of one another, so that emotional stimuli can be presented to the child as independent elements, and the child will respond to them as such. Indeed, it is the same kind of assumption that a physicist makes when measuring physical phenomena under different physical conditions. The physicist would, for example, measure the speed of a laser beam in different gases and would repeat such measurements under different physical conditions. A laser beam, however, does not have conscious experience and therefore the assumption that one measurement is independent of another is justified. Human beings, on the other hand, cannot be manipulated in the same way as a laser beam because they are self- and other-aware agents, who try to make sense of their experiences, not as separate stimuli but as meaningful wholes.

Second, the authors assume that the stimuli will evoke a *particular kind* of emotion in a child. The stimuli are constructed to elicit happiness, sadness, anger or fear in the experimental children. Since the researchers encode these constructed stimuli in a particular way, they expect the child to encode these stimuli in the same way. Having made such an assumption the authors code the child's responses to the stimuli as either 'correct' or 'incorrect'. But let us consider the following: having heard a short story about a boy who has lost his dog, a child might think about his or her own little puppy who has not been lost and says 'I am happy'. Such a response would, of course, qualify as non-empathic. But this does not mean that the child is unable to empathize, for the child might have encoded the stimuli differently from the experimenter's expectations. The child might have the ability to feel the happiness, sadness or anger of other people, but not display such emotions every time he or she encounters such emotions in others. We all, both children and adults, often encounter happiness, sadness, fear or anger in others, but probably none of us empathizes on every such occasion. First, human beings are not equipped to withstand all the sorrow in the world, and, second, we are not able to change our emotions as frequently as we encounter different people and perceive their emotions. One is selective as to the conditions and the extent to which one empathizes with other people. It would be a mistake to conclude, from the fact that a child does not empathize with some fictitious child, that he or she is unable to empathize with a real-life child. Feshbach and Roe found that children's empathy scores were lower than their social comprehension scores. In other words, although the children did understand the feelings of the story child, they did not feel what, supposedly, the story-child felt. However, this does not provide sufficient grounds for the authors' proposition that social comprehension is a prerequisite for empathy (Feshbach and Roe, 1968; Feshbach, 1978), for there could be various reasons for the children's low empathy scores.

Third, even if a child gives an answer which the experimenter records as a 'correct' response, the question still remains: did the child actually empathize with the story-child? In fact, although he or she has given a 'correct' answer, the child might, in reality, have empathized more with the experimenter than with the child in the story. The children might simply give answers which they considered *socially desirable*. They might answer in a particular way because they know that a certain situation requires a certain kind of response: the whole process of socialization is geared towards being sympathetic to those who suffer, towards helping people in need, and complying with the wishes of superiors. The children, therefore, might give responses which they considered to be correct and desirable in a given situation while not feeling anything at all for the story-child who has lost his dog.

Fourth, there is yet another problem with children's verbal responses to experimental stories. People often describe emotional situations by saying 'she was so overwhelmed by emotion that she could not speak'. Yet Feshbach and Roe assume that the more children empathize the better they can express their feelings explicitly, thus contradicting people's everyday experience. An additional problem is that children may obtain low empathy scores not because of lack of empathy but because of their low ability to express themselves verbally, that is, because they have low *communicative competence*. This problem applies to all studies in which the person's expressive ability might interfere with the assessment of another psychological characteristic. Feshbach and Roe (1968) partially realized this problem when they introduced different kinds of scoring for empathy and social comprehension.

Finally, we should consider the question of the *ecological validity* of the Feshbach and Roe experiment, i.e. the extent to which a lack of empathy with the story-child can tell us anything about the child's empathy in real life situations. The answer to this question is that we do not know. It is conceivable that a child showing no empathy or social comprehension when presented with laboratory situations might react empathically to emotions involving members of his or her family and other people who are important in his or her life; it may be that such a child might respond to *more intense* emotions even if these were emotions of strangers or of story-children. Feshbach (1978) is aware of these problems, saying that naturalistic and longitudinal research on empathy is specifically required so that the 'subtle and transient affective transactions that characterize family interaction' can be identified (ibid., p. 40).

In conclusion, laboratory experiments designed to study child empathy claim to have demonstrated that as children grow older they are more and more able to understand and feel the emotions of others. Unfortunately, however, the majority of these studies have been based on theoretical and methodological assumptions more suited to the exploration of the physical properties of a mechanism than the ever-changing characteristics of human beings. Therefore, the specific conclusions of such studies must be interpreted very cautiously. It is essential that future studies of empathy be based on the assumption that empathy is a process that unfolds in the person's life experience. Consequently, such studies should employ longitudinal and naturalistic studies, and ensure the ecological validity of such research (Iannotti, 1985).

The nature of empathy: cognition and affect

It was pointed out at the beginning of this chapter that there is little agreement among psychologists about the nature of empathy and how it should be defined. Let us now, first, discuss the reasons for this lack of agreement, and second, let us attempt to resolve the problem as to whether the nature of empathy is cognitive or affective.

Although empathy has been defined in a number of ways, two basic kinds of definition stand out very clearly: empathy defined as *cognitive response* to the emotions of others, and empathy defined as *affective response*. Examples of definitions of both kinds and the sort of research to which they have led will highlight the problematic nature of this issue.

With respect to empathy as *cognitive response*, Freud (1921), in his attempt to distinguish empathy from identification, said that empathy plays an important role in our understanding of 'what is inherently foreign to our ego in other people' (p. 108). According to Freud, then, while identification is based on one's emotional closeness with other people, one empathizes in order to understand those with whom one is not emotionally tuned. For Sarbin (1954), to empathize means to imagine oneself in the role of the other person. It is *as if* behaviour. Each person, in his or her life, enacts a number of roles (e.g. one and the same person is a mother, a wife, a teacher, a friend, and so on), and in order to take on these different roles one uses one's *as if* ability. Sarbin points out that this *as if* behaviour can be treated in the same way as an academic aptitude or a skill. An earlier scale for empathic ability, developed by Dymond (1949), is also based on the principle of *as if*. A person's ability to empathize is assessed by his or her ability to imagine himself or herself in different situations. Finally, the studies by Borke (1971, 1973, 1975), mentioned earlier in this chapter, are also based on the concept of empathy as a cognitive response, since the child participating in such studies is given tasks of *understanding* the feelings of others.

Those who claim that empathy is a purely *emotional response* point to a different kind of evidence than the cognitivists. Thus, Sullivan (1953) refers to emotional unity between the mother and her baby as an example of primitive affective empathy. Earlier in this chapter we pointed to an affective cry as a response to a distress cry in other infants. Escalona's observation of the disruption in feeding of the babies of imprisoned mothers also serves as an example of, presumably, pure affective empathy. Stotland (1969) and his students (Stotland *et al.*, 1971), too, define empathy as emotional reaction to another's emotion. And finally, Feshbach and Roe (1968), as we have already seen, have distinguished affective empathy from social understanding.

Although it may seem obvious, it is important to realize the effect of these different conceptualizations upon the research methods utilized in the study of empathy. Those who view empathy as a cognitive response devise experimental situations in which one is given the task either of assessing another person's feelings (Mood *et al.*, 1974; Deutsch, 1974; Chandler and Greenspan, 1972; Rothenberg, 1970; and others), or of imagining oneself in another person's situation and as acting on the basis of this *as if* situation (Dymond, 1949; Stotland, 1969). In contrast, those who conceive of empathy as an emotional response utilize physiological measures (Stotland, 1969; Krebs, 1975; Berger, 1962), verbal reports as to how the empathizer feels (Mehrabian and Epstein, 1972; Novak, 1974; Bryant, 1982), and facial expressions of the observers of emotional situations (Hamilton, 1973; Zuckerman *et al.*, 1976; Buck *et al.*, 1972). In other words, those who claim that empathy is a cognitive response explore empathy in situations in which a cognitive response is required, while those who claim that empathy is an affective response explore empathy in situations requiring an affective response. Consequently, the gulf between the cognitively and affectively orientated psychologists remains since there is no way in which the one could demonstrate to the other that his or her position was correct and the other's was wrong. The researchers' theoretical assumptions about the nature of empathy determine the kind of method they use to explore it, and consequently the evidence they obtain simply supports their own assumptions.

The inseparability of cognition and affect

Those who adopt the cognitive definition of empathy often refer to authorities such as Piaget or Mead. Since both Piaget and Mead emphasized the role of cognition, Piaget with respect to the transformation of the child's *egocentrism* into his or her ability to *decentre*, and Mead to the role of the other, there appears to be a shortcut to saying that, for these two researchers, empathy is a cognitive response (Feshbach, 1978; Deutsch and Madle, 1975). Such an interpretation of Piaget and Mead, however, is misconceived because, as a matter of fact, both for Piaget and for Mead, cognition is impossible without emotion and every emotion is at least partly cognitive. Thus, Piaget makes it clear, on a number of occasions, that 'the affective dynamics and cognitive structuring represent two inseparable aspects of all behaviour regardless of whether relationships to people or to things are involved' (Piaget, 1965, p. xiii; see also Inhelder and Piaget, 1958; Piaget, 1967). For Mead (1934), too, the abilities of the self to feel what the other person feels and to take the role of the other person, are two indissociable aspects of one and the same process.

In contrast to the Piagetian and Meadian view according to which cognition and affect are inseparable, such questions as 'is empathy a cognitive or an affective response?', and those methods which attempt to explore either the cognitive or the affective 'component', assume that a particular empathic response *could be either one or the other*, or at least that cognitive empathy could be separated from affective empathy. Such an assumption implies special compartments of the mind, one dealing with cognition, the other dealing with emotion: perhaps they can influence each other, but we should still conceptualize them as distinct entities and, indeed, explore them as distinct entities. This view, moreover, makes it possible to ask such questions as whether one of the components, cognition or affect, is a prerequisite for the other. For example, Feshbach (1978) concludes from her own studies that empathy and social comprehension are both closely interrelated and at the same time independent. According to her, social comprehension appears to be a prerequisite for empathy (ibid., p. 25). Staub (1978) makes a similar claim when he says that 'role-taking may be a pre-condition for but not a guarantee of experiencing empathy' (ibid., vol. 1, p. 44). However, the claim, that before people can emotionally empathize, they must already have the cognitive ability to take the role of the other, contradicts the developmental nature of empathy, a subject to which we shall now turn our attention.

We mentioned earlier (cf. Chapter 1) that the development of empathy can be compared to the development of an apple from a bud, to a blossom, and finally into the fully grown fruit, which can be conceptualized as a process in which the potentiality of a bud, in interaction with the environment, transforms into the actuality of a ripe apple. Let us now use this analogy to obtain a better understanding of the development of empathy. Empathy, too, should be conceptualized as a process in which certain potentialities, i.e. the precursors of empathy proper, in their interaction with the individual's environment, transform into the actuality of a mature empathic relationship. The research studies discussed earlier in this chapter have shown that the responses of a very young child to the emotional processes of other people are, originally, global and diffuse, and often involve the whole of the child's body. Only later does the child not only become able to *separate* his or her own emotions from those of other people, but also become *aware* of his or her own and of other people's emotions (see Chapter 4). The research thus suggests that the global and undifferentiated responses of the young child to the emotions of others undergo a gradual transformation into particular cognitive–affective, empathic processes, which become progressively more and more complex as the child matures. These suggestions, of course, await further theoretical and empirical exploration. One example of the conceptualization of empathy as a developmental cognitive–affective process that has already been discussed is Hoffman's (1978b) four stage model of empathy. This model is, in fact, based on the assumption that empathy is a process in which affective precursors of empathy, found in young infants, gradually transform from mainly affective processes into cognitive–affective ones as children grow older.

If one accepts a developmental conceptualization of empathy in which cognitive–affective processes become progressively more differentiated, questions about possible relationships between various levels of such cognitive–affective processes come to the fore. Is there, indeed, any relationship between the cry of an infant in response to another infant's cry, on the one hand, and the more advanced levels of responding to other people's emotions, such as the empathic relationship between a clinical psychologist engaging in a therapeutic dialogue with a person in a state of anxiety, on the other? What are the conditions under which cognition and affect can appear as two, virtually separate, components of the cognitive–affective process? For example, a person coolly speculating on another person's emotion, presumably, employs his or her cognitive ability to understand the other's emotions, without actually feeling what that person feels. It is, probably, such instances of an apparent divorce between cognition and affection that have led some psychologists to argue either that the two are independent or, indeed, that role-taking is a precursor of affective empathy.

The suppression of emotion

Bearing in mind that empathy is a developmental process involving gradual, cognitive–emotional, transformation of the lower stages of empathy into its higher and more complex stages, we can now argue that the cases of apparent divorce between cognition and emotion signify a *suppression* of emotion rather than its independence from cognition. Human emotions are, essentially, cognitive–emotional processes. To a considerable extent, people can control their emotions by volition, and can *reflect* upon their feelings. Reflexion, as we shall see in Chapter 4, is the ability to stand back and assess one's emotion, to evaluate it and to come to terms with it. In order to reflect upon one's emotion one must be able to observe it like any other object. Reflexion involves the distancing of emotion from cognition, and therefore may appear as a separation of cognition from emotion. Indeed, the conceptualization of an emotion may serve a therapeutic purpose. Psychotherapy aims, basically, to explain emotions cognitively, whether by bringing to light unconsciously suppressed emotions as Freudian psychotherapy does; or by explaining emotions as attributional therapy does; or by conceptualizing and acknowledging emotions as humanistic therapy does. Through these processes emotion becomes less harmful; in being conceptualized it becomes intelligible.

It follows from this discussion that there is one important difference between cognition and emotion. 'Too much' cognition, at least in the present western culture, does not seem to be harmful to an individual and there seems to be no limit as to how much new information one can accept (Neisser, 1976). 'Too much' emotional involvement, on the other hand, is often thought to be harmful and a number of mental disturbances are defined in terms of high emotionality and emotional imbalance. Such disturbances can be treated cognitively, as we have pointed out. In order to get better the patient must cognitively distance him- or herself from the oppressive emotions, reflect upon such emotions and manage them cognitively. A similar process applies to the therapist. Although, as Rogers (1961) says, the therapist, in order to help the patient, must *feel* what the patient feels, it is also important that the therapist distances him- or herself cognitively from the oppressive emotions. According to Rogers, the therapist must enter into the client's moment by moment experience and accurately understand the emotional states of the patient. The psychotherapeutic process is based on the ability of both participants, first, to feel the oppressive emotions, second, to distance themselves cognitively from them and to explain and acknowledge them, and third, to communicate these cognitively transformed emotions to each other. It is empathic understanding that has a therapeutic effect. As the patient communicates his or her emotional problems to the therapist and finds that the therapist's regard remains unchanged, the patient is on the way to recovery (Rogers, 1961). If it were not for this intellectualization of emotion, if all the therapist did was to identify him- or herself with the emotions of the client, no help would be possible for the patient because, quite probably, the impact of the oppressive emotion would be the same for the therapist as it was for the patient. Counselling and psychotherapy are possible only because human beings are capable of reflexion, and are able to distance themselves cognitively from their own emotions and from the emotions of others.

Another possible reason for supposing that cognition and emotion are independent of each other, is to be found in the fact that society, itself, socializes people so that they are able to control their emotions and suppress them. Ekman (1971) has described four kinds of techniques people use to control expressions of emotion: intensifying and deintensifying emotion, neutralizing emotion, and masking emotion by 'putting on a face' appropriate for another emotion (see also Chapter 6). Most social situations proceed smoothly because people know the *display rules* appropriate for various situations. Such display rules specify the behaviour appropriate to particular social roles in such situations as funerals, weddings, job interviews, or transient interaction regularities such as talking, listening, or leaving a room. Display rules are used instantaneously:

Rarely will a person pause to consider what display rule to follow; such a pause would indicate that there is no display rule, or that something is ambiguous in the situation and the person does not know which display rule to follow (Ekman, 1971, p. 226).

For example, in a number of western countries it is a rule that anger and sadness should be neutralized or masked in public places, and that 'the winner should deintensify expressions of happiness, while the loser should deintensify, neutralize, or mask with happiness the facial expression of sadness' (Ekman, 1971, p. 226).

Finally, there are considerable individual differences among people with respect to their ability to control and to mask emotion and in how they do this. Since the ability to distance oneself from one's emotion and to be rational are usually associated together in present western society, many people opt for presenting themselves as rational persons undisturbed by strong emotions. In addition, some life circumstances require, primarily, a cognitive involvement, such as learning situations.

On the other hand, some situations, such as intimate relation-ships, are primarily emotional. For example, if a little girl witnesses an accident involving her friend, her terrifying shriek in response to her friend's being hurt may appear to have virtually no cognitive component. Such a response appears to be spontaneous and emotional. On the other hand, there can be situations in which emotion is almost completely suppressed and empathy may appear to be entirely cognitive: thus, a person may speculate as to how to manipulate another person's feelings and even predict what emotions his or her deeds will arouse in the other.

As people grow up and mature they gain greater ability to understand and to feel the feelings of others. This does not mean, however, that they always use this ability because, as we shall see in the next section, there are a number of factors that modify a person's empathy in particular situations. For example, in a war-like situation, although one may be perfectly capable of understanding the position of the other, one's own circumstances are of paramount importance, and in attempting to justify one's own actions one may undervalue and misinter-pret the position of the other. Or, in order to alleviate one's own emotions and to facilitate one's own understanding of the other's position one may distort the other person's position or project one's own aggressive intentions on to one's opponent.

We can thus see that in all the situations mentioned so far the apparent separation of cognition from emotion arose from either the suppression of emotion or the conceptualization of emotion. At various stages of child development it may *appear* that one 'component' of empathy is a precursor of the other, namely, that the cognitive component is a precursor of emotional empathy. However, there is no psychological evidence that empathy consists of two independent components, one of which may sometimes be missing. In addition, since human development is neither unilinear nor continuous it may appear that one capacity is the precursor of the other because such a capacity may, at a particular stage of development, be more observable than another.

Empathy and related phenomena

Having explored the nature of empathy as a cognitive–emotional process, let us briefly consider some of the phenomena related to empathy such as *sympathy*, *projection*, and *identification*.

As Feshbach (1978) points out, in the psychological literature the notion of empathy has often been used interchangeably with the notion of sympathy. Indeed, Mead (1934) used the term 'sympathy' to refer to the process of feeling as the other person feels, that is, to what we now call empathy. So is empathy any different from sympathy and if so, in what respects? Feshbach (1978, p. 8) points to an important distinction between the two terms. While empathy implies a *match* between the feeling of the empathizer and the person with whom he or she empathizes, sympathy does not assume such a match. For example, if empathizers experience anger in another person, they themselves feel anger. Those who sympathize, on the other hand, when experiencing anger in another person, might feel sad rather than angry; that is, they might be sorry for the other person, rather than experience an emotion that would be an accurate match with the emotion of the victim. Sympathy, just like empathy, means taking the role of the other person, that is, understanding the other person's situation together with his or her emotion, but one's own emotions might be different if one is empathizing rather than sympathizing. However, one must not be too rigid in labelling emotions as either sympathy or empathy. We must not forget that both sympathy and empathy are processes and the one who is experiencing an emotion may be empathic at one moment and sympathetic at the next moment or even be empathic and sympathetic at one and the same time. Making a clear distinction between these two emotions in empirical research may be very difficult and, perhaps, non-productive. It is certainly not clear, in Feshbach and Roe's (1968) study, whether it was empathy or sympathy that the authors identified in the young children. Certainly, if we consider their broad coding of such responses of the children as 'I feel bad', such responses might refer both to empathy and sympathy, in contrast to their specific coding in which the child's response had to match accurately with the emotion of the story-child.

While sympathy implies a clear distinction between the sympathizer and the sympathized, *projection* and *identification* lack such a clear distinction. *Projection* refers to a process in which people attribute their own characteristics to someone else. It is the extending of oneself into another person rather than treating the other person as an independent individual.

Projection may arise through one's inability to make a clear distinction between oneself and the other person because of immaturity, as we have seen, for example, in the case of a child in Hoffman's stage one in the development of empathy. Projection, therefore, can also be conceived of as a stage in the development of empathy. In addition, projection may arise through the Ego's defences, as Anna Freud (1937) explained. Unconsciously, one may not wish to attribute certain characteristics to oneself because they are undesirable, and therefore one projects these characteristics on to another person. In his analysis of distorted perception of the self and of others, Ichheiser (1950) makes a conceptual distinction between two types of false social perception: *projection* and *mote-beam mechanism*. By projection Ichheiser means attributing certain characteristics, quite falsely, to other people. However, while the 'others' in question actually do not have the attributed characteristics, the attributor himself or herself does. For example, an angry person may project his or her own anger on to others who actually are not angry. The second type of false perception, mote-beam mechanism, means *perceiving* certain characteristics in others, but not in oneself. In this case the other person does actually possess the characteristics attributed to him or her by the perceiver; but so also does the perceiver. As Ichheiser points out, we often do not have insight into our own weaknesses, although we perceive them, quite clearly, in others. For example, we perceive others as prejudiced, aggressive or unfriendly, but we do not recognize the very same traits in ourselves.

Identification, in contrast to projection, is a conscious or subconscious relationship of regard and admiration for another person, in which the admirer may affectively imitate the model. For example, a girl may identify with her mother, a boy with his older brother, members of a political party with their party, and a member of a nation with that nation. We can say that in child development identification is very important for the emergence of a mature form of empathy: since identification is affective imitation, it is, in a sense, practising the role of the other person. For example, when a girl affectively identifies with her mother in play, she is practising the role of a mother.

Modifiers of empathy

It has been claimed already that as children grow older, their ability both to understand other people and to feel the feelings of other people increases, and the research data available on the subject supports this claim. The study by Feshbach and Roe (1968) shows a significant increase in the ability to empathize between the age groups 4–5 and 6–7: similar findings have been reported by others (Feshbach, 1978; Marcus *et al.*, 1979; Bryant, 1982).

In spite of these findings showing a positive correlation between age and ability to empathize, one has to bear in mind that empathy, just like any other process, does not occur in a vacuum but is modified by other processes and social pressures imposed upon the individual in the process of socialization. Any research exploring the relationship between empathy and other variables such as age, sex, prosocial behaviour, aggression and so on, should take the modifying factors and processes into consideration. In this section we shall consider some of the modifiers of empathy.

First, and as already pointed out, in the process of socialization one learns to control emotions by using display rules. Display rules are mostly directed towards neutralizing and masking emotion rather than towards presenting it.

Second, as children grow older they not only acquire other-awareness but also self-awareness. A feeling for others is often in opposition with a feeling for the self. The relationship between empathy and selfishness is presumably different at various stages of child development, though such relationships still await exploration.

Third, the ability to empathize may be modified by one's life experience, and by one's own, and other people's suffering. For example, people who have someone handicapped in their family may be more empathic than those who have not had such an experience. Indeed, Shakespeare (1975) reports a way of teaching non-handicapped children to empathize with the disabled. The older school children each spent a day either being blindfolded or confined to a wheelchair while otherwise continuing their normal school life. As a result of such an experience they developed a much greater understanding of how a chronically handicapped person may feel.

Continuing the same line of argument, there is considerable research evidence that people empathize more with those who are similar to themselves. Thus, it has been shown that girls empathize more with the girls in experimental stories than with the story-boys and that boys empathize more with story-boys than story-girls (Feshbach and Roe, 1968). Klein (1971) found that black girls empathized more with black girls while white girls empathized more with white girls. Krebs (1975), in his study of the relationship between empathy and altruism, found that his subjects empathized more if they thought the person was similar to themselves in personality than if they were told that the person was dissimilar in personality. Hoffman (1978b) points out that the findings of research into the relationship between empathy and the similarity of observer and observed, reflect the tenets of evolutionary theory with respect to the survival of the species. Thus, on the basis of evolutionary theory one would expect more empathy and pro-social behaviour among members of the same species than among members from different species. The question, though, is whether the findings on the effect of similarity in empathy amount to more than just a convenient metaphor. One could say just as easily that people empathize more with those who are similar to them because it is easier for them to take the role of others who are like them: if something bad can happen to someone who is like you it can also happen to you. In this case, empathizing with those who are similar to the empathizer might reflect an effort for personal survival rather than for the survival of the species.

The problems of empirical research in this field are: what counts as similarity? How can similarity be measured? For example, one might assume that similarity with respect to age would prove important, and that a child would empathize more with another child than with an adult. However, a study by Shaw (1979) demonstrated that such an expectation is a gross simplification. Young children, in the process of socialization, not only learn to empathize with others but also acquire values and moral codes, they learn to judge responsibility and other characteristics in people, and their relationships with others are partly determined by all these factors and not just by similarity. Thus, if a child witnesses an act in which an adult is hurt because the culprit, another child, was careless or had bad intentions, the observing child, although supposedly similar to the culprit, might empathize more with the adult who, with respect to age, is clearly dissimilar.

Perceived similarity, moreover, is only relative. For example, in one context the inhabitants of an island may empathize with each other more than with the inhabitants of the mainland. In another context, however, the members of a particular political party on the island may empathize more with the member of the same political party on the mainland than with their neighbours on the island.

With respect to sex as a modifying factor in empathy, as Hoffman (1978b) pointed out, females, according to the sex-role stereotype, are more emotional, and therefore more empathic, than males. In his own studies Hoffman found that, in every single case, females obtained a higher score on empathy than did males. Similarly, studies with preschool children using the Feshbach and Roe (1968) test all found that, on the whole, girls empathized more than boys.

Summary

Empathy is a cognitive–affective response of the individual to the emotions and to emotion provoking situations of other people. It involves both feeling and understanding how the other person feels in particular situations. The early expressions of empathy in child development are global, often involving the whole of the child's body. At this stage there is no evidence that the child differentiates between him- or herself and the other person. As the child grows older, evidence begins to emerge pointing to the child's awareness of his or her feelings as being different from those of other people.

Empathy is a cognitive–affective process that develops throughout the whole of an individual's life. Under some conditions, however, the emotional aspect of this process can be suppressed, either partly or almost completely. Thus the process appears to be decomposable into two components: the cognitive and the emotional. Various modifiers of empathy, for example display rules, perceived similarity, awareness of one's own self, and the individual's life experience, may neutralize or, on the other hand, amplify the expression of empathy.

3 Awareness of human agency

Events that are perceived as having a physical cause often have a different psychological impact than those perceived as caused by human beings. The difference between these two kinds of event in their psychological impact is due to the fact that physical causality is usually viewed as deterministic, and therefore more or less inevitable. Events that causally involve human beings, on the other hand, are perceived as intentional or as resulting from some intentional activity, and therefore as optional. If events occur because of human involvement, various questions arise for the perceiver. For example, why the others did what they did, what their motives and intentions were, what they were trying to achieve, whether they were trying to benefit or harm someone, and so on. Events may, of course, be viewed as interactions between environmental causes and human actions, but here again the question of the human contribution to the event arises.

In this chapter we shall explore some of the factors that are important in people's awareness of themselves and of others as agents. We shall first discuss the ways naive perceivers analyse action. Second, we shall be concerned with some developmental aspects of the awareness of agency, and with the self's and with the other person's point of view in their awareness of action. Finally, some questions will be raised about the meanings of words with respect to the analysis of action.

People as perceivers and as perceived

There are both similarities and differences in the ways human beings are aware of physical objects and of people. Concerning the similarities, both physical objects and people are entities affecting our senses, occupying space, having particular physical properties, and so on. Nevertheless, there are at least two fundamental differences in the ways human beings are aware of physical objects and of people. First, objects are

67

perceived as manipulanda, i.e. they can be picked up and dropped again, destroyed, made use of, decomposed into their parts and turned into something different. In contrast, people are perceived as agents trying to control and predict events, and to alter their environment (Heider,1958). Second, the perception of physical objects is a *one-way flow*, in the sense that people are aware of physical objects but objects are not thought to be aware of people. The perception of people, on the other hand, is a *two-way flow*. The perceiver is not only aware of the other person, but he or she is also aware of the awareness of the other person directed towards the perceiver himself or herself. Being mutually aware of each other, the perceivers interact with each other.

In the process of perception as mutual interaction, people can manifest two of their basic characteristics. First, they have the power to recognize or confirm each other *as* human beings rather than just as physical objects. Second, in the process of interaction in general, and of social perception in particular, they seek recognition or confirmation of themselves by others. Among psychologists, it was probably James (1890, p. 293) who first pointed to the importance for people of being recognized by others as human beings. He remarked that 'no more fiendish punishment could be devised, were such a thing physically possible, than that one should be turned loose in society and remain absolutely unnoticed by all the members thereof'. Recognition of one person by the other is realized in every single act of interpersonal perception. We shall briefly consider the process of recognition, first from the point of view of the perceiver and then from the point of view of the perceived.

It is the privilege of the perceiver that he or she has the power to indicate to the other person, whether by a look, a smile, a word, or a gesture, that he or she invites the other to participate in interaction. Alternatively, the perceiver may indicate that he or she does not wish to enter into interaction: no gesture may be made, or, if made, it is such as to discourage the other from interaction. Moreover, the perceiver also has the power to look at the other just as he or she wishes, such as to stare at the other, to look on while the other, for instance in a wheelchair, struggles with a heavy door. Or the perceiver can look closely at the features of a sufferer from Down's syndrome totally ignoring the other's obvious embarrassment. The perceiver can, therefore, through perception, invade the other's privacy, as Heider (1958) made clear. In sum, the perceiver has the power either to enter into or refrain from interaction with the other by making a gesture, or may pass by another without any gesture as if the other did not exist.

People are not, however, divided into perceivers and perceived, but every human being is both perceiver and perceived, often at the same time. In the role of perceiver one is in control of one's visual field, deciding for oneself the focus of one's attention. In the role of the perceived, in contrast, one is at the mercy of others, being now oneself the object of the others' senses and cognition. As the perceived, one is awaiting an invitation to participate in interaction; as the perceived one may remain ignored, indeed, invisible, even if the perceiver stares into his or her face. Moscovici (1984) quotes the following passage from a black writer, illustrating this point:

I am an invisible man. No, I am not a spook like those who haunted Edgar Allan Poe; nor am I one of your Hollywood-movie ectoplasms. I am a man of substance, of flesh and bones, fibre and liquids – and I might even be said to possess a mind. I am invisible, understand, simply because people refuse to see me. Like the 'bodiless' head you see sometimes in circus sideshows, it is as though I have been surrounded by mirrors of hard, distorting glass. When they approach me they see only my surroundings, themselves, or figments of their imagination – indeed anything except me (Ellison,1965, p. 7, quoted by Moscovici, 1984, p. 4).

In cases like this the perceiver may genuinely not see the other person as a human being, having adopted a prejudice against minority groups based on colour or skin, race, or other visible and invisible criteria. As Goffman (1968) maintained, people with such a *stigma* are believed to be *not quite human*. In the same vein, the belief that people with a stigma, like those with a mental handicap, 'do not have the same feelings as we have' still prevails even among those who care for them. It is through such 'genuine ignorance' that stigma affects the dynamics of interpersonal interaction and thwarts the life hopes of the one perceived as stigmatized.

Watzlawick *et al.* (1967) have distinguished three basic kinds of response of one person to the other in interpersonal interaction: confirmation, rejection and disconfirmation. In normal interpersonal interaction people confirm each other at least to some degree by responding to others as agents. They listen, nod, comment, interrupt and look at each other. Watzlawick *et al.* say that mutual confirmation is likely to be the greatest single factor contributing to personal development and a stable self-concept. It is not just exchange of information that human beings need for their development, for it is, above all, through communication with others that self-awareness, in mutual relationship with other-awareness, develops. The second possible response of one participant towards the other is rejection. Rejection does not necessarily mean outright negation of the other's definition of himself. Since, as Watzlawick *et al.* say, rejection presupposes at least some recognition of what is being rejected, it assumes, to some degree, the agency of the other person. For example, parents may reject a child's request, but since the request is rejected it is, at least partly, taken seriously because it has been responded to. Indeed, rejection can sometimes be constructive. Rejection of a patient's self-definition by a therapist may lead to the patient's redefinition of his or her self-concept, and thus to an improvement in the patient's health. Rejection can also be destructive. It may mean depriving others of their agency, that is, of their ability to influence their environment and to do things for themselves, by saying to them 'you cannot' or 'you must not'. For example, children, and mentally and physically handicapped people, due to over-protection by their parents, may find themselves in situations of not being allowed to do certain things, although fully able to do them. The third kind of response of one participant in interaction towards the other is disconfirmation or non-recognition. While rejection can be expressed as 'you are wrong', Watzlawick *et al.* point out that disconfirmation actually means 'you do not exist'. While rejection can be an attempt to deprive the other person of agency, disconfirmation actually denies the other person the reality of agency, indeed, of existence as a human being.

Non-recognition in interpersonal interaction can be displayed in a variety of ways, for example:

1   The listener does not respond to the speaker. Questions are left unanswered, utterances are not commented upon, there is even no recognition that a message has been sent.

2   A person may be excluded from interaction. He or she is not looked at, not asked questions or involved in any way. His or her actions are not acknowledged in either a positive or a negative way.

3   Comment on the speaker's utterance may be irrelevant or tangential. Laing (1961) gives an example of a boy of five years running to his mother and holding a big fat worm and asking her

to look at it. The mother replied: 'You are filthy, go and wash your hands.' By giving this response she disconfirmed the message since she did not respond in any way to the child's request. She could have rejected the message by saying, for example, 'I do not like worms' which would mean that the message was listened to. Instead, the message was treated as not worthy of response.

4   The message may be deliberately interpreted in a sense which was not intended. For example, metaphors may be taken literally or a message may be interpreted metaphorically. Jokes and wit may be part of such devices.

It is thus obvious that social perception can follow different patterns. In many situations, people treat each other *as* human beings and at least to some degree recognize each other's agency. In some situations, however, they treat each other in the same way that they treat physical objects, not attending to each other's agency. The perceiver simply ignores the fact that the perceived is also a perceiver because for his or her purpose the fact is irrelevant. In such cases, the two-way flow of mutual exchanges characterizing *social perception* is substituted by a one-way flow from one of the perceivers to the other, just as in the case of perception of physical objects.

Awareness of actions and intentions

Under normal circumstances people are aware of each other as agents whose actions are guided and organized by intentions to achieve particular goals. Perception of others as agents is so natural to people that they quite automatically perceive human behaviour in terms of meaningful actions rather than as sheer movements of bodies and their parts.

In a series of demonstrations, From (1971) showed moving pictures of short behaviour sequences to experimental subjects. Such sequences involved a man sitting and writing, lighting his pipe, smoking a pipe, putting his coat on and then sitting and writing again. The subjects were asked 'to look at the film and to take an interest in what the acting person does and why he does it' (From, 1971, p. 86). The results were not at all surprising. Subjects had no difficulty in describing the behaviour of the man in terms of purposeful actions and intentions, and readily provided reasons for his actions. The subjects demonstrated that an action such as a man lighting his pipe does not need any further explanation: it is obvious that if a man is to have a smoke he must light his pipe. Similarly, the action involving the man writing was perceived as an ordinary action which did not need any special reason (From, ibid., p. 91). In general, people view themselves and others as performing actions, and not just as mechanisms producing successions of physical events. If a man wants to light his pipe, the observer does not see his hand first moving down his thigh, then up under the bottom of his jacket, then finally down again into his pocket where it grasps a box of matches. The observer simply sees him putting his hand into his pocket to get his matches (From, 1971, p. 5).

However, From hardly needed to perform a series of apparently trivial experiments in order to arrive at such a simple point. The purpose of his experiments was to bring home the fact that the movements people perform are perceived as meaningful actions. We perceive directly people's intentions and actions, their drinking, smoking a pipe, caressing or slapping another. Only when, for some reason, an action is experienced as ambiguous, do we have to decide whether it was caressing *or* slapping that we saw. From has shown, moreover, that actions are not perceived as sequences of *isolated* happenings but as meaningful wholes. If a perceiver is provided with incomplete information, he or she fills in the gaps using his or her past experience and knowledge to impute meaning to what he or she perceives.

The fact that people search for meaning and fill in gaps if not enough cues have been provided, has been demonstrated forcefully by the experiment of Heider and Simmel (1944). These researchers designed a cartoon film in which three geometrical figures, such as a large triangle, a small triangle and a disc, were moving in various directions and at various speeds in a rectangular enclosure, with a movable section in the upper right-hand corner. The experimental subjects were given the instruction to 'write down what happens in the picture'. Almost invariably the experimental subjects perceived animated beings chasing one another, rather than just two triangles and a circle changing their positions in time and space (see Figure 2). Most of the subjects perceived the changing positions of the geometrical figures as purposeful actions, in most cases of people, in two cases of birds. Only one subject out of twenty described the film in geometrical terms. An example of an average kind of story went like this:

a man planned to meet a girl but the girl came along with someone

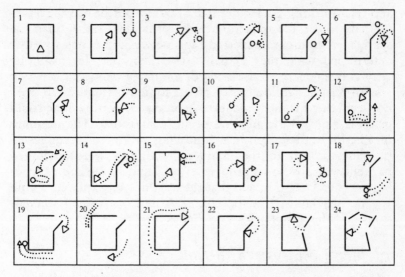

Figure 2 Outline of story in a picture film. Broken lines indicate path of movement
Source: Heider, F. (1967), *American Psychologist*, 22.

else. After some mutual persuasion a fight started between the two, while the girl, worried, raced in to the far corner of the room. The first man made approaches to the girl who eventually succeeded in getting out of the room and looked for the help of the second man. They ran around the room chased by the first man. Finally they escaped him while the first man got back into the room and could not get out since the door had locked itself. So he got into a rage and broke one wall after another.

In a variation of this experiment subjects were asked the following question: What kind of person is the big triangle? 97 per cent of the thirty-five subjects described the 'person' using the following adjectives: aggressive, war-like, quarrelsome, troublesome, mean, ugly, bully, villain, taking advantage of his size, picking on smaller people, dominating, power-loving, possessive.

It was not simply the changing positions of the geometrical figures with respect to each other that instigated experimental subjects to tell stories about animated beings. Rather, they actually *perceived meaningful actions* of chasing, fighting and hating. They interpreted a potentially ambiguous experimental situation according to their knowledge of social interactions and relationships. As Heider (1958) points out, it was the *meanings* that the subjects attributed to situations, rather than the spatial and temporal relationships between the objects, that determined what they actually saw. Consider, for example, why subjects perceived *chasing* of animated beings rather than just mechanical following of two geometrical figures. It does not seem that the movements of geometrical figures alone could provide clues to the answers of such questions. The meaning of 'chasing' rather than just 'following' seems to be suggested by the fact that to the geometrical figures were attributed particular dispositional properties (see later, p. 75) and psychological characteristics, and that their actions were placed within a particular environmental context based on societal conventions and the individual's knowledge and experience.

Heider's analysis of action

Having made the point that people perceive themselves and others as agents, we shall now explore the basic constituents of people's naive conception of action which they use in cognizing whether someone is trying to, wants to, or is unable to do something. Heider was concerned with ordinary people's awareness of their own and of others' actions rather than with armchair philosophizing, and consequently called this approach a naive analysis of action. In order to explore this issue, consider first the example Heider (1958) gives of the following event: a person is sitting in a boat lying on the surface of a lake, and moving the oars with a rowing action. Different people watching this person in a boat may see different things:

> He is *trying* to row the boat across the lake
> He *can* (i.e. he has the power and ability to) row the boat across the lake
> He *wants* to row the boat across the lake
> *It is difficult* to row the boat across the lake
> *Today is a good opportunity* for him to row the boat across the lake
> *It is sheer luck* that he succeeded in rowing the boat across the lake

The italicized words in the above sentences, i.e. *trying, can, wants, it is difficult, today is a good opportunity*, and *it is sheer luck*, refer either to the person involved in the action in question, or to the environment relevant to the event. Thus, *trying, can*, and *wants* all refer to the person moving the oars while *it is difficult, today is a good opportunity*, and *it is sheer luck*, all refer to the environment. Moreover, some of the words or phrases refer to relatively stable characteristics of the human agent or the environment such as *can* or *it is difficult*. Others refer to changeable characteristics of the acting person, e.g. *trying, wants*, or of the environment, e.g. *today is a good opportunity*, and *it is sheer luck*. In sum, Heider's example draws attention to two important dichotomies in people's everyday analysis of action: stability/variability, and person/environment.

Stability/variability

In order to make sense of the sheer amount of information impinging upon the senses and cognition, people search for the relatively unchanging characteristics in their environments that make the world more or less predictable. Such relatively unchanging characteristics of phenomena that display themselves whenever suitable conditions obtain, are known as *dispositional properties*. For example, brittleness, a dispositional property, is displayed by a sheet of glass when it fractures under a sharp blow; solubility, another dispositional property, is displayed when sugar or salt is stirred in water, and so on.

With respect to the awareness of other people's actions, dispositional properties are more or less permanent characteristics of a person, such as personality traits, abilities and attitudes. For example, a person is perceived as intelligent if he or she is able to cope with given tasks better than the majority of those with whom the perceiver compares that person. A person is perceived as helpful if in situations characterized by the needs of others he or she offers a hand more than others do in similar situations, and so on. While dispositionality in physical objects is subject to natural laws, dispositionality in a person is dependent on the meaning attributed to his or her characteristics by the perceiver. While the solubility of salt or sugar displays itself in more or less the same way whenever in contact with water, friendliness, a dispositional characteristic of human beings, can be conveyed in a number of ways depending on the personal and situational factors that obtain at the time.

Person/environment

Although in Heider's example of a person in a boat the outcome of the event is attributed either to the person or to the environment, the attributions one makes about actions, events, and their consequences are usually more complex. Quite commonly, the outcome of an event is perceived as an interaction of personal and environmental forces, for example:

> She succeeded because she tried hard and the task was not too difficult.
> He failed because he was not motivated to work for the examination and it happened to be quite difficult.

These examples show that the person's success depends both on an *effective personal force* and an *effective environmental force* (Heider, 1958). The effective personal force itself is the result of the person's ability (CAN) and effort or motivation (TRY). CAN is mainly a dispositional property concerning the person's ability to control his or her environment. TRY has two components: *intention*, organizing the direction of action, and *exertion*, referring to how hard the person tries. Ability and motivation have different statuses in the analysis of action. If a person tries but cannot do what was expected, then it is not considered to be his or her fault. On the other hand, if the person can but does not try, the responsibility is on him or her. Thus, people are held responsible for their motivation, i.e. intention and exertion, but not for their abilities. Accordingly, intention is the essential concept in the naive analysis of action.

So when does one say that a person is *responsible* for his or her action? Analysing the concept of responsibility, Heider shows that there are at least five different levels of meaning that people attach to the word 'responsibility'. At one level people attribute responsibility globally to the person for everything with which he or she is considered to be connected. For example, the perceiver may be prejudiced against the perceived on the basis of the latter being a member of a nation that had started a war although the perceived might have had nothing to do with the affair. In this case, being a member of a nation that had started a war is enough for being attributed with responsibility for it. At another level the perceived may be held responsible for the outcome of his or her action although the outcome was not intended or even foreseeable. For example, the perceived may be blamed for the accidental death of another person in a car crash which, given the circumstances, he or she could not have prevented. At still another level responsibility is attributed to a person only for the after-effects of his or her action. Although such after-effects may not in any way have been intended or desired, responsibility is attributed to the person for his or her negligence, ruthlessness, and so on. Fourth, a person is held responsible only for outcomes that were intended and planned beforehand. If the person did not intend the particular outcome, he or she is not held responsible for it. Finally, a person may be held responsible only partly or not at all for what he or she intended if the circumstances were believed to have been such as to force him or her to act in a particular way. For example, a person may intentionally hurt someone in self-defence and be excused for his or her act. In general, Heider's five levels of the concept of responsibility represent a continuum on which the relative contribution of the environmental forces towards the outcome of an action increases as one progresses from level one to level five, while the contribution of the individual decreases: the greater the contribution attributed to the environment, the less responsible the person is held to be (Heider, 1958, p. 113).

The above analysis, in terms of stability/variability and person/environment, however, represents only the *basic* constituents of an action, as was pointed out earlier in this section. What is just as important as these basic constituents that are used to *cognize* people's involvement in an event is the *emotional* impact that every action has on the agent and on the others. For example, actions are beneficial or harmful to agents and others, whether individuals or groups. Therefore, the analysis of action in terms of the basic constituents of stability/variability and of person/environment does not represent a full account, although it has been by far the most influential in generating research (Kelley, 1967; Jones and Davis, 1965; Jones and Nisbett, 1972; Kelley and Michela, 1980). Heider himself maintained that underlying the basic constituents of action are affects, liking, power and status relationships, and the obligations people have towards each other. These social psychological factors have yet to become a meaningful part of research into human action.

Development of awareness of action

Investigation of the child's awareness of agency has developed within different research traditions, including studies of the perception of the self and of others, the development of moral judgement, and the attribution of responsibility. We shall attempt to draw these different traditions together following Heider's two dichotomies in his analysis of action, stability/variability, and person/environment.

The child's awareness of stability and variability in the analysis of action

Psychological research has been concerned with the question as to whether young children are aware of relatively stable, i.e. of dispositional characteristics of people such as friendliness, helpfulness, and so on. In order to explore this issue, Livesley and Bromley (1973) carried out studies with 320 children 7–15 years old. The children were required to write down their free descriptions of eight people they knew: four people they liked and four people they disliked, in each case a man, a woman, a boy and a girl. These descriptions were then content analysed and the authors identified two main kinds of statement, a *central* and a *peripheral*. Central statements referred to psychological qualities of people and personality traits, dispositional characteristics, general habits, motives and attitudes. Peripheral statements referred to non-psychological qualities such as the physical characteristics of a person and his or her environment, the appearance, age, sex, possessions, social roles, likes and dislikes of the person in question, and to general information about his or her life and past history. The study has shown that the number and proportions of central descriptions increase with the child's age. Moreover, children of all age groups and of both sexes described males more in terms of dispositional characteristics, friendliness, helpfulness, and so on, than they did females. Children were described more in terms of dispositional characteristics than adults. The greatest increase in the number of categories that children used to describe others occurred between the ages of 7 and 8 years. This fact led the authors to conclude that the age 7–8 years is critical in the development of conceptual competence in person perception. Describing people in terms of peripheral characteristics probably means that perceivers are unable to discern the diverse factors involved in people's actions and environmental effects. Prediction of the behaviour of others, based on peripheral, i.e. non-psychological characteristics, is not likely to be adequate for the satisfactory development of interpersonal relationships. Central statements, on the other hand, provide perceivers with predictive cues and thus enable them to adjust to other people, and to their characteristics, much more efficiently. A study of descriptions of others made by popular and unpopular children 8–10 years old, carried out by Aydin (1976), supported Livesley and Bromley's suggestions. Aydin has shown that unpopular children make fewer psychological descriptions of others than popular children.

A similar study of children's free descriptions was carried out by Peevers and Secord (1973). In this study, eighty children, ranging from pre-school to college ages, were asked to describe, in their own words, three peers they liked and one they disliked. Descriptions were then categorized, and evaluated on each of four dimensions. The first of these dimensions was *descriptiveness*, i.e. the ability to differentiate the other person from his or her environment. For example, at the most primitive level the child described the other only in terms of his or her environment, making statements such as 'John has a lot of toys' or 'she lives in a big house'. At a more advanced level the child described his or her peer in terms of temporary differentiating characteristics, e.g. 'John is confused right now'. At the most advanced level, descriptiveness represented the child's ability to express dispositional characteristics, e.g. 'John is talkative'. The second dimension was *personal involvement*, which included descriptions in which the perceived related himself or herself to other people. Third, *evaluative consistency* referred to the extent to which the perceiver expressed desirable qualities in people he or she liked, and undesirable qualities in those he or she disliked. This dimension enabled the researchers to explore the child's ability to appreciate that the liked and the disliked both have positive and negative characteristics. Finally, *depth* referred to the extent to which personal characteristics were recognized as being dependent upon both situational circumstances and on the internal states of a person. For example, the child might offer an explanation for the person's characteristic, such as 'because he is black he is very defensive'. The authors found that as children grew older they used more dispositional statements in the dimensions of both descriptiveness and depth; they used fewer egocentric statements in the dimension of personal involvement, and they were able to perceive others as having both positive and negative characteristics at the same time.

In conclusion, studies of free descriptions of others all confirm that as children grow older they use more psychological characteristics in describing others, just as they use psychological characteristics to describe themselves (see also Chapter 4). However, a word of caution is necessary: at least two issues must be raised. First, in studies of free descriptions, failure of a child to describe others in terms of dispositional characteristics is not necessarily evidence that the child is unaware of such characteristics. It could be that the child, while interacting with others, is well aware of the psychological characteristics of others and uses such awareness effectively in natural situations. However, to verbalize such awareness may require additional conceptual and language skills which the child may not yet have developed. Second, it is possible that the instruction 'say what the person is like' may be interpreted differently by younger and older children. Shantz (1975) suggests that younger children may interpret the instruction as a *referential* task demanding an identification of the person in question, such as where the person lives, what the person does or what the person possesses. Bearing in mind these problems it is important that researchers explore children's awareness of dispositional characteristics using other means in addition to verbal descriptions.

The child's awareness of personal and environmental factors in the analysis of action

The development of the child's ability to consider intentions in evaluating the actions of others has been explored within two traditions: Piagetian focusing on moral judgement, and Heiderian focusing on attribution processes in the analysis of action.

Piaget (1932) suggested that the child's development of moral judgement is based on the judgemental shift from objective to subjective responsibility occurring at the age of about 7–9 years. At the age of objective responsibility the child blames others on the basis of what they did rather than on the basis of what they intended to do, or what their motives were for doing something. The child at the stage of subjective responsibility, on the other hand, takes into consideration intentions and motives when evaluating actions. The following two stories from Piaget's research exemplify the point:

1 There was once a little girl who was called Marie. She wanted to give her mother a nice surprise and make a piece of sewing

for her. But she didn't know how to use the scissors properly and cut a big hole in her dress.

2   A little girl called Margaret took her mother's scissors one day when her mother was out. She played with them for a bit. Then as she didn't know how to use them properly she made a little hole in her dress.

When younger children, under the age of 7 years, were asked which of the two girls was naughtier, they said that they thought it was Marie because she made more damage than Margaret. In other words, younger children, under the age of 7 years, attribute responsibility to others on the basis of *outcome* rather than *intention* or *bad luck*. Piaget did not argue that a young child is totally unaware of intentions in others. Rather, he suggested that a child's cognitive limitations coupled with his or her respect for adult authority and adult justice explain children's responses to such moral dilemmas. A young child evaluates actions with respect to whether they please or annoy adults, and whether they lead to punishment or praise. Following Piaget's ideas on the development of morality, research on the child's moral development has been prolific (see, for example, Karniol, 1978).

In the last twenty years, however, the development of the child's perception of intentions has also been explored within the tradition of attribution research, derived from Heider's (1958) five levels of attribution of responsibility mentioned above. Heider himself pointed out that his second and fourth levels were, in fact, what Piaget called *objective* and *subjective* responsibility, respectively. However, Heider has not, as far as I am aware, suggested that children, in their ontogenetic development, progress from level one to level five. Indeed, it is quite clear from Heider's examples that the attribution of responsibility at the five different levels refers to *adults*. Moreover, Heider discusses the factors involved in people's analysis of action in the context of his exploration of interpersonal relationships, alongside motivation, emotion, belonging, social control and the awareness of the person's life space. In contrast, research into attribution of intentions in children, while appealing to Heider, has been carried out in a purely cognitive framework resembling the Piagetian tradition in this respect, rather than in a broadly based social psychological tradition in the spirit of Heider.

Work on attribution of intentions in children was probably

initiated by Shaw and Sulzer (1964) who set out to test empirically Heider's levels of attribution of responsibility as stages in child development, although, as pointed out, there is no evidence in Heider's writing that he actually considered them as such. The authors devised a series of short stories with the central character, a boy called Perry, acting in all of them. The events told in the stories were described with only the minimum information for the story to be categorized by the researcher at one of Heider's five levels. The levels of responsibility were given the following names: global association, extended commission, careless commission, purposive commission, and justified commission. Twenty stories were constructed, four at each level, two with a positive and two with a negative outcome. They were presented to children 6–9 years old, and to adult college students, aged 19–38 years. Here are some examples of the experimental stories:

1 *Level 1, global association, negative outcome*: A boy hit another child with Perry's toy gun. Is Perry responsible for the child being hit?
2 *Level 2, extended commission, positive outcome*: When Perry rang the doorbell it made the baby drop a sharp knife he had picked up when his mother wasn't looking. Is Perry responsible for the baby dropping the knife?
3 *Level 4, purposive commission, negative outcome*: Perry opened the door so that the wind blew the children's papers all over the room. Is Perry responsible for the scattered papers?

Just as they predicted, the authors found that children, on the whole, attributed more responsibility than adults, in particular at the levels of global association and extended commission. Second, as they predicted, they found that attribution of responsibility increased from level one to level four and dropped back at level five, justified commission. Moreover, both children and adults were more likely to attribute responsibility to the actor if the outcome of the described event was negative rather than positive. As Shaw and Sulzer put it, 'apparently, individuals are more willing to blame another than to give him credit for his actions' (1964, p. 44). Shaw, Sulzer and their colleagues have subsequently carried out further investigations using various age groups, cultures and personality characteristics (for example, Shaw, Briscoe and Garcia-Estéve, 1968; Shaw and Iwawaki, 1972; Shaw and Schneider, 1969). These studies have confirmed the authors' original finding that as children grow older they attribute less responsibility to the person involved in the event, and more to his or her environment.

Methodological criticism of research into children's cognition of intentions

In recent years the majority of studies into the child's cognition of intentions and attribution of responsibility that have been carried out, both in the Piagetian and Heiderian traditions, have expressed concern over various methodological problems of the earlier research. In both cases the criticism has been particularly focused on the adequacy of the experimental stories.

Piagetian stories have been criticized on several grounds. First, in paired stories (see pp. 80–1) presented to the child, high damage outcomes always occur together with good intentions on the part of the actor in the story. On the other hand, low damage outcomes appear together with bad intentions or clumsiness. As a result, it is difficult to identify which factors exactly are responsible for the child's judgement of the events (Shantz, 1975; Karniol, 1978). Second, some stories do not make it clear whether an unfavourable outcome results from an accident, i.e. the manner in which the act has been carried out, such as negligence or clumsiness, or from a primary bad intention (Karniol, 1978). Third, since in some stories the experimental child is not explicitly told that a bad outcome was due to a bad intention, clumsiness, negligence, or lack of knowledge on the part of the actor in a story, the researcher has no way of determining how exactly the experimental child interpreted the story. Karniol (1978) has reviewed studies which actually remedied some or all of these methodological defects, and these studies suggest that if children from 4 years onwards are presented with clearly defined distinctions between bad-intention actions and accidents, they tend to evaluate the behaviour of the story-child as more naughty if the act is intentional than if it is accidental (King, 1971; Armsby, 1971; Buchanan and Thompson, 1973; Farnill, 1974).

Criticism of the stories used within an attributional framework was, perhaps, best summarized by Fincham and Jaspars (1979). First, it is uncertain whether the stories actually reflect the levels of responsibility they are supposed to represent. Second, the perceived effort of the actor may influence judgement of responsibility. Third, it is probably insufficient to use only two stories at each level since the level of responsibility and the content of the story may become confused. Fourth, the use of the same story character is inappropriate because the child may not respond to individual stories discretely but may form a continuous story about the boy Perry, so that the response to one story may influence the response to another story.

However, although criticism of the original Piagetian and Shaw and Sulzer stories has been very important in detecting methodological shortcomings and has led to considerable methodological improvements, it has not addressed two major issues in these studies: first, their cognitive bias, and second, their *ecological validity* (see pp. 53–4 for an explanation of this term).

Piaget clearly viewed the transition from objective to subjective morality in cognitive terms, and Heider's levels of responsibility have been conceptualized in terms of 'cognitive representations' and 'cognitive functioning' (Sedlak, 1979; Fincham and Jaspars, 1979). Cognition, however, is only one aspect of the awareness of agency. Although one may sometimes be presented with a moral dilemma at a level of pure problem-solving, it is unlikely that anyone would solve such a problem while totally suppressing his or her emotions, life experience, societal conventions, and so on. And no moral problem can be solved in the absence of some sort of moral code. Concerning ecological validity, when one is faced with the problem of making a moral judgement or of attributing responsibility, one is not usually presented with a little story with a minimum of information. Instead, real life problems provide so much information that the perceiver may have difficulty in extracting the essence of the problem. One may be hurt by the action of the other, one has to interact with the agent personally and so is personally involved. The question that both Piagetian and attribution research must ask is what exactly does one learn from studies based on judgements of the story-deeds of a story-child.

A refreshing innovation in studies of child responsibility is a recent investigation by Walton (1985) carried out in a natural setting. She argued convincingly that judgement of a hypothetical actor in Piagetian and attribution traditions may have little in common with actual situations in which a child is accused of something, or accuses someone of something, has to defend him- or herself or another, take sides, and resolve conflicting accusations in interpersonal interaction. Walton carried out observations of children in an open classroom setting. In this setting, the children worked on their tasks whenever they chose as long as they completed the work by the end of the day. They were encouraged to help each other and could talk freely so that their interactions with peers were quite natural. Analyses were made of detailed records of samples of 'remedial' interchanges, i.e. 'interpersonal events in which the behaviour or character of one of the participants is challenged by direct accusation or by subtler communication of disapproval' (Walton, 1985, p. 726). These interchanges were then divided into conversational moves and categorized as challenges, remedies, defiances, no responses, reliefs, endings, clarification requests, or ambiguous moves. Walton has analysed the data from the points of view of three different approaches to the study of responsibility: Piagetian, attributional, and symbolic interactional. Symbolic interactionism is an approach in social psychology and sociology, arguing that one acts on the basis of the meaning one attributes to the act of the other person (Meltzer, 1964; Blumer, 1966). Walton's study revealed the following: first, there was no evidence of any judgemental shift from objective to subjective responsibility, as defined by the Piagetian approach. Second, results showed limited support for the attributional approach, although there was no evidence of judgements at the level of global association and there was no clear pattern in the attributions made at other levels that would suggest developmental progression. Walton found most support in her data for the symbolic interactionist approach, which is particularly concerned with negotiations between interactants as to how a situation is to be defined. An example of such an attempt to define a situation is clear in the following extract from Walton's research:

Boys are working on various workbook tasks. Kerry is just returning to the table and finds John sitting where he had been before he left.

Kerry: John, that's my seat.
John: How do you know?
Kerry: 'Cause that's my stuff. (He nods toward the papers on the table in front of John).
John: How was I supposed to know that?
Kerry: It has my name on it. (He points to his name on the papers).

John: How do you expect me to see that?
            (Kerry stands over John, as though expecting him to
            leave the seat).
John: Scott, were you saving his place?
Scott: No.
John: Were you? (He looks towards Omar).
Omar: No.
John: I have every right to sit here. 'Cause no one was saving
            your place. Just as I thought.
Kerry: My paper was saving my place.
John: Your paper?! Your paper doesn't even have your name
            on it!
            (Kerry sits down in the chair, forcing John to scoot over
            and the two boys share the chair) (Walton, 1985, p. 735).

One can feel from this example the emotional and interpersonal involvement of the participants. In this case they are agents rather than observers. They make decisions, justify and defend them. Mistakes in their judgements have personal and interpersonal consequences. In situations of this kind children learn what is expected of them, and what their rights and obligations are. Learning such rules of interpersonal commitment and the accepted moral code is often painful. If one is unable to define problem-situations, one's recognition by others as a worthy partner in interaction may be at stake.

What conclusions should we draw from this discussion? Should we suggest that laboratory experiments based on hypothetical stories should be abandoned? Not at all. However, it is important to clarify what exactly psychologists learn from such studies. Well designed hypothetical dilemmas can prompt a child to reveal the internalized repertoire of existing societal conventions into which he or she has been socialized. One can assume that such a repertoire of generalized solutions plays some role in the child's solutions of actual moral dilemmas. However, it is questionable how much one can learn about the child's actual level of awareness of agency from such research. In the solution of hypothetical dilemmas the child tries to find out the right solutions to problems in terms of given social conventions. In contrast to the solution of hypothetical dilemmas, in real life interpersonal dilemmas the child may confront the very conventions that he or she took for granted before. As an agent the child may try a totally new solution at a qualitatively new cognitive and emotional level. Alternatively, the child may regress to a solution at a lower cognitive and emotional level if the strain of the interpersonal situation is excessive. Or the child may challenge the existing social conventions, and so on. In sum, laboratory research and research in a natural setting explore different kinds of things with respect to the individual's awareness of agency. Laboratory research can give some answers to the ways a child reflects upon established social conventions. Research in a natural setting, in contrast, can answer some questions about the cognitive, emotional, and experiential level of the human agent.

The different perspectives of the perceiver and of the perceived in their awareness of action

Our discussion of Walton's research brings into focus another important issue pertaining to the perceiver and to the perceived: their different points of view with respect to their awareness of action. This issue is related to a subject, known in social psychology as the 'divergent perceptions of the causes of behaviour by actors and observers', that has been extensively explored in the attributional approach that we have already discussed. The student should note our change in the use of terminology: attribution theory uses the terms 'actor' and 'observer' where we use the terms 'perceived' and 'perceiver'. However, it will shortly become clear that the terms 'actor' and 'observer' on the one hand, and 'perceived' and 'perceiver' on the other, express more than just terminological differences. More importantly, underlying the differences between the two pairs of terms are conceptual differences between the attributional and human awareness approaches.

The interest of the attributional approach in the divergent perceptions of actors and observers with respect to causes of behaviour, is largely due to an influential paper by Jones and Nisbett (1972). In this paper the authors argued that actors attribute the causes of their behaviour to the stimuli inherent in the situations, i.e. to the variable aspects of the environment in which their behaviour occurs, while observers, when viewing the *same* behaviour, attribute it to the dispositional characteristics of the actor, i.e. to the relatively stable aspects of the person (Jones and Nisbett, 1972, p. 93). For example, if a person fails to keep a promise it is likely that an observer will explain it as a *personal* failure of the actor, rather than attributing the failure to environmental circumstances. The actor, on his or her part, is more likely to explain the failure of keeping the promise in terms of situational constraints. The tendency of observers to attribute reasons for action to relatively stable personality traits and dispositions, rather than to situations, was discussed by Ichheiser (1949), on whose ideas Jones and Nisbett partly base their own theory. Ichheiser, however, was not concerned with the divergent perspectives of actors and observers. The focus of his exploration was the study of bias in social perception, and the study of the reasons for such a bias. He suggested that the tendency of observers to overestimate personality characteristics and to underestimate situational factors can be sought in cultural and historical societal conditions. Such conditions, Ichheiser argued, developed in Europe in the nineteenth century. The dominant, though largely unspoken, presupposition in the nineteenth century was that it is the inner personal characteristics of an individual that determine his or her success or failure in life. (For a discussion of individualism in modern Europe, culminating in the Romanticism of the nineteenth century, see Chapter 1.) This ideology, based on the conception of the individual's personal responsibility for his or her success or failure in life, also became, quite unnoticed, part of the basic assumptions of scientific social psychology. As Ichheiser (1949, p. 49) puts it, 'We see the experimental laboratory psychology of the nineteenth century investigating the individual as divorced from his all-important social setting and disregarding the role of situational factors in human behaviour.' He goes on to say that nineteenth-century scientific psychology misconceived personality characteristics in the same way that a contemporary layperson does, 'in a more naive way, in his everyday life relations'. One should add, however, that much of Ichheiser's criticism of nineteenth-century psychology is equally valid today. The environment in which a person lives, and the social context of human actions and interpersonal relationships, are still ignored in much contemporary psychology (see also criticism of laboratory experiments in Chapters 2, 3 and 4).

Although Jones and Nisbett draw on Ichheiser's ideas concerning the observer's overestimation of the personality characteristics of the actor, they nevertheless develop their views along different lines. Their main concern is with the *divergent perceptions of actors and observers* from the point of view of their cognitive and motivational perspectives. According to them, actors know much more about their own behaviour than do observers; actors perceive differences between, and variability of, situations that escape observers' attention. Motivational influences on information processing, such as a desire to maintain self-esteem, are also different for the actor who is personally involved, and the observer who is 'neutral affectively and morally' (Jones and Nisbett, 1971). Most of the research instigated by Jones and Nisbett's ideas has, indeed, supported their claims that the actor and observer have divergent perceptions of the causes of behaviour. Accordingly, such divergent perceptions are claimed to be due to cognitive factors, such as perceptual and information-processing differences, and motivational factors, such as self-evaluation and self-presentation (Kelley and Michela, 1980).

I have deliberately introduced Jones and Nisbett's (1972) ideas on attribution research using their own terminology. For example, they use such terms as 'causes of behaviour' (rather than 'reasons' and 'motives' for action), 'actors and observers' (rather than 'perceived and perceivers'), 'cognitive factors' and 'information-processing' (rather than 'human awareness'). As mentioned already, these terminological differences highlight underlying major conceptual differences between Jones and Nisbett's approach, on the one hand, and the one adopted in this book, on the other.

First, although attribution theory is currently one of the dominant approaches in *social* psychology, it does not take a truly social psychological point of view in its analysis of the divergent perspectives of actors and of observers. Thus, it treats the actor and the observer as two *different*, and *mutually independent*, individuals. Just as the world is inhabited by different things such as houses, animals, and so on, so it is inhabited by actors and by observers. It was Farr and Anderson (1983) who, in their important paper, drew attention to this misconception of actor and observer. In addition they pointed to the fact that such a conceptualization represents a basic misinterpretation, on the part of the attributional approach, of Heider's (1958) ideas. For Heider, 'perceived' and 'perceiver', or in his own terminology, 'person (P)' and 'observer(O)', are *relational*, rather than just *different*, terms. Relational terms, in Heider's case 'person' and 'observer', must not be treated in separation from each other because such a treatment would be meaningless. There is no perceived without a perceiver, and vice versa.

Let us consider in some detail why, quite apart from logical considerations, it is important to conceptualize 'actor' and 'observer', or 'person' and 'other', as relational, rather than as different, terms. There are, of course, situations in which some people *act* while others *observe*. However, although this fact is obvious, one must not forget that those who today are actors, may tomorrow be observers and vice versa. To be sometimes an actor and sometimes an observer is more than to play different roles at different times. Each of these roles interacts with the other because people are self- and other-aware agents. Moreover, there are occasions in which the one who acts is also a reflexive observer of his or her own action, in which case the actor and the observer are one and the same person. In this case the self both acts and evaluates his or her action (cf. Chapter 4). The self's evaluation of his or her action is partly determined by the ways in which *others* view it (Mead, 1934). As a result, the self is aware of him- or herself not just as a *subject*, i.e. as the actor, but also as an *object*, as an observer. This position will be discussed in considerably greater detail in Chapter 4.

One consequence of treating actors and observers as different rather than relational social phenomena is a simplified view of their divergent perspectives. The attributional approach discusses the divergent perspectives of the actor and observer in terms of the differences in the amount of information available to them for cognitive processing when perceiving the same action. This point has been made particularly clearly by Harvey and Weary (1981, p. 33). They emphasize that the importance given in attribution theory to informational, as opposed to motivational, sources of biases in the perspectives of actors and observers has been solidly established in social psychology for a good many years now. Harvey and Weary maintain that Ross (1977) also suggested that 'we *abandon* motivational concerns and concentrate on informational, perceptual, and cognitive factors' (see Harvey and Weary, ibid.). It is obvious that the information-processing approach was not established by Heider, for whom motivation and emotions are an integral part of social perception. Farr and Anderson (1983) argue that the different perspectives of the self and the other person must not be reduced to differences in sheer cognitive information-processing. Rather, the differences between the two perspectives relate to differences between the self's and the other's levels of awareness, i.e. the self's awareness of him- or herself *as agent*, and the self's awareness of the other person *as agent*. Awareness of the self and of the other as agents involves differences with respect to their commitment to an action, to their feelings and motives, to differences in the directness of contact with action, to differences in their fears, hopes, and defences: any attempt to reduce the richness of such social experiences to sheer cognitive information-processing is misconceived.

Usually, one takes it for granted that the action of which the agent and the other person have divergent perspectives is one and the same. But that is not the case. The view that one can identify stimuli in the environment or in oneself that are the *same* for everybody is common in psychology. However, such a view is totally mistaken. There is no such thing as an 'objectively' defined stimulus from which information flows towards the perceiver or is selected by the perceiver (Markova, 1982). Just as there is no self without the other person, *in the psychological sense* there is no object of perception without a perceiver. However, the claim that the perceiver and the object of his or her perception must be conceived as *interdependent* must not be misunderstood. Under no circumstances should it be confused with the claim of some philosophers that the world is just a fiction and that its existence depends on the individual's imagination. Rather, one can conceive of the interdependence between the perceiver and the object of his or her perception in the psychological sense of every person perceiving the 'same' thing according to his or her own experience, and according to his or her idiosyncratic level of awareness. This does not mean, however, that every person lives in a totally different and individualistic world. People's experiences overlap considerably, not only because they are very similar biologically, but because they share the same physical and social environments at the more basic level. Consider, however, John's and Kerry's perception of the interpersonal conflict situation in the above study by Walton (1985). They are not simply extracting different information from the same action, but for each of them *the situation itself* is different. For each of them, the situation is defined with respect to their own selves, and therefore they extract different information because *their situations* are different. A similar point was made by Maher (1972) with respect to patients with schizophrenia. Maher points out that schizophrenic delusions have usually been explained in terms of an underlying thinking disorder. Thus, it has been assumed that the information available to the patient with schizophrenia is the same as to everybody else but that the patient is unable to make valid inferences from such information. Maher contests this view, arguing that it may be that the information available to such patients is different, while their inferential processes may proceed in a perfectly logical manner. Maher argues that distortion of the information may occur at the sensory level because of some malfunction of the central nervous system.

Finally, let us return to Jones and Nisbett's hypothesis concerning the divergent perception of action by actor and observer. Questions such as 'Why did you do x?' and 'Why did he or she do x?' are not the same questions with the single exception of the pronoun. The meanings of these questions are radically different for actor and observer because the actions in question themselves have different meanings for the two, as argued above. The actor, or better, the agent, may understand the question, for example, as a request for an explanation of the process involved, or for justification. If understood as the former, the question calls for a description of the procedure for getting from A to B; if the latter it calls for the agent's account of his or her action as in the case of Walton's experiment, so that the other person comes to understand that the agent behaved consistently with his or her previous action and has integrity. For the observer, i.e. the other person, while the request may likewise be understood as a request for an explanation of the procedure, it may also be taken as a request for the other's opinion as to why the agent involved himself or herself in an action that harmed or benefited others. In other words, the question itself may be understood by the actor or agent as a request for a situational account while the observer or the other person may interpret it as a request for an account in terms of the actor's dispositional characteristics.

Language and awareness of action

In our discussion of Heider and Simmel's (1944) experiment it was noted that the meanings of such words as *move, follow* and *chase* reflect different attributions concerning the intentions of the agent. In general, attributions of causes, intention with respect to actions, and moral judgements are all built into the meaning potentialities of words in ordinary language (Rommetveit, 1968). Thus, words such as *accusation, blame, criticism, forgiveness, praise, condemnation* and many others, are used by the person to diagnose social situations, to evaluate the action, and to qualify the relationships between the perceiver and perceived (Fillmore, 1971; Markova, 1978a, 1978b). For example, *accusation* is associated with a harmful action, and it presupposes that the person, rather than the environment, caused the event in question; moreover, it assumes particular interpersonal power relationships that allow one to make an accusation against one or more of the people involved. At the same time the perceived, i.e. the agent, is aware that the perceiver has the power to administer the accusation. The *accusation* would have no effect if administered by someone who is of inferior status with respect to the agent, for example, a physical object, an animal or even a human being belonging to a category unnoticed or unrecognized by the agent. For an accusation to be effective it must produce changes in the accused's mental state, for example it must make him or her feel guilty, embarrassed, unworthy or ashamed. By accusing someone one presupposes that the person in question has performed the action of which he or she stands accused, and it is up to him or her either to accept this presupposition, or to provide evidence that it was someone else who was responsible for the act.

Consider another example. Verbs such as kill, murder, execute, assassinate, all mean cessation of life of a human being. It is with respect to intentions, motives and reasons that the meaning potentialities of these verbs differ. While in English it is appropriate to talk about a person *and* animal being killed, *murder, execution* and *assassination* refer to human beings only, because of the unique kinds of intentions involved in killing human beings in these particular ways. Only people can be killed as a punishment, or to achieve particular political aims, and such purposes are only intelligible in human society.

Summary

In the process of social perception people display two basic characteristics. First, they have the power to recognize other human beings as agents rather than mere physical objects. Second, they seek the recognition of themselves by other people. Recognition of others as agents implies the attribution of intentionality. People's everyday analysis of action is based on two essential dichotomies: stability and variability, and person and environment. People are usually held responsible for their motivation, i.e. what they try to do and how hard they try, but not for their abilities. The concept of responsibility can be analysed at several levels according to the perceived relative contributions of the personal and environmental factors. Development of the child's awareness of action has been explored in psychology in the Piagetian and attributional frameworks using hypothetical dilemmas to which children of different age groups have been asked to respond. This research has shown that on the whole as children grow older they judge actions more on the basis of the agent's intentions than on the basis of the outcome of an action. However, most of this research has suffered from numerous methodological shortcomings, some of which have been overcome by better designs, more explicit instructions and improvements in the contents of experimental stories, while more essential methodological improvements still await reconceptualization of actions in terms of human awareness. Research has demonstrated that an agent tends to explain his or her action in terms of environmental factors, while the other person tends to explain them in terms of the dispositional characteristics of the agent. These divergent perspectives of action by the agent and other person can be attributed to different levels of awareness of the agent and other person with respect to the action in question. Social attributions such as causality, intentionality and responsibility, and judgements and evaluations of actions are built into the meaning of words.

4 Self-awareness

Awareness of the self as an agent, as an experiencer and a social being, does not emerge suddenly in the individual at the time of his or her birth, or at a particular moment during his or her life. Instead, it develops gradually from its precursors into more and more complex forms, never accomplishing any final state in the course of a single human life. The conception of self-awareness discussed in this chapter is based on the hypothesis that the self has two components, the *I* as an agent and experiencer, and the *Me* as a socially formed object. This conception was first proposed in psychology by James (1890) and elaborated by Mead (1934), and just like any other conception of self-awareness it is historically and culturally determined, and therefore transient. We shall start this chapter by clarifying the two concepts, the I and the Me, and their mutual relationships.

The I – the experiencer and agent

The I component of the self emerges and develops in mutual relationship with the individual's environment. It is first through basic needs, such as hunger, thirst, coldness and other kinds of discomfort, Mead (1934) argued, that a baby posits himself or herself as an experiencer in the world. In other words, the individual experiences himself or herself as an entity separate from the rest of the world through satisfaction and dissatisfaction of his or her basic biological and social needs.

Very soon, however, the baby learns that he or she can exert a certain amount of control over the world. For example, his or her crying, smiling, or moving around evokes responses from people and brings physical objects under closer surveillance. Testing the limits of his or her ability to control events and to explore things becomes essential if the child is to define the boundaries between himself or herself on the one hand, and the environment on the other. That such boundaries are not innately defined became clear in our earlier discussion in which the example was given of a young boy who in his distress pulled his father's ear while sucking his own thumb (cf. Chapter 2).

Mead (1934) constantly pointed out that one's awareness as an agent arises from situations in which one's train of ordinary, automatic activities is interrupted for some reason, and one cannot carry on with them habitually as before. The lower animals, when finding themselves in a problem situation or in an unusual environment, continue to behave as if no change has occurred because their behaviour is determined by rigid instincts. In contrast, a human being, when facing a problem, will stop, think, consider the available options, choose one, and act accordingly.

One's awareness as an agent develops from impulsive and spontaneous goal-directed activities at a very early stage in one's life. Lewin *et al.* (1944) refer to observational evidence and to experimental studies pointing to the growth of *aspiration* in very young children. The term 'level of aspiration' (Dembo, 1931) means the degree of striving towards a goal one has set up for oneself (cf. also p. 110). Observational evidence demonstrates that, very early in their lives, children strive to be independent in such activities as walking, putting on their clothes, handling and manipulating objects, and so on. Lewin *et al.* (1944) refer to experiments by Fales and Anderson specifically designed to explore levels of aspiration in very young children. Thus, Fales (1937) found that 2 year olds in a nursery school actively refused help from an adult when putting on and taking off clothes. Jucknat (1937) showed that 11 and 12 year olds reach the same level of aspiration in setting standards for themselves as adults. Finally, Anderson (1940), using a ring-throwing task with 3 to 8 year olds, corroborated Jucknat's findings by demonstrating that as children grow older their level of aspiration increases, with the 8 year olds reaching the same level of aspiration as adults.

In a number of ingenious studies, Lewin and his colleagues (see Lewin, 1935) explored the ways in which the individual behaves in his or her *psychological environment* when confronted with various problems interfering with his or her activities. By 'psychological environment' Lewin meant the environment as it exists for, or is related to, the particular individual rather than as defined objectively in physical terms. Lewin emphasized that a psychological environment arises from mutual interaction between the self and the characteristics of the physical environment. For example, one and the same physical object may have different psychological significance for different children or even for the same child at different ages or in different circumstances: a wooden stick may at one moment be a horse, at another a gun and at yet still another a castle. A psychological environment, rather than the objectively defined physical environment, is the one within which a person actually lives and which he or she tries to understand and control. A psychological environment presents one with various kinds of challenge. For example, objects a child wants to reach may be placed too high up or too far away, steps may be too steep or too narrow to manage, a pencil tip may break and not draw on paper, and things may be forbidden by an adult and therefore be inaccessible. Some of Lewin's excellent films of young children were recently rediscovered at the University of Kansas at Lawrence. They show children's tremendous persistence in their attempt to climb stairs or reach for an object behind a barrier, or in trying to sit on a stone without realizing that one must turn one's back to the stone if one wants to sit on it.

Within the context of psychological environment, Lewin and his colleagues were particularly concerned to explore the various issues involved in the resolution of psychological tension caused by individual psychological need, motivation or intention to perform particular activities while the possibility of carrying them through is prevented. For example, Zeigernik (1927) designed experiments in which people were presented with various tasks but were not allowed to complete them. Zeigernik found that if people are motivated to perform particular tasks and prevented from completing them, their recall for such tasks is much better than for those that were completed. Moreover, what in this context is meant by completion or lack of completion of a task is decided by the participant in an experiment rather than by the experimenter. Once again, it is the individual's psychological environment rather than the physical environment that matters in deciding how he or she will perform.

In sum, Lewin's studies of psychological tension and of the ways in which it is reduced, are an important contribution to our understanding of the formation of the I, a process of gradual differentiation from the psychological environment, through facing and overcoming obstacles in the world.

The I also forms itself through its experience in situations in which it cannot control its fate. For example, when one's life is threatened, when one experiences the death of a close friend or relative, or when one's basic needs are denied, the boundaries between the I and the environment may become sharply clear: things that previously were taken for granted may suddenly appear to be the greatest possible trophy one could achieve. Severe or chronic illness, too, may lead to greater self-awareness. For example, in a study of patients with haemophilia, a blood clotting disorder, patients were interviewed concerning their self-perception (Markova *et al.*, 1980a). It was found that patients who were able to hold jobs in spite of problems caused by their chronic disorder felt that they were more independent than 'normal' people because, in contrast to 'normal' people, they had been compelled by the restrictions imposed upon them by their disease to work harder for their personal and social independence. As a result, they felt they had become exceptionally aware of themselves as individuals, and that they had learned to take care of themselves more than had others. Moreover, these patients thought that they themselves would be more dependent upon others if they did not have haemophilia because they would not then have the insight that the illness had given to them. Although their beliefs could be justifications of a situation over which they had no control, nevertheless they still reflected on their insight and awareness of their potentialities as human beings. Similarly, parents of mildly affected haemophilic children (Markova *et al.*, 1980b) gave more sophisticated answers with respect to their child-rearing practices than did parents of children who were either not affected by haemophilia or who were severely affected. Perhaps, if the strain of the illness on the parents is not excessive the experience of having a mildly affected haemophilic child makes them more aware of various aspects of child-rearing, motivates them to take precautions and to consider possible dangers for the child, and may result in generally increased self-awareness.

Finally, the I manifests itself through the individual's creative actions. Human beings not only solve problems that their environment presents to them, but they themselves, in their attempt to control, construct and create their environment, pose new problems for themselves and for others. People become aware of their I's in the process of moulding their environment, shaping objects with their hands and using their own ideas.

Among the numerous possible examples of human creativity, let us choose the one of the child's creative play with language.

Garvey (1977) was interested in various forms of a child's play with language, such as spontaneous rhyming, play with fantasy and nonsense words, and play with speech actions and discourse conventions. She points out that in order to play with language the child must have grasped the basic grammatical structure and conventional meanings of words. Moreover, the child must believe that the other people with whom he or she interacts share with him or her this knowledge about structure and meanings in language. Only when the child has internalized the shared social reality can he or she distort it in play, and temporarily create a new reality. In his classic article 'The sense of nonsense verse' Chukovsky (1963) analyses nonsense verse in Russian. He points out that many nonsense verses seem to make a special effort to throw into confusion much of the established social reality people take for granted. In order to respond to nonsense verse the child must have a knowledge of the real order and relationships between things, so that he or she will regard such verse, for example

> In the sea the corn kiln burns
> while the ship runs in the cornfield,

as nonsense and find it amusing. Chukovsky emphasizes that children are particularly attracted by incongruities in language, and that it is through experimenting with language, creating incongruities and combining words that distort the order they have learned, that they reflect upon their own thoughts and language, i.e. become actively aware of the established order. Thus, distortion and play with language leads the child to a greater awareness of language and of the self as the I. Cazden (1976) points out that in playing with language the child focuses his or her attention on language as a means of expression, rather than on the message. He hypothesizes that such play with language may be important for attaining literacy.

The Me – the experienced

While the I is the *spontaneous* and *acting* component of the self, the Me is the *reflexive* and *evaluative* component. While the acting self focuses on the present and future, the reflecting self turns back towards the past to evaluate its own action (Mead, 1934, p. 134). Evaluation of one's actions is a social, rather than an individual process. In order to evaluate and reflect, the individual must be able to take the attitude of *others* towards him- or herself. It means that one must be able to perceive oneself as others do, and thus to look at oneself from the outside, as an *object*. One learns to take the attitude of others towards oneself as one learns to understand other people's thoughts and feelings and feel others' emotions (cf. Chapter 2).

Mead maintains that it is through *play* and *games* that the child gradually acquires the ability to take the attitude of others towards him- or herself, just as he or she learns to take the role of others. The essential feature of play is a reality–appearance distinction. Some sense of a reality–appearance distinction exists already in animals. Dogs, cats, and monkeys make a distinction between biting each other while playing and while fighting; while playing, they never bite *really*. In order to play the role of others, a child must have a firm grasp of what it is to play, i.e. what is not 'for real'. Garvey observed that children in their play provide a great deal of evidence of making such a distinction, and assure each other of their awareness that they are making such a distinction, in particular by using words such as 'really' and 'pretend', as in the following example:

> (X sits on three-legged stool that has a magnifying glass in its centre).
>
> X. I've got to go to the potty.
>   Y. (turns to him) Really?
> X. (grins) No, pretend.
>   Y. (smiles and watches X)
> (Garvey, 1976, p. 576).

It is evident that both participants must be aware that a state of play is established so that they can interpret each other's gestures and language. As Garvey points out children often open and close the play explicitly, e.g. 'pretend you called me on the telephone', or 'I'll be the mommy and you be the daddy, O.K.?', or 'I'm not playing any more'.

To play a particular role a young child must, at least in a very simple form know the sort of things that are involved in taking that role. For example, in order to play the role of a mother, the child must know the kinds of thing a mother does: she bathes, dresses, feeds, cuddles and punishes the child; she has particular kinds of relationships with other people; she has rights and duties. When the child plays at being a mother, a knowledge of the rules, conventions, and obligations with respect to the role of a mother is necessary in order to carry out the particular play activities, and to anticipate responses from the others involved in the play.

In contrast to play, *a game* is an organized social activity in which a child has to learn to follow the rules of the game and restrain his or her fantasy and imagination. Rules must be obeyed and are created for the particular purpose of a particular game. As Mead points out:

Children take a great interest in rules. They make rules on the spot in order to help themselves out of difficulties. Part of the enjoyment of the game is to get these rules. . . . The game represents the passage in the life of the child from taking the role of others in play to the organized part that is essential to self-consciousness in the full sense of the term (Mead, 1934, p. 152).

Moreover, rules allow one to exclude a disliked person without this being unethical and make it possible to include the favourites. The rule becomes a force which strips the individual of responsibility for unpopular decisions: it becomes the force controlling the individual, allowing and forbidding things. It is a censor exercising social control. It prescribes what one *ought* and *ought not* to do.

Every individual is a member of various social groups, such as the family, peer groups, clubs, political parties, religious groups, and nations, all of which exert various kinds of obligation on the basis of which the individual evaluates himself or herself as the Me. The stability of such a group can be preserved only if the individual members adopt the group's beliefs and rules and behave accordingly: anyone who offends or deviates breaks the group's unity.

The group's beliefs and attitudes must be organized and consistent so that individuals can respond to them unambiguously. Such organized sets of attitudes Mead calls the *generalized other* (Mead, 1934, pp. 152–64). Mead explains the concept of the *generalized other* by the example of the notion of *property*. In order for this notion to have any meaning it has to be accepted by all members of the community. For the claim 'this is mine', to have any sense everybody must have the same attitude towards it, including the individual in question. From this common attitude the rights and obligations of individuals follow: if someone has property, it is his or her right to control it and nobody else can. It follows from this common attitude that one may covet another's property, and may accept or give gifts but taking another's property is not permitted: it is stealing. By having this common attitude the *generalized other* exercises control over individual members.

The *generalized other* takes on different forms as the individual takes on the rights and obligations of different groups and social relations. Thus, as the individual identifies with a political party or a local club the *generalized other* represents itself as the set of organized social attitudes of this group. Some of the groups of which the individual is a member are temporary, others are long-lasting, some are so important that the individual defines him- or herself in terms of his or her relationship to them, whereas others are just on the fringe.

Membership in and identification with different kinds of group can lead to a conflict at different levels of the Me. Having identified oneself with a particular group and having accepted one's duties and obligations with respect to that group, one may personally oppose the group's rules if they are in conflict with the rules of another group of which one is a member, or with one's own personal views. The more one identifies with the two groups the greater the conflict experienced. One's conscience or sense of duty, the most basic forms of the *generalized other*, may then provoke one to call for changes in a group and for the institution of new values and new practices, or to leave the group totally. The intensity of an experienced conflict between different levels of the Me is determined both culturally and individually, but may be missing in some thought systems, as shown in Chapter 1.

The I and the Me as relational concepts

We pointed out in Chapter 3 that the concepts of perceiver and perceived are *relational* in character. This means that they must not be treated in separation: the concept of the perceiver is meaningful only with respect to that of the perceived and vice versa. Similarly, the I and the Me can be understood properly only as mutually relational concepts. While the I is practically involved in the world, whether as an agent or as experiencer, its immediate involvement with the psychological environment makes it difficult for it to reflect on and evaluate itself at the same time. It is only when the act or experience has passed that one can look back, reflect on it, and interpret it. In other words, in reflexion, the I becomes Me. As Mead (1934, p. 174) puts it:

We can go back directly a few moments in our experience and then we are dependent upon memory for the rest. So that the 'I' in memory is the spokesman of the self of the second, or minute, or day ago. As given, it is a 'me' which was the 'I' at the earlier time.

For example, while playing, a boy may tear his shirt and even continue tearing it when his peers laugh at his appearance. The boy does it as an agent, as the I. His act is finished when the boy realizes that his mother will have to work hard to earn the money to buy him a new shirt. He now feels guilty and ashamed of his earlier performance, the I becomes the Me as he reflects on, and evaluates what he has done; in a similar way his mother will evaluate his action when she comes home from work. The boy is an object of the evaluation of others and in a similar way he becomes an object to himself. In other words the Me is *its-self*. About the term 'itself', involving the self both as subject and object, Mead (1936, p. 74) says:

The word 'itself', you will recognize, belongs to the reflexive mode. It is that grammatical form which we use under conditions in which the individual is both subject and object. He addresses himself. He sees himself as others see him. The very usage of the word implies an individual who is occupying the position of both subject and object. In a mode which is not reflexive, the object is distinguished from the subject. The subject, the self, sees a tree. The latter is something that is different from himself. In the use of the term 'itself', on the contrary, the subject and object are found in the same entity.

Our earlier example of a child playing with language also demonstrates a constant switching from the I to the Me and from the Me to the I. In playing with language, creating incongruities and new words, the child acts as the I. Having created incongruities and new words the child reflects upon them as the Me, comparing them with the ordinary meanings. As the I transforms into the Me and the Me again becomes the I, both components of the self become modified through their mutual interaction. In this process the I, being checked by the Me, becomes less spontaneous and less impulsive while the Me through the relationship with the I becomes less subdued to and more critical of the authority of the 'generalized other'.

Indeed, it is through the self-aware individual that the 'generalized other' undergoes change (cf. Chapter 7).

Mead's and Freud's theories of the self

We have shown that, although the nature of the I component of the self is originally spontaneous and impulsive, as the child develops his or her activities become progressively more goal-directed. Thus, the I expresses itself in actions designed to master its environment. The Me component of the self, in contrast, evaluates, checks, and restrains the activities and impulses of the I. The self develops through the interaction of the I and the Me, of which it is composed.

Students may, at this stage, wonder whether one can, in any way, relate Mead's conception of the self to Freud's theory of personality based on the *id, ego*, and *superego* (Freud, 1923). In this theory, the id comprises uncontrolled urges, spontaneous activities and instinctive drives, many of which are unconscious. The impulsive id does not recognize the dictates of time, the release of unconscious desires and urges being entirely uncontrolled. The id's desires are not logically organized, and the id may attempt to satisfy incompatible urges at the same time. The ego, although not strictly separated from the id, represents reason and common sense. It seeks to be in contact with the external world, to influence the id, to restrain it and to substitute rationality for the unrestricted passions of the id. The ego is the product of socialization and education. As the child grows up, its ego strengthens, and by adulthood it should be able to control the impulses of the id. The ego functions mainly at the level of consciousness, although some of its aspects are also unconscious. The most important of the processes by which the ego is in contact with the outside world are perception and language. They organize and systematize the ego's functions. Freud describes the relationship between the ego and the id by comparing them to a man on horseback trying to control the strength of the horse. If the horse, the *id*, is too wild, the rider, the ego, in order not to be thrown from his saddle, must guide the horse in its choice where to go, rather than trying to make the horse go where the rider wants. In this way, the ego transforms the id's will and impulses into actions as if such will and impulses were those of the ego. The ego rationalizes the irrational urges of the id (cf. Freud, 1923, p. 25). The superego represents forces of morality derived from the ego's efforts to master the Oedipal conflict (for more details see, e.g., Kline, 1984). For the individual, the superego manifests itself primarily as criticism of the ego and as a feeling of guilt. The functions of the superego are performed unconsciously, as the individual's *conscience*. However, they can also become conscious (cf. also Jahoda, 1977).

What, then, is the relationship between Mead's and Freud's theories of the self? Miller (1973, p. 6) suggested that 'the Freudian id corresponds to the Meadian I, and that the superego corresponds to Mead's generalized other', although he also points to some essential differences between Freud's and Mead's theories. Thus, Miller mentions that while Mead's I emerges out of the relationship between the individual and society, Freud's id exists apart from the superego; and that while the superego mainly functions as a censor of the id and ego, the generalized other has a variety of functions.

It is my view that any attempt to map Freud's components of the self on to those of Mead, without careful analysis of the two theories, is dangerous. Such an analysis, to the best of my knowledge, has not yet been made. Freud and Mead worked in different conceptual frameworks, and their perspectives on the self were quite different as a result. Mead was concerned with the evolution of the mind and the ways in which originally unconscious aspects of interaction between individuals, and between individuals and society, become conscious. Freud, on the other hand, was concerned with the pathological consequences of the individual's inability to express his or her impulses, drives, and instincts, and to bring them into consciousness. For these reasons, it would be an undesirable simplification, based on a superficial similarity between the contents of the respective concepts, to map Freud's id, ego, and superego, on to Mead's I and Me. In his paper on 'Mead and Freud', Swanson (1961) maintained that these two psychologists focused their attention on quite different aspects of behaviour, and therefore that their work is complementary. For example, the subject of self-control plays an important role in the work of both Freud and Mead. In Freud's theory, self-control is induced by societal pressures that prevent the id from expressing its natural instincts. In this case self-control is achieved through a variety of defence mechanisms, such as projection, repression, denial or rationalization, and through fear of punishment, guilt and anxiety. If the individual, torn between the drive to express its natural instincts and at the same time to yield to the societal pressures, is unable to cope with the experienced conflict, pathological reactions result. In Mead's theory, too, self-control is induced by societal pressures. However, self-control is achieved through the individual's increasing ability to take the role of other people and, eventually, of the generalized other. The growth of self-control is achieved through the growths of self- and other-consciousness. It is a process of self-knowledge in which the individual is educated, through action and reflexion about his or her capacities and limitations. In reality, of course, self-knowledge and self-defence (or self-deception) are part of the same life-process (Markova, 1987), and thus Freud's and Mead's conceptions do in fact complement each other.

It is my view, moreover, that both the I and the Me actually change their very nature throughout the life of the individual. Although the child's I is originally spontaneous and impulsive, in the process of socialization, and in its relationship with the Me, the I learns to restrict itself and loses its original spontaneity and impulsiveness, as already pointed out above. The I, originally a pure drive, becomes goal-directed and creative under the influence of the Me (see also Lewin *et al.*, 1944). It is, perhaps, only under the conditions of frustration and inability to master one's environment that the I may regress to its original impulsive and spontaneous expression and become similar to the id (see pp. 191–7 on aggression). Bearing on the same issue, Lewin *et al.* (1944) refer to experiments in which a regression to lower developmental forms of levels of aspiration occurs as a result of frustration.

Self-awareness and related notions

In recent years there has been a proliferation of terminology in social and developmental psychology, starting with the prefix *self-*, which is associated with the growing interest in the study of self-processes. One of the consequences of such rapid development is that, very often, terms are used without any clear definition and distinction from one another, and they reflect the authors' language biases and preferences. It is important that students should be aware of this problem, and not be too concerned by this terminological variability, though it can be rather bewildering at times. However, in spite of such variability there are some general trends in the use of self- terms. For example, some terms with the prefix *self-* express cognitive biases while others are associated with motivational aspects of the self; and still others refer to the self in terms of the dichotomy of action and reflexion. This section is not intended to be a terminological review but an outline of the basic groupings of self- terms, serving to heighten students' awareness of this problem. Students should not be alarmed, though, if they find a difference between the way the term is used here and in other literature.

Terms referring to the self by way of the dichotomy between action and reflexion

Terms belonging to this group usually, though not always, reflect James's (1890) and Mead's (1934) distinction between the I and the Me. Mead (1934) himself used the term 'self-consciousness' to explain the relationship between these two components of the self, and to refer to the individual's ability to conceptualize himself or herself as both subject and object. Since Mead's conception of self-consciousness, or self-awareness, to use the term applied in this book, has already been discussed in the first part of this chapter, and will also be referred to in Chapter 5, we do not need to dwell on it now.

Duval and Wicklund (1972) use the term 'self-awareness' in a rather different way, although they too postulate a theory based on the distinction between the self as object and the self as subject. According to their theory, one may focus one's attention in either of the two dichotomous directions, either *inwards*, i.e. towards oneself, one's own actions, experience, body and personal history; or *outwards*, i.e. towards one's environment. In the former case one is an *object* of one's own attention, that is, one is *objectively self-aware*. Objectively self-aware individuals are likely to monitor their own behaviour and adjust it so that it is consistent with social norms, and to evaluate themselves in terms of these norms and standards. If, on the other hand, one focuses one's attention *outwards*, one is aware of oneself as a *subject* exerting effects upon one's environment. For example, someone grasping a microphone, or standing with hands thrust into pockets, is exerting an effect upon his or her environment, and is *subjectively self-aware*. Duval and Wicklund conceive of subjective self-awareness as focusing away from oneself. In being involved in an activity, the authors argue, the self's attention is occupied by that activity and not by itself. There is, however, an important distinction between Mead's, and Duval and Wicklund's conceptions of self-awareness. In Mead's conception the two components of the self, the I as a subject and the Me as an object, undergo transformation of the one into the other during the individual's life-process. In contrast, in Duval and Wicklund's theory it is not clear as to where, if at all, subjective and objective self-awareness meet, or what their relationship is. Although the authors assume that the self may shift focus from objective to subjective awareness and vice versa, the two kinds of self-awareness are treated as mutually independent. There is nothing in the theory to suggest any relationship between the two which would lead to the development of qualitative changes in the levels of awareness in the sense discussed in this book.

Harré (1979, 1983) studied the relationship between the individual's rational and co-ordinated action and societal moral orders. For Harré, to be an agent means also to be reflexive, that is, to have self-control, the ability of self-mastery and self-monitoring. An agent not only acts but also has the power to control his or her impulses and obsessions, and thus to achieve freedom with respect to his or her environment. In this sense, Harré's position is close to the one adopted in this book.

Terms referring to cognitive aspects of the self

This group of terms focuses on the self as knower and the self as an information-processing system, and includes notions such as self-knowledge, self-perception, and self-understanding. Both philosophers and psychologists have been preoccupied with the clarification of the concept of self-knowledge (e.g. Hamlyn, 1977; Toulmin, 1977; Gergen, 1977, 1984, 1987) and with the processes by which individuals gain knowledge and awareness of their strengths and weaknesses. However, Lewis and Brooks-Gunn (1979) use the term 'self-knowledge' in a different sense, referring to the basic and concrete knowledge that preverbal children have about their bodies and about themselves. The authors distinguish such self-knowledge of preverbal children from *awareness of the knowledge of self.* Damon and Hart (1982) use the notion of self-understanding in their discussion of the development of social and cognitive awareness in children.

The term 'self-perception' has been used by Bem (1967, 1972) in his analysis of attitudes, emotions and other internal states.

Bem argued that individuals come to know these mental states through observation of their own overt behaviour and the circumstances under which it occurs. Bem derived his position from Skinner's radical behaviourism according to which internal states are just as observable as anything else. According to Bem, if the individual's internal stimuli are ambiguous and unspecific, he or she is in the same position with respect to such stimuli as any *outside* observer. In such a case the individual must rely upon some external cues, i.e. his or her own overt behaviour, in order to infer his or her own internal states. For example, according to Bem's self-perception theory, one first observes one's response to a particular stimulus, i.e. one's crying as a response to a disaster, and second, one infers that one is sad. Changes in self-perception may occur as a result of a particular kind of experience being repeated over a period of time. For example, a person with a mental handicap may change his or her self-perception as a result of living independently in a community.

In contrast to Bem, Rogers (1951) uses the term 'self-perception' in a different manner. According to Rogers, changes in one's self-perception are essential for successful psychotherapy. As therapy progresses there is a tendency for the patient to perceive him- or herself more positively and to develop self-regarding attitudes towards him- or herself. On the other hand, if the therapy is unsuccessful such improvements in self-perceptions and self-regarding attitudes do not occur. Improved self-perceptions, according to Rogers, take three different forms. First one perceives oneself as a more adequate person; second, one allows experience to play a greater role in one's awareness; and, finally, one realizes that values do not lie in objects in the external world but in one's relationships to such objects. Such changes in self-perception resulting from psychotherapy are conceived primarily as cognitive changes.

Terms referring to affective and evaluative aspects of the self

Self-evaluation, self-esteem, and self-regard are all concerned with whether one feels superior or inferior when compared to others or to one's ideal self, both in general terms, and in some special respects such as intellectually, socially, morally, and so on. Empirically, there have been two main methods in social

and developmental psychology to explore affective and evaluative aspects of the self. First, self-evaluation has been extensively explored using self-evaluative scales, tests with multiple
choice responses, and tests based on the individual's own statements about himself or herself, such as 'Who am I?' (Kuhn
and McPartland, 1954). Self-evaluation obtained through such
tests can be either positive or negative in terms of categories,
attributes, and values. Very often self-evaluation has been
identified with self-concept proper, although such a position
has recently been criticized (e.g. Wylie, 1979; Damon and Hart,
1982).

Second, there is a tradition of research on self-evaluation
stemming from experimental social psychology. This work
derives from the studies of Lewin, his collaborators and
students, on goal-directed behaviour and levels of aspiration,
to which we referred on p. 90. This tradition of research is
based on the view that since human beings are self-aware
agents, they tend to set goals for themselves, and aspire to
attain these goals. The degree of striving towards a goal has
been called a *level of aspiration*. The individual's level of aspiration is determined by a variety of characteristics specific to
the individual in question, by temporary situational and general
cultural factors. Competitive societies, in which goal setting
and the attaining of higher and higher goals is one of the main
values, constantly pressurize individuals towards improvement
of their performances. However, the individual's feeling of
success or failure with respect to a particular performance does
not depend primarily on the actual level of his or her achievement. Such a feeling is determined both by subjective factors
and by the individual's perception of his or her position as
compared to those of others. The individual's standards can be
set with respect to a group of which he or she is a member,
or with respect to the standards of some other groups. The
groups themselves may have aspirations that the individual
adopts as his or her own. The individual then evaluates him-
or herself in terms of these standards. Subjective factors such
as motivation, interest in the goal, competitiveness or lack of
it, all interact with the group pressure and determine the level
of aspiration.

Festinger (1942, 1954), who was one of Lewin's students,
developed his theory of *social comparison processes* on the basis
of level of aspiration research. The fundamental hypothesis of
his theory is that human beings have a drive to evaluate their

own opinions and abilities, and that to do so they compare themselves with others. For example, to evaluate one's own ability to write poems or to swim fast one compares oneself with others who engage in such activities. The drive for self-evaluation makes people join groups which, in their opinion, enable them to make appropriate self-evaluations. Thus, Festinger argues, people do not tend to evaluate their opinions and abilities by comparison with those who are too divergent from themselves. A student would tend to evaluate him- or herself with other students rather than with, say, people in mental handicap institutions or with prison inmates. Festinger's theory of self-evaluation by social comparison has had important implications for the study of social influence processes, group pressure, and changing membership of groups.

Just as people have a drive to evaluate their own opinions and abilities, so, Schachter (1959) suggested, they also have a need to evaluate their feelings by means of social comparison processes. If a person's emotion is different from that of the group, there should be indications, either of changes in the person's own emotions, or of attempts to influence others and bring them closer to the person's own emotion. If discrepancies in emotional states exist among the members of a group, the deviants tend to be rejected. Schachter has obtained experimental evidence demonstrating that increasing anxiety leads to affiliation. In other words, people who experience anxiety have a greater need to be with others, and to evaluate their own emotions by comparing them with those of others. Studies on level of aspiration have shown that if an individual is unable to compare his or her opinions and performance with relevant others, his or her self-evaluations are unstable (Gould, 1939; Lewin et al., 1944; Sears, 1940). In a similar vein, Schachter has shown that ambiguous situations or ambiguous emotions lead to a desire to be with others so that one can evaluate others' emotions and decide which emotions and reactions are appropriate for oneself.

In his search to identify the determinants of emotions Schachter (1964) then extended his theory to include physiological and cognitive aspects of emotion. He suggested that emotional states are functions of physiological arousal and of cognition appropriate to that state of arousal (Schachter, 1964). For example, a person being told the diagnosis of his or her illness by a doctor may experience a state of arousal that he or she identifies as fear. In this case, a person has an adequate explanation for his or her fear; he or she understands the meaning of the diagnosis, and that the particular emotion, in this case fear, results from cognitive and physiological processes. Schachter suggested that a person in a state of physiological arousal for which he or she has no immediately available explanation, needs an explanation of this arousal. If no explanation is immediately available, he or she will seek one in terms of whatever cues are at hand. Schachter's own experiments, in which he manipulated the extent to which a participant in an experiment had an appropriate explanation for his or her arousal, confirmed his hypothesis (Schachter, 1964; Schachter and Singer, 1962). A series of experiments followed in which people's beliefs about their physiological arousal were manipulated, and their self-evaluations of their emotional states were altered accordingly (Nisbett and Schachter, 1966; Valins and Nisbett, 1972). The results of these studies have had important implications for attribution therapy of emotional disorders. The emotional disorders of many people arise from people's faulty beliefs about their problems. If a person is unable to compare his or her emotions, attitudes, or behaviour with those of other people because he or she assumes that these feelings, attitudes or behaviour are shameful, bad or inappro-priate, this person may ascribe to him- or herself mental abnor-mality and personal inadequacy that may have a debilitating effect upon him or her (Valins and Nisbett, 1972). In such cases the person may benefit from reattribution, i.e. a change in his or her beliefs about the causes of his or her particular problem leading to self-evaluation of his or her emotions.

Self-identity

Although the concept of self-identity is sometimes equated with self-concept (Turner, 1971), most often two kinds of self-identity are recognized, following Goffman (1968). First, *personal identity* refers to the characteristics on the basis of which one recognizes oneself as a unique being. For example, the individual expects others to recognize him or her as the same individual and expects particular reactions from others towards him- or herself to be relatively consistent over time. The indi-vidual learns to attach particular kinds of personal attributes towards himself or herself and expects others to identify him or her using these. *Social identity*, on the other hand, refers to a system of social relationships in which the person is located with respect to other people. Social identity determines the person's place within various social groups, such as a family, a club, a political party, and one defines and evaluates oneself as a member of such groups (cf. also the discussion of the 'generalized other', p. 102). Therefore, situations that might result in change or loss of social identity are experienced by people as threatening and the individual develops various strategies to cope with such threats (Breakwell, 1986). Since one defines and evaluates oneself in terms of social identity, threats to one's identity challenge one's self-concept and self-evaluation. Breakwell uses the case of unemployment as an example of threatened identity. Unemployment means exclusion of the individual from the existing work membership and moving into a social category that has been stigmatized for various reasons, whether material, social or of competence. Being in a state of unemployment forces the individual to revise his or her self-definition in terms of a lost social identity.

The growth of self-awareness

Recently, interest in the development of self-awareness in children has been rapidly increasing and excellent reviews of this field have appeared (Lewis and Brooks-Gunn, 1979; Anderson, 1984; Damon and Hart, 1982), and thus some repetition and overlap in our account of this work is inevitable. This section will be divided into two parts. In the first part we shall discuss the development of self-recognition in very young children. In the second part we shall focus on the development and growth of self-awareness. It will become clear that the development of self-awareness occurs hand in hand with the development of other-awareness, indeed, each process makes sense only in relation to the other.

Recognition of one's reflected image

Research on human self-awareness starts with infants. Since infants cannot communicate verbally researchers have focused on the use of indirect means to identify instances of self-awareness or its precursors. The methods for this have involved observing infants' reactions to their own images in mirrors, pictures and video-recordings. Reviews of the literature refer to Darwin's (1877) observation of his 9 months old son's mirror self-recognition and Preyer's (1893) observation of child self-recognition at the age of 14 months as the earliest records of the phenomenon. Since that time other reports of mirror recognition by very young children have appeared here and there. Systematic exploration of the recognition of mirror images by children younger than 2 years started in the early 1970s, inspired by Gallup's (1970) study of chimpanzees and other non-human primates mentioned earlier. (p. 21). Papoušek and Papoušek (1974) explored the reactions of 5–10 months old infants to their videotaped and filmed images. The infants were shown images of themselves that were either contingent on their immediate behaviour, or non-contingent, i.e. they had been filmed earlier. The authors analysed the amounts of various kinds of behaviour, such as the infant's eye contact with the televised and filmed image, looking at objects, amount of smile and motor activity. It was found that 5 months old infants responded more to eye contact than to contingency. However, in the course of experiments the infants started to respond to contingency, probably due to a training effect. There was clearly no evidence in any of the analysed behaviours that infants recognized themselves at this age.

Amsterdam (1972) investigated self-recognition in children under 2 years of age using a technique similar to that of Gallup (1970). In her study, Amsterdam placed a spot of rouge on the children's noses and then allowed them to observe themselves in a mirror. She inferred self-recognition if the children touched the red spot or used the mirror to examine their nose. However, in contrast to the above mentioned observations of Darwin and of Preyer, she found that it was not until the last part of the second year that the majority of the children showed self-recognition. Amsterdam's studies have been followed by numerous investigations. Most of them support her finding that the majority of children recognize themselves in the mirror in the second half of the second year (Schulman and Kaplanowitz, 1977; Berthenthal and Fischer, 1978; Johnson, 1982), although Lewis and Brooks-Gunn (1979) have identified self-recognition slightly earlier, at about 15 months. The difference between the earlier reports on self-recognition by Darwin and by Preyer, those by Amsterdam and her followers, and those by Lewis and Brooks-Gunn could be due to methodological differences, and the stringency of the criteria for self-recognition. Various methodological considerations revealing some limitations of the mirror-recognition studies have been discussed by Anderson (1984).

Self-recognition in infants using different methods have been systematically explored by Lewis and Brooks-Gunn (1979). The importance of their approach consists in their exploration of self-awareness (or self-knowledge, using their term) in its relationship to other-awareness. The researchers presented children with contingent and non-contingent images of themselves and of others using photographs, videotapes and mirrors. While mirror images are always contingent with the individual's behaviour, photographs are not contingent and videotapes can be used either contingently or non-contingently, as in the case of Papoušek and Papoušek's (1974) study.

In a study using photographs designed in accordance with the previous studies (Brooks and Lewis, 1976; Lewis and Brooks, 1974), Lewis and Brooks-Gunn inferred self- and other-recognition from differential responses, such as smiles, frowns and fixation times, to photographs of the self and others. Their results suggest that infants 9–12 months old are capable of some differentiation between the self and others, although this ability becomes much greater in their second year. It was found that although children recognized pictures of themselves as opposed to those of others at the age of 18 months, correct verbal labels of a photograph of the self appeared much later. The children started using their own name first, while using a personal pronoun did not appear until about 2 years of age.

The purpose of Lewis and Brooks-Gunn's (1979) videotape studies was to explore self- and other-recognition in young children using contingent images varied systematically. In the two studies, with children 9–24 months old and 9–36 months old, the children were shown videotapes of the self contingently and non-contingently, and of another person non-contingently. The results showed that the children were responsive to contingency. Responses to contingency tended to increase during the second year of age. It appears that children find contingent images an interesting phenomenon at an early age, a finding also documented by Papoušek and Papoušek (1974).

Concerning self- and other-discrimination, it appears that children distinguish between self-images and other-images at an age of between 15 and 18 months, and that such differentiation is based on learning the facial features specific to the individual. However, clear differential responses involving different vocalizations, affective responses, turning towards the image and contingent play do not become established until somewhere between 2½ and 3 years of age. Lewis and Brooks-Gunn provide a great deal of evidence that awareness of the self emerges at the same time as awareness of the other. Children are born into networks of social relationships in which they actively participate from the start. They not only learn to differentiate people from physical objects and interact with them accordingly, but they also learn that their interactions with other people differ according to their relationships with them. Lewis and Brooks-Gunn (1979) maintain that, of the whole complex of interactions with others, differentiation on the basis of familiarity, age, and gender appears to be the most important in the development of early other-awareness. Differentiation on the basis of familiarity, such as between mother, father, and stranger, starts before 3 months of age (Bronson, 1972). As for gender, 6 month olds were found to respond differently in terms of vocalizations to male and female photographs, and by 18 months children label adults correctly most of the time using words such as 'mommy', 'lady', 'daddy' or 'man' (Lewis and Brooks-Gunn, 1979; Brooks-Gunn and Lewis, 1979). In conclusion, the three social categories, namely familiarity, age, and gender, form the basis of the child's construction of a very complex social world, the details of which are still to be explored. The authors emphasize, however, that

Whatever the construction, the knowledge of other and the knowledge of self are parallel, and the task of understanding early social cognition must be the task of studying self, other and their interaction (Lewis and Brooks-Gunn, 1979, p. 240).

In the field of self-recognition, the developmental psychologist is primarily concerned with answering the question as to whether one recognizes one's own image in a mirror, in photographs, or on a video screen. The social psychologist, on the other hand, focuses his or her attention on the study of the consequences of the recognition of one's self-image, and on the consequences of one's awareness that other people, too, recognize it. In many respects this issue is similar to that of the relationship between perceiver and perceived discussed in Chapter 3. In both cases the perceived is aware of the perceiver's power to denigrate or praise the object of his or her perception. There are, however, important differences between social perception as it occurs in face-to-face interaction, and in the perception of a person in a photograph. In face-to-face interaction, one adjusts, both consciously and unconsciously, to the other party. For example, when one talks to a child, to a lover, to a friend or to a prime minister, one not only alters one's vocabulary, pitch or dialect (see Chapter 5), but one also adjusts one's facial muscles and posture in subtle ways in order to achieve the expression one desires. Such adjustments constitute both conventionalized responses to particular social situations, and idiosyncratically monitored responses to the other participant as a unique human being. Thus, in face-to-face interaction one continuously changes one's image in accordance with the responses of the other participant. In contrast, when one's picture is taken, a single image out of many possible images appears on the photograph in a frozen form, and it is this single image that is seen by different people in a variety of contexts (Milgram, 1977). How, Milgram asks, can we create a facial expression that is generically acceptable? What do we do when we pose in front of a camera? Answers to such questions are not universally valid but are culturally and historically determined. Different cultures and sub-cultures have different preferences as to what should and should not be displayed on photographs (Milgram, 1977; Beloff, 1985).

In a photograph, one becomes an object of one's own perception, the Me, more than at any other time. It is through the 'image freezing machine' (Milgram, 1977) that one sees oneself in exactly the same way as others do. Perhaps this is why, Milgram says, so many unflattering snapshots are rejected. People often believe that they look much better than the picture shows, and are unwilling to accept their mirror images. Quite often a photograph allows the perceiver to assess the kind of mask the person photographed is wearing.

Just like language, photographs have tremendous persuasive power, focusing attention on particular aspects of the person which then take the place of the original. Just as a word or a sentence can be taken out of its context and given a meaning different from the one intended by the author, so a photographer can select particular aspects of reality for his or her picture. This selected aspect can then, out of its context, be presented as the whole reality, as a fact, and therefore as an evidence of truth. As Beloff puts it

It is possible to lengthen the neck of a film-star, to show poverty as noble rather than sordid, to denigrate or flatter a political leader.

Like the computer, the camera is an instrument of human intelligence (Beloff, 1985, p. 18).

Milgram (1977) remarks that studying the manner in which people pose for pictures, and the way the manner of posing changes over time in different cultures and sub-cultures, just as much as throughout the lifetime of an individual, is an exciting subject still awaiting future research. The study of the manifold aspects of photography has not, as yet, attracted enough imagination from social psychologists.

Developmental stages in self- and other-awareness

In recent years, considerable effort has been made to describe developmental stages in child self- and other-awareness. The most significant work in this area has been done by Selman and his colleagues. Central to Selman's approach is his call for the integration of developmental, social, and clinical concerns in the study of self- and other-awareness. Thus, Selman and Jaquette (1977) emphasize that in the past social psychologists have paid little attention to developmental psychology and vice versa. Cognitive-developmental approaches have attempted to describe the social and moral development of the child without considering that there are a variety of social and psychological factors that may have significant influences on the levels of a child's awareness. They also treat the development of cognition without taking account of the child's social environment. Social psychologists, on the other hand, have carried out investigations of social psychological phenomena without paying attention to variations in the child's self- and other-awareness due to his or her cognitive stage or age. In order to bring the point home Selman and Jaquette discussed a classic study by White and Lippitt (1960), carried out originally in 1938 under the direction of Kurt Lewin. In this study, three types of leadership, democratic, laissez-faire, and autocratic, were manipulated in small groups of 11-year-old boys in order to discover which type of leadership was most effective. The study demonstrated that democracy was the most effective type of leadership. Selman and Jaquette rightly point out that since the cognitive levels of that age group were not taken into consideration, the value of this very interesting study is limited. Thus, the 11 year olds fall within the age group 8–12 years, i.e., according to Piaget, the stage of autonomous morality (i.e. subject to their own moral code), which is based on respect for the reciprocity and equality characteristic of democracy. Children under the age of 8 years, on the other hand, might actually prefer autocracy, being at the stage of heteronomous morality (i.e. subject to another person's code). Selman and Jaquette's call for the integration of social and developmental psychology has been repeated by Gallup (1983) and Anderson (1984).

Equally important is Selman and Jaquette's call for the integration of developmental and clinical concerns. For such an integration to take place, it is important to evaluate the relation of the child's capacity for social adaptation to his or her cognitive-developmental levels. Since the sources of both pathological and normal development are functions of the reciprocal interaction of self and societal structures, integration of the two approaches should lead to understanding of the relationships between maturity of reasoning processes and socially adaptive behaviour (Selman and Jaquette, 1977, p. 263).

In their attempt to initiate such an integration of developmental, social, and clinical interests of human awareness, Selman and his colleagues have carried out a series of longitudinal and cross-sectional studies over several years using two basic methods of exploration, one based on *reflective thought* and the other based on *'real-life' thought*. Concerning the former, Selman, like Piaget (1932), has employed a clinical interview technique, a hypothetical dilemmas method used by Kohlberg (1969), and a series of semi-structured questions in order to follow and to probe people's ideas. Data have been collected from children and adolescents attending normal schools, from adults of various socio-economic backgrounds, and from children and adolescents suffering from severe emotional and interpersonal problems and attending special treatment schools. The second method, based on 'real-life' thought, involved naturalistic observation of social reasoning occurring during class meetings in a special treatment school for teaching the disabled and emotionally disturbed children. In these class discussions children solved their own interpersonal conflicts and set their own group goals. Thus, the problems the children had to solve by their spontaneous actions were their own, rather than hypothetical laboratory dilemmas.

Selman's reflective type of research with children, adolescents and adults included four kinds of content areas: individual self-awareness, conflict resolution in friendship, leadership in peer groups, and parental punishment of their children. On the basis of this research Selman defined five levels in child development of self- and other-awareness.

In order to present Selman's five levels I shall use an example of a hypothetical dilemma that was presented in one of the content areas, that of individual self-awareness. In addition, in describing each of the five levels, I shall give examples of questions from clinical interviews from the four content areas. The example of a hypothetical dilemma in the study of individual self-awareness is as follows:

Eight-year-old Tom is trying to decide what to buy his friend Mike for his birthday party. By chance, he meets Mike on the street and learns that Mike is extremely upset because his dog, Pepper, has been lost for two weeks. In fact, Mike is so upset that he tells Tom, 'I miss Pepper so much I never want to look at another dog again'. Tom goes off, only to pass a store with a sale of puppies; only two are left and these will soon be gone (Selman, 1980, p. 94).

The presentation of such a dilemma was followed by the question as to whether Tom should buy a puppy for Mike, and by a series of questions exploring the child's awareness of Mike's psychological problems, e.g. 'Mike said he never wants to see another puppy again. Why did he say that?', and the level of the child's awareness of his or her feelings and states of mind, e.g. 'Can you ever fool yourself into thinking you feel one way when you really feel another?' Selman's five levels of the development of self- and other-awareness are as follows:

Level 0: *Undifferentiated and egocentric perspective taking*, at about the ages of 3 to 6.

At this level children do not differentiate between the physical and the psychological characteristics of people, between intentional and unintentional actions, and between their own perspective and those of other people. The self and the other are differentiated in terms of their physical characteristics but not in terms of subjective features. Like Piaget (1932) Selman calls this level egocentric because, he argues, the child does not recognize that different individuals may view one and the same thing in different ways. At the undifferentiated level of self-awareness the child does not appear to be aware of possible differences between inner experience and outer expression. For example, the child would believe that if Mike says that he does not want to see any dog ever again, he really does not want to, and all other possibilities are excluded. In the domain of conflict-resolution in friendship, here again the child's conception is physicalistic, what is out of sight is out of mind. Interpersonal conflicts appear to be resolved if the people involved do not interact physically. Psychological perspectives are not considered. Leadership is seen as undisputed physical power over others, the leader being obeyed unquestioningly by his or her followers. Accordingly, punishment by parents is viewed as an inevitable consequence of disobedience and as reactive physical enforcement. For example:

WHY DO PARENTS SOMETIMES PUNISH THEIR CHILDREN?
Because they don't do what they are told to do.
BUT WHY PUNISH THE CHILD?
To make them do it   (Selman, 1980, p. 123).

Level 1:   *Differentiated and subjective perspective taking*, at about the ages of 5 to 9.

At this level the child is able to realize that one and the same action or event can be viewed differently by different people. The child is aware that every person has unique subjective experiences. However, the child's perspective is unilateral, that is, it is in terms of the impact that one person has on another. For example, the child does not realize that one can hide one's feelings, although he or she knows that one can hide facts from others or deny that one has done something when one has. If the child is asked whether Mike can say something and not mean it, the only possible explanation for his doing so would be that he was lying. The child does not see the possibility that Mike might be depressed or confused about his feelings. Level 1 is not truly self-reflective, and 'fooling oneself' for the child means actually changing one's subjective feelings rather than being unaware of them:

WHAT DOES IT MEAN TO FOOL THE SELF?
You do something and then you disagree with it. You find out you didn't want to do it   (Selman, 1980, p. 97).

The child is not aware of active self-deception. Instead, at this level one does something and then realizes one's error. In conflict-resolution in friendship, in leadership and parental punishment, a one-way unilateral perspective dominates the child's awareness of situations: conflicts between friends are caused by one party while the other party feels it; the leader is the one who is most knowledgeable, the best, so that knowledge is transmitted downwards from the leader and what he or she says is gospel truth; children are punished to teach them a lesson.

Level 2: *Self-reflective/second person and reciprocal perspective taking*, at about the ages of 7 to 12.

The child is now able to see him- or herself as an *object*, as the Me. The child is able to reflect on his or her thoughts and feelings and see him- or herself from the perspective of others. A two-way reciprocity of thoughts and feelings, and not just actions, takes place. Concerning the domain of self-awareness, the child realizes the possibility of putting on an outer façade in order to hide one's inner feelings. Moreover, the child now believes that one can monitor one's feelings and thoughts. For example, self-deception is no longer a matter of changing opinion because of error of judgement, but of persuading oneself to believe what is not the case:

IS IT POSSIBLE TO FOOL YOURSELF?
Yes, sometimes.
HOW CAN YOU FOOL YOURSELF?
You can say to yourself, I didn't really care and keep on saying you didn't care, and when someone brings up the subject, you say I didn't really care and sometimes it works and you don't really care about it   (Selman, 1980, p. 99).

Both friendship and leadership are now reciprocal relationships. Conflicts in friendships should be resolved by the attempt of both parties; a leader is now an 'arbitrator' and not a 'dictator', although his or her perspective still dominates the group. Punishment by parents is seen as a method of facilitating a self-reflective process, to make the child think about his or her actions in order to monitor behaviour.

Level 3: *Third-person and mutual perspective taking*, at about the ages of 10 to 15.

At this level of awareness a person now has the ability to detach him- or herself from the I and Me relationship and from the I and You relationship and to take up the position of a 'third person'. While at level 2 the person was aware of reciprocal relationship, the reciprocity was just to and fro, like a pendulum. At level 3 the relationship between the two parties is not just reciprocal, but there is an aspect of mutuality between the participants in the interaction. One is able to look at oneself, now as an agent, now as an object, these two aspects of the self forming a unit. Similarly, the I and You relationship is now viewed as a unit, as we-ness. For example, one can do things for the sake of friendship, 'the team has to work together as a unit'.

At this level the child is aware that one has some control as to what one wishes to keep in consciousness (e.g. 'you just put it out of your mind and you don't want to know about it'), although it is not always possible (e.g. 'if I did something wrong, I can't make myself forget'). The person now views himself or herself as actively trying to monitor and control inner experience, rather than just hiding it from outside view or forgetting about it.

In the other three domains explored by Selman, i.e. conflict-resolution, leadership, and parental punishment, the 'third person' perspective again dominates the child's self-awareness. Concerning the resolution of conflicts in friendship, the child can now understand that '*each* side must feel that *both* he or she, and the other, are truly satisfied with the resolution and would be satisfied if in the other's place' (Selman, ibid., p. 111). The child also recognizes that some friendship conflicts may occur because of people's personality characteristics, and that such conflicts may be resolved only if people actually change their personalities. It is the commitment of both partners in a friendship to work through a conflict and to strengthen their friendship through genuine resolution of the problem. As already pointed out, at this level the value of the relationship itself, the we-ness, makes it worth all the effort. The role of the leader now is to strengthen solidarity in the group, to give it structure and purpose. Finally, in accordance with the 'third person' perspective, parents and children are viewed as two separate parties and punishment as a means of control:

Parents have their lives too. If a kid is always screwing up, it's not just the kid who needs to see the light. The parents don't always want to be bailing him out of trouble   (Selman, ibid., p. 128).

But corporal punishment is not seen as the optimal way of obtaining obedience; just as in friendship, it is important 'to talk things through'.

Level 4:   *In-depth and societal-symbolic perspective taking*, from about the age of 12 to adult.

At level 4 one is aware that subjective perspectives of the self and others are determined by psychological processes functioning on multiple strata, both conscious and unconscious, and reflected and unreflected. People are viewed as sometimes doing things they themselves do not understand rather than doing them because they want to. The self and the other are now seen as determined not only by their traits, dispositions, beliefs and personal values, but also by their group membership and by their functioning within particular social networks and under societal constraints. It is now understood that communication may proceed at different levels with superficial understanding and sharing of common interests and, at the same time, with misunderstanding at deeper levels. The legal, moral, conventional and societal functioning of the 'generalized other' (cf. earlier pp. 101–5) are now understood in their full complexity and their implications, both for the self and the other, are comprehended.

Concerning the domain of self-awareness, the person understands that some thoughts, motives and feelings are totally resistant to self-analysis and the individual engages himself or herself in a form of self-deception that is hard to overcome. People behave on the basis of unconscious motives and no conscious effort can break into such processes. An extract from an interview with a 16 year old exemplifies this point:

SO MIKE MAYBE DOESN'T KNOW HOW HE FEELS?
He is just talking out of emotions. He may think that at that instant he doesn't want to see another puppy, but he will get over the initial loss.
IF MIKE THINKS ABOUT WHAT HE SAID, WILL HE REALIZE THAT HE REALLY WOULD LIKE ANOTHER DOG?
Maybe, but maybe not. He might not be aware of his deeper feelings.
HOW IS THAT POSSIBLE?

He may not want to admit to himself that another dog could take Pepper's place. He might feel at some level that it would be unloyal to Pepper to just go out and replace the dog. He may feel guilty about it. He doesn't want to face these feelings, so he says, no new dog.
IS HE AWARE OF THIS?
Probably not   (Selman, ibid., p. 106).

Selman describes the resolution of conflicts in friendship at level 4 in terms of autonomous interdependence between the participants and their symbolic action. By this he means that while at level 3 friends must really talk a conflict through, at level 4 they are aware that it is not always necessary because 'you do certain things and each of you knows what it means'. Friends understand that each of them has his or her own problems and that these may sometimes be the sources of conflict. In other words, intrapersonal conflicts may lead to interpersonal ones. One has to understand this, and a good friendship helps one to solve such intrapersonal problems. Therefore, people should be aware of each other's deep feelings and they should establish routes by which these can be overtly discussed. An ideal group leader is now seen as embodying the spirit of a group. It is understood that the group functions at multiple levels, cognitive, emotional and organizational, and an ideal leader should be able to cope with the various demands of such a multiple group structure. At level 4 the person is aware that parent–child interaction also functions at multiple conscious and unconscious levels. These multiple levels of interaction affect the ways in which punishment given is understood, and often misunderstood, by both parties.

The meaning of Selman's developmental levels of self-awareness

It was pointed out earlier in this chapter that Selman's five levels of self-awareness are defined on the basis of reflective research, i.e. on the data obtained from clinical interviews, the solution of hypothetical dilemmas, and from semi-structured questions concerning self- and other-awareness. Thus, these levels represent the child's ability to consider various factors in personal and social problems, to reflect upon his or her own solutions of such problems and to offer explanations for his or her own thoughts and reflections. In this sense the developmental levels represent the child's *potentiality* for understanding issues involving self- and other-awareness. One cannot, however, make inferences about the ways in which the child would *actually* solve such problems in real life. Selman was well aware of this and, as already mentioned, he and his colleagues have also carried out research involving real-life situations with a small sample of emotionally disturbed children (Selman and Jaquette, 1977; also in Selman, 1980). The results of this study have shown that although children in real-life situations generally performed at all five levels of self-awareness, their naturalistic real-life understanding of interpersonal problems was more superficial than in reflective research, and their responses often regressed to lower levels, and oscillated between different levels. Such regress to lower levels of awareness and oscillation between levels, found in naturalistic situations, was related to the child's state of stress, to the content of the problem, to varying conditions in the group such as perceived status, and to the specific content of the issues discussed. Thus, situational factors interacted considerably with the particular psychological or psychodynamic concerns of individual children and so distorted the pattern of the reflective research.

Although results from naturalistic research do not diminish the value of reflective research, it is important to clarify the meaning of the levels of self-awareness obtained in reflective research. These levels appear to demonstrate the quality of thought a human being is capable of under ideal conditions of Socratic questioning and reflection in a relatively relaxed state of mind, which may or may not obtain in actual involvement in interpersonal issues. We have already encountered a similar kind of problem in Chapter 3 when we discussed the child's awareness of agency. Selman's results actually show a regression of thought to lower levels of self-awareness in naturalistic conditions. Although stress, anxiety, or particular kinds of intrapersonal, interpersonal and societal problems may lead to regress in self-awareness both in children and in adults, it is equally plausible that results from naturalistic studies might show higher levels of awareness than those obtained in reflective research. Since people acquire higher levels of self-awareness in the process of practical involvement in the world, as was shown earlier in this chapter, one can also hypothesize that further research with children would show higher levels of self-awareness under certain naturalistic conditions than are achieved in reflective research.

Moreover, it can be assumed that some people, for a variety of reasons, will never reach levels 3 and 4 of awareness. It could be that poor family socialization, social frustration, and mistrust in other human beings or simply lack of social experience, may prevent them from forming close relationships so that the sense of we-ness will never be experienced. In addition, even if a person reaches level 4 in one situation, he or she might not reach it, or might not wish to employ it, under other conditions. One may actually prefer to maintain superficial relationships at level 1 or 2. For example, with strangers or casual acquaintances one may remain only at the level of reciprocity of actions, perhaps calculating costs and gains. Some people, of course, fluctuate in their social reasoning more than others. The question for researchers is to identify the interactive processes involved in social reasoning and to generate information that will help to characterize either typical or abnormal degrees of fluctuation, consequently providing information as to the relationships between action and reflexive thought.

Other research on the development of self- and of other-awareness

In addition to Selman's comprehensive studies, other researchers, using cross-sectional and longitudinal designs, have also attempted to identify the stages and levels by which the child's self- and other-awareness proceeds. The methods of these studies have been mainly clinical interviews, self-descriptions and other-descriptions. Guardo and Bohan's (1971) exploration of children's knowledge of the self, and Broughton's (1978) study based on clinical interviews studying children's naive epistemology, both support Selman's claims of a developmental shift from physicalistic to reflective self-awareness. Studies using children's self- and other-descriptions all assume that self- and other-awareness can be revealed through verbal accounts, and that these can identify changes in descriptions due to the child's maturity (Livesley and Bromley, 1973; Peevers and Secord, 1973; Keller et al., 1978; Bernstein, 1980). Peevers (1984) studied four aspects of the self in 6 to 21 year olds: *continuity*, i.e. the sense of a self-existing over time; *distinctness*, i.e. the sense of the self as unique and different from others; *the self as agent*, i.e. the ability to make decisions and act purposefully; and the *self as object*, i.e. self-reflexivity and explanations of self-attributes and of one's own behaviour. Peevers found that continuity was the only aspect of the self that had emerged by the age of 6 years and existed in all the age groups involved in her study. Both distinctness and awareness of agency first appeared in children's descriptions at the age of 9 years, increased up to the age of 17 years and then dropped. Presumably, once distinctness and awareness of agency become established there is no need for people to describe themselves in terms of these categories. Self-reflexion, on the other hand, appeared in children's descriptions at the age of 9 years and had increased dramatically by the age of 21 years.

Damon and Hart (1982), in their summary of research on the development of self-understanding, refer to four widely replicated findings in this area: first, the shift from physicalistic to psychological levels of understanding; second, the emergence of stable characteristics of the self; third, the increasingly volitional and self-reflexive nature of self-understanding; and finally, the tendency to integrate diverse aspects of the self into a unified self-system. It should be added, of course, that all of these four findings apply equally well to other-awareness.

The I and the Me in self-awareness research

Although the distinction between the I, the self as agent, and the Me, the reflexive component of the self, was clearly made in psychology by James (1890) and Mead (1934), both the theoretical and the empirical research following from this conception have consistently favoured the Me, the reflexive component of the self. This bias concerning the emphasis on the Me is probably partly due to Mead's repeated claims that the individual becomes self-conscious to the extent that he or she can and does take the attitudes of others towards himself or herself and acts on such attitudes (cf., for example, Mead, 1925, 1934, p. 138). As a result of Mead's own bias, psychologists have often ignored the other component, the I. For example, Wicklund (1982, p. 209) says that Mead defined self-awareness 'solely in terms of reflecting on oneself through the perspective of others'. In addition to paying less attention to the I, Mead also defined it less clearly than the Me, and this has led to a great deal of argument with respect to the I's role in the concept of the self.

On the theoretical side the focus on the reflexive component of the self, the Me, has led to the notions of *symbolic interactionism* (see p. 85) and *social construction of self-knowledge*. Both emphasize that the concepts of self, self-consciousness, and self-knowledge, arise from comparison of oneself with others through observation, communication and learning. In the process of social interaction and commitment to group membership one learns to take the attitudes of others towards oneself and to evaluate oneself in terms of the adopted social criteria. Opponents of these approaches, however, have been critical of the overemphasis of passive reliance on the regard of others, with human agency totally ignored. Among the critics, Hamlyn (1977) argued that self-knowledge arises through the individual's practical involvement with things and people. In being actively involved people make decisions about themselves and their futures, and monitor their own actions. Their new decisions often lead to reinterpretations of their past decisions: things that only yesterday might have been marginal, may in the view of new decisions, be seen in a different light, and consequently may now be regarded as essential. For example, a housewife who takes up a job for 'financial reasons' may, as a result of her decision, realize how bored and dissatisfied she had been before, with her life reduced to looking after her family without being able to express herself in any other way. Her new understanding of her past as a dependent woman may now give new meaning to the job that has enabled her to be independent. Following the same argument, some psychotherapies, e.g. psychoanalysis or insight therapies, in their procedures search to rediscover significant and forgotten events in patients' lives. Having become aware of such events, patients are helped to re-live them and to re-interpret them as significant. Through a new understanding of the past these patients are able to understand more about themselves and about significant others, and so can take more adequate decisions about their future.

On the empirical side, James (1890) was among the first psychologists to suggest that it would be difficult to explore the I because of its elusive and ever-changing nature. In accordance with James's prediction, Wylie (1979), in her comprehensive review of research on self-concept, found that an overwhelming majority of empirical studies had focused on self-evaluation, and so on the Me. A similar bias in favour of the reflexive component of the self has already been noted in the previous section concerned with the developmental aspects of self-awareness. In general, a great proportion of empirical research in this area has been based on the use of self-esteem and self-evaluation scales. The purpose of such scales is either to explore overall self-evaluation seeking agreement or disagreement with such statements as 'on the whole I am satisfied with myself', or to focus on some specific characteristics, such as 'I am a friendly person', 'I am reliable', and so on (Wylie, 1979; Damon and Hart, 1982; Harter, 1982). As Wylie points out the nature of this research has been largely correlational, studying the various relationships between self-evaluation, and age, race, sex, interpersonal attraction, creativity, and so on. The results of these studies, however, have, on the whole, been disappointing, showing null or very weak relationships between variables. Wylie argues that the research instruments chosen to explore self-evaluation have suffered from numerous conceptual and methodological shortcomings. Conceptually, the statements used in self-evaluation scales are too crude to explore the psychological subtlety of self-evaluation. Moreover, they do not allow for the differing socio-cognitive levels of children of different ages, the motivational and emotional aspects of people from different socio-economic backgrounds, or the relevance of such statements to the individual's self-evaluation. In addition, self-evaluation is determined by multiple personal and social factors, from which it follows that the analyses of data must be based on multivariate methods. However, Wylie makes it clear that it is at the stage of theorizing and research design that the multivariate nature of self-evaluation must be taken into consideration. It is no use applying complex statistical procedures to data that have been collected in a simplistic fashion. Bearing upon Wylie's criticism of the present state of research, Damon and Hart (1982), in their review of studies concerned with the development of self-understanding, argue that the self-evaluation approach is too narrow and that social and cognitive investigation of self-understanding is required, based on both the I and the Me. Peevers (1984) endorses this criticism, pointing out that study of the I component has received so little attention for two reasons: first, it is logically impossible for the individual to observe his or her I since in doing so the I becomes the Me; and, second, psychologists are, on the whole, reluctant to consider people's ordinary language, or their verbal accounts of events, as actual data. Instead, they tend to transform what people say into categories, or use ready-made multiple-choice response sheets, thus minimizing the possibility of studying direct self-expression of the I.

Can the I be studied empirically?

One might infer from the above discussion that the I cannot be studied empirically, either because it is ever-changing as James remarked, or because it is logically impossible for the individual to observe his or her I, as Peevers maintained. Nevertheless, Peevers points out that the I can be studied through the verbal accounts which people give of their subjective processes in actions in which they are involved. Broughton's (1978), Selman's (1980) and Peever's (1984) own researches have all been based on the analysis of either free language descriptions or interviews concerned with the nature of the mind and the self.

However, although one can infer subjective processes from verbal accounts of self-descriptions, the research discussed above still studies them at the level of the Me rather than the I. Whenever one is required to describe oneself or one's states of mind or feelings, one is requested to reflect and to put one's thoughts into perspective, which, once again, concerns the Me. The I can be studied only through actual actions, decision-making and experiencing here-and-now, or through non-reflexive speech actions. Any standing back, observing or describing oneself, involves evaluation and reflexion, and there-fore takes us back to the Me.

The crucial point in the answer to the problem as to whether the I can be studied empirically is that both the I and the Me must be explored *jointly* because they are two relational components of the self, one having no meaning without the other. Therefore, any adequate study of self-awareness must be concerned with both spontaneous action or involvement in personally relevant issues, *and* evaluation of, and reflexion on, such action and personal involvement. Theoretically and methodologically such research is time-consuming and expensive. On the positive side, it provides more adequate data for the understanding of such a complex phenomenon as human self-awareness.

There have been some studies, although very limited ones, pointing in this direction. Attributional (Weiner, 1985), locus of control (Phares, 1976) and cognitive dissonance (Aronson, 1968) research all refer to the relationship between success in various kinds of performance and self-esteem. Laboratory experiments exploring such relationships usually manipulate subjects' beliefs about the causes of success or failure in their performance, these being attributable either to the person or to the environment. The results of such studies have shown that if people attribute success in laboratory tasks to themselves rather than to environmental factors, their self-esteem increases. In the same vein, there has been considerable research showing correlations between achievements in various tasks and self-esteem (Wylie, 1979). Although this research has been restricted to the laboratory, to the use of self-esteem scales rather than full verbal accounts, and to the study of self-esteem rather than to self-awareness as such, it is still important from the point of view of the connection between action and reflexion. Such a connection between the I and the Me needs to be explored fully, in socially relevant settings, in natural situations, and over extended periods of time. So far, people's actions, important life events, speech actions, decisions taken and coping with problems, all of them concerned with the I, have largely been studied in isolation from reflexion upon such activities, i.e. without the Me, just as self-understanding has been investigated without the I. However, the self is a process in which the I transforms into the Me and the Me into the I, leading continuously to more complex levels of self-awareness. Therefore any adequate research on self-awareness must explore the one in relation to the other.

Summary

Awareness of the self develops in a life-long process in mutual relationship between the self and its psychological environment. It involves a gradual transformation of the two components of the self, the I and the Me, into their more complex forms. One is aware of the I as a subject, agent, and experiencer that affects its psychological environment. And one is aware of the Me as an object, a reflecting and self-experiencing being that evaluates its activity against societal standards, norms, conventions and morals. The I and the Me are relational phenomena, developing through their mutual inter-action and interdependence.

Research into the development of self-awareness in very young children has been concerned with the child's self-recognition in mirror and video images. The development of self-awareness in older children and adults has focused on the description of developmental levels in self- and other-aware-ness. The research has established four main findings. First, as children grow older they become aware of themselves and others in terms of psychological, rather than just physical, characteristics. Second, as children grow older they become aware of some relatively stable characteristics of the self. Third, they become aware of their own and others' self-control, self-monitoring, self-reflexion and self-understanding. Finally, they develop the ability to integrate diverse characteristics of the self into a unified self-system. Most of the research on self-aware-ness has been carried out reflectively, focusing on the Me, and in laboratory conditions. It is important that more real-life studies be designed, involving action and not just reflexion. Since the I and the Me are relational phenomena, it is essential that awareness of the I and awareness of the Me be investigated jointly.

5 Communicative awareness

Interpersonal communication is one of the most significant expressions of self- and other-awareness. Its quality and kind depends very largely on the participants' ability to assess each other's feelings, thoughts and intentions, and on their reactions to each other's messages. Moreover, the quality and kind of interpersonal communication are also determined by the knowledge and experience that participants mutually share. However, while interpersonal communication is an expression of human awareness, the participants in communication are often unaware of much that they convey to each other. This claim is not paradoxical. On the one hand, in order to master language and become competent in verbal and non-verbal communication, one has to learn to be aware of the other's feelings, thoughts, and intentions. On the other hand, as language and rules of verbal and non-verbal communication are passed from generation to generation, they turn into conventions and institutions. Having been socialized into such conventionalized and institutionalized forms of communication, people adopt them as part of their social reality, unaware of the effect they exert upon them (Chapter 7). In addition, as one masters one's language and becomes competent in interpersonal interaction, one often acts habitually and automatically. Just as when mastering a piano piece or driving a car one is no longer aware of the position of one's fingers or the movements of one's arms, so in communication one says certain things and makes certain gestures, quite unaware of their impact on the other person. It is only when, for some reason, the flow of communication is interrupted and when one reflects upon one's performance that one finds it difficult to continue, either because one has been thrown out of gear, or because of the sudden awareness of the effect of one's action on the other person. Interpersonal communication proceeds at different verbal and non-verbal levels. Saying something is accompanied by a variety of non-verbal messages expressed by voice, facial muscles, gaze and so on. One and the same utterance expressed in a sarcastic voice will be immediately comprehended as the opposite of what would be understood if expressed in a 'normal' voice (Rommetveit, 1974). One may try to hide one's feelings by putting a mask upon one's face, that is one may try to *express* something in order to make a particular kind of *impression* upon the other person (Chapter 6; Ichheiser, 1949). Moreover, one and the same communicative act can mean different things to the speaker and to the listener, just as one and the same action can be interpreted differently by the actor and the observer, or by the perceiver and the perceived (cf. Chapter 3). One can thus see that interpersonal communication is a very complex phenomenon. Only a part of it is performed with full awareness, and this part represents the tip of the iceberg. A much greater part remains under the level of awareness.

In this chapter, we shall first explore interpersonal communication as a mutual adjustment of the participants to each other, and then discuss the development of communicative awareness in children. Second, we shall focus our attention on verbal and non-verbal communication as a highly open and flexible means of interaction dependent on the social situations in which it is used. Some social situations may require the use of full and explicit messages, while in others the use of ellipsis and various other forms of incomplete sentences and implicit messages indicate a high degree of communicative awareness of the participants.

Communication as co-operation and the mutual adjustment of participants

In order to explain the nature of interpersonal communication we shall start our discussion with Mead's (1934) notion of a *social act*. Mead defines a social act as a set of behaviours that involve the co-operative adjustment of the interacting individuals. These behaviours can be accounted for in terms of two *interacting individuals as a dyad* rather than of the *interacting individuals as individuals*. Let us consider this definition in some detail, using Mead's classic example of two interacting dogs. The behaviour of one dog, or 'gesture', using the term Mead adopted from Wundt, has a stimulating effect on the other dog. For example, the first dog, let us call it dog A, may make a gesture that signals to the other dog, let us call it dog B, the readiness of A to attack B. As a result, dog B adjusts itself to the gesture of dog A. Such adjustment can be of different kinds. Dog B may simply imitate A's gesture, i.e. take a posture of readiness to attack. Or, B may run away, or itself start to attack, or it may growl. However, whatever gesture dog B makes it becomes, in turn, a stimulus for dog A, and dog A now adjusts itself to the gesture of B, and so on. Thus, 'a conversation of gestures, a reciprocal shifting of the dogs' positions and attitudes' (Mead, 1934, p. 63) arises, and an inter-individual interaction becomes established.

When Mead talks about adjustment of the participants in the process of interaction, he does not mean that gestures are performed by the participants because they *intend* to perform them or because they are aware of them. Indeed, according to Mead the beginnings of a social act can be explained without bringing in intentionality or awareness. In our example of interacting dogs the notion of intention is not necessary at all. However, although gestures in such interaction can be explained without appealing to awareness, those gestures, nevertheless, serve *as social stimuli. They are social in the sense that they start interaction going, and thus are parts of social acts.*

Gestures produced without the individual's realization of the impact they might have upon the audience Mead (1934) called *non-significant gestures.* For example, babies start crying when they feel discomfort; they may be hungry, or wet, or be in pain. At first they do not cry for their mothers to give them food, or to change their nappies or to soothe their pain. In other words, their gestures are non-significant because they signify nothing to the agents who produce them. They do, of course, signify something to the child's mother, which is a different matter altogether.

It is not until babies start crying *in order* to attract the attention of their mothers that their gestures become significant. In other words, for a gesture to be significant, it must convey to the attender the meaning that the agent intends. A significant gesture stands for a certain idea in the agent's mind, and the agent can predict the kind of response such a gesture will evoke in the attender. In Mead's words, a gesture, which could be a sound, a look, a movement, and so on, becomes significant when it has the same meaning for both participants, for the one who is making it and for the one who is responding to it. That it is a significant gesture indicates that there is a common object in the attention of both participants. A significant gesture is a more efficient and adequate means of interpersonal interaction than a non-significant gesture. Its most important property, *reflexivity* (cf. Chapter 4), which is responsible for the efficiency of interaction, is absent in non-significant gestures. This claim can be explained as follows.

To say that a significant gesture stands for an idea is to say that a significant gesture is carried out with *awareness* of the meaning of that gesture for both parties in the interaction: for the one who is making the gesture and for the one who is attending to it. When interpersonal interaction is based on such an awareness, the following feature of the interaction comes to the fore. Communication is not just a two-way process from one participant to the other and back again in which process the participants mutually adjust to each other. Rather, we must account for such a process in terms of *three steps*. Let us consider, as an example, two people interacting with each other. One participant says something that he or she considers to be pleasant to the other participant. The other, however, instead of responding with an expression of appreciation for the pleasantness of the first speaker, looks offended and responds offensively. The first person is puzzled. In order to understand what has happened, he or she *reflects* upon his or her previous turn, and on the response of the other, before taking the next turn. In other words, an elementary unit of communication involves three steps. The first speaker *acts*, the other speaker *responds*, and the first speaker *reflects* upon the turns of both of them. Of course, we could as well start with the turn of the second speaker and complete the elementary unit with the reflexion of the second speaker. The important point is that to communicate with awareness means more than a shifting of positions and attitudes, to and fro. To communicate with awareness means acting, accepting a response, and reflecting on that action and response.

Reflexive communication is more efficient than non-reflexive because it enables people to respond to each other as *individuals*. To respond to someone as an individual means to be aware of that individual's specific characteristics, and to alter his or her response should the characteristics of the other person change. Thus, reflexive communication is flexible, adaptable to situations and to individuals. This does not mean, of course, that every act of communication is carried out with careful consideration of each single step one takes, and of the point of view of the other person. As we shall see later in this chapter, and in the next chapter, we are often insensitive to each other, whether consciously or unconsciously. However, to discuss what one *can* do, and what one *actually does*, are two different matters. The point of the present discussion is that people have the ability to co-ordinate action and reflexion while communicating with each other. Therefore, *conceptually*, a communicative act must be conceived as a *three step process*, although in practice not every act of communication proceeds in this manner.

If one defines communicative awareness in terms of a three step process, the transition of I into Me, discussed in the last chapter, can be seen in a new light. This transition, too, can be accounted for in terms of our three step process. For example, the person acts as an agent, as the I. His or her social environment, i.e. a parent, a lover, or a peer group, responds to that individual's act. As a result, that individual reflects, as the Me, upon both his or her action and on the response of his or her social environment. It is in this sense that the I transforms into Me. The social environment, however, does not need to be *physically* present for such a transformation to take place. The agent, having performed his or her act, may *experience* the response of the generalized other in imagination, or may experience the response of his or her own conscience representing the generalized other. One's own conscience, or various forms of the generalized other internalized in the individual, act on behalf of the other person as the response component in a three step process.

In general, socio-developmental processes consist of sequences of elementary three step processes embedded in each other. While at one level of analysis, an act of a person may be defined as gazing at the other, at another level of analysis that gazing may only be part of a more complex act, e.g. an act of loving, or an act of hostility. It is up to the researcher to specify at which level of analysis he or she is approaching the issue in question.

Synchrony and turn-taking in communication

It is a well-established fact that synchrony and rhythm are essential characteristics of various biological functions. Indeed, irregularities and asynchrony in such functions as heart beat, brain waves and breathing may be signs of severe bodily disorders. Synchrony and rhythm are also essential, at various levels of functioning, to human communication. Psychological research has demonstrated that, in the process of speech, different parts of the speaker's body move in time with each other and with the articulation of syllables, words and phrases. For example, while speakers articulate particular syllables they may also move their heads, their hands and legs in particular directions, their eyebrows may go up and down, and so on (e.g. Scheflen, 1968; Birdwhistell, 1970; Kendon, 1972). While studying the micro-organization of human behaviour, using a frame-by-frame analysis of sound films and videotapes, Condon and his co-workers (Condon, 1970; Condon and Ogston, 1966; Condon and Brosin, 1971) discovered synchrony in the behaviour of young babies. Micro-analysis of sound films of newborn babies has demonstrated that the movements of a baby are not uncoordinated and disorganized as many people had assumed, but are self-synchronized and well organized.

Synchrony of various parts of the body during communication has been discovered not only *within* a single individual but also *between* communicating individuals. It is to interactional synchrony, both at the micro- and macro-levels, that we shall now turn our attention.

Micro-synchrony in interpersonal interaction

The most surprising finding is that interactional synchrony exists very early in human life. In a series of studies Condon and Sander (1974a, 1974b; Condon, 1977, 1979) found that interactional synchrony between the human voice and bodily motion exists as early as twenty minutes after birth, and the authors suggest that it may even exist in utero. The authors obtained sound films of sixteen neonates 1 to 4 days old. The neonates were filmed while being addressed by male and female adults or while recorded human speech was presented to them. The presentations included a Thai nurse talking to American babies in her native language, and tapes with Chinese speech. In all of these cases marked synchronization of bodily motions with the human voice has been observed: infants' bodily movements followed certain patterns during the sound of a voice and were altered into new patterns with changes of sound, or where silence followed vocalization. Condon and Ogston (1971) refer to this 'isomorphism of pattern of change between the speaker and hearer' as interactional synchrony. Martin (1972), characterizing interactional synchrony, pointed out that the listener does not simply follow the speaker when synchronizing with him or her but, rather, actively enters into the speaker's tempo having been given some initial cues. Similarly, Kempton (1980) maintains that interactional synchrony is not a reaction to the sound or a reflex, or a simple following of the speaker by the listener. Instead, Kempton hypothesizes that synchronization is a result of the participants sharing 'mutually known rhythmic patterns'. Thus, the participants anticipate changes in articulation or movement on the basis of their knowledge of the rhythmic patterns of language and by employing their experience of previous changes: 'We move together in all everyday interaction by using the same ability that allows us to dance with someone, or sing in time with another person's song' (Kempton, 1980, p. 71). If the explanation in terms of mutually shared rhythmic patterns is correct, then interactional synchrony must play an important role in the child's learning of language. These rhythmic movements, co-ordinated with the speech structures of the culture into which they are born, enable children to participate in sociobiological entrainment processes from the very beginning before they actually speak. Since these rhythmic patterns are continuously repeated, by the time children start speaking they have already acquired the structure and the form of the language (Condon and Sander, 1974b, p. 462).

However, Condon and Sander's work has recently been subjected to severe criticism. Rosenfeld (1981) points out that in spite of considerable interest in and enthusiastic acknowledgement of the phenomenon of interactional synchrony, there have been virtually no attempts to replicate the study. McDowall (1978) made such an attempt but totally failed to demonstrate the phenomenon. Rosenfeld points out a number of logical and methodological considerations according to which Condon and Sander's findings appear to be an artefact caused by errors in measurement rather than a genuine effect. Thus, he argues that in order to obtain what he calls the deterministic microsynchrony of infant movements and adult phonemes which Condon and Sander claim to have found, phoneme and movement boundaries would have to be scorable within time intervals of $1/24$ to $1/48$ second, which the judges of

Condon and Sander's films could hardly have achieved. An error of $^1/_{30}$ second in coding would totally demolish the claimed findings. Another attempt to replicate Condon and Sander's study, by Dowd and Tronick (1982), was also unsuccessful (see also Miller and Byrne, 1984). Rosenfeld (1981) points out, however, that even if the findings of Condon and Sander's studies do prove to be an artefact, interactional synchrony at a macro-level is certainly not disproved and he encourages a search for interactional synchrony at different levels. The phenomenon of early interactional synchrony, as claimed by Condon and Sander, awaits replications using more sophisticated equipment that can capture reliably the fractions of a second required.

As Condon and Sander point out, the child is entrained into a culture by sharing from the very beginning the rhythm of speech and communication. The child learns the meanings of messages just as much from rhythms and intonation as from the actual meanings of words. In addition, as Kempton (1980) says, the acquisition of synchronization patterns in speech at an early stage of socialization integrates two aspects of language acquisition: learning the language and learning how to interact with others. The process of entrainment is not language specific, and a child has equal receptivity to different languages and can start learning any language equally well (Chomsky, 1962). Children can originally produce all the sounds necessary for learning foreign languages, but it is when sounds become associated with exact meanings that children lose this ability (Jakobson, 1941; Kempton, 1980).

Inspired by Condon's studies, Byers (1976) also explored micro-synchrony in interpersonal interaction. Byers was particularly interested in explaining the relationship between brain waves and interactional synchrony and in bridging the gap between biologically and socially defined levels of interactional synchrony. As an anthropologist, Byers acquired copies of films from three cultural groups: the Netsilik Eskimo, the Bushmen of the Kalahari Desert in Africa, and the Maring of New Guinea. Analysing the films of the Maring, he found that as the speakers talked the listeners moved rhythmically in relationship to the speaker. Another example of interactional synchrony in Byers's work comes from story-telling among Bushmen. The cultural habit of story-telling among Bushmen consists of one speaker giving a 'story-line' while the other participant imitates some of the speaker's gestures, adds comments and repeats the syllables of the speaker at the end of particular speech units. Byers found very fine interactional synchrony at 10 cycles per second. Finally, he refers to a most interesting case of self-imposed interactional synchrony in controlled violence among the Yanomamo, who live on the upper Orinoco in South America. Chagnon (1968), in his work on Yanomamo culture, described ritual greetings which require a display of fierceness but avoid actual violence. The speakers start shouting at each other, a process in which they achieve full synchrony with each other: one person begins, shouts two or three syllables, and is followed by the second person almost exactly one-tenth of a second later also shouting two or three syllables, this being repeated for some time. Byers points out that such close synchronization may create a state which is such as to preclude violence; synchrony, biologically regulated, brings all the participants into the same state of consciousness through a process of mutual entrainment. Byers maintains that a similar kind of entrainment is involved in shamanistic curing ceremonies, as reported by Coberly (1972). The patient is cured by becoming entrained, synchronizing with group dancing, movement, clapping, and thus reaching the same level of consciousness as the others.

Macro-synchrony in interpersonal interaction

Research into early child development has demonstrated that synchrony and reciprocity in child–adult interaction operates in various social contexts and at different levels. Kaye (1977, 1982; Kaye and Wells, 1980) focused on the study of mother–infant interaction during feeding periods. Babies' sucking consists of patterns of bursts and pauses during which the mother and the baby adapt to each other's tempo. During bursts the mother is passive while jiggling the baby, stroking his or her mouth area, retracting the nipple and talking to him or her during the pause. Kaye calls such interactional patterns 'dialogues' in which both baby and mother play their respective parts.

Synchrony and reciprocity in mutual gazing and visual co-ordination has been widely explored (see Schaffer, 1977, 1979). Fogel (1977) investigated mutual gazing between baby and mother in which patterns of interaction changed from attention to withdrawal in a co-ordinated manner. Collis and Schaffer (1975) and Collis (1977) pointed to visual co-orientation of mothers and babies, showing how babies' interests in various objects lead their mothers to follow the direction in which their babies look. Scaife and Bruner (1975), on the other hand, demonstrated that infants follow the gaze direction of adults. Brazelton *et al.* (1974) observed that interaction between a mother and her baby consisted of cycles of on-looking and non-looking, or attention and non-attention. The interaction operated on several levels, even with infants only a few weeks old. If the mother responded to the baby in a particular way the mutual interactional activity of the mother–child dyad increased (see Figure 3). If, on the other hand, the mother responded in other ways, the infant turned away and the interactional activity decreased. Moreover, the same applied to mothers' responses to their babies' behaviour. Brazelton *et al.*'s (1974) study showed that while some mothers were sensitive and able to synchronize interaction with their babies, others were not. For example, in their study one baby started the cycle of interaction by looking at her mother who followed by smiling, touching the baby and talking. The baby responded briefly and turned away. The mother, however, continued with her part, not giving the baby time to reciprocate so that the cycle of interactions became unsynchronized and a break-down of communication occurred. In sum, from a very early stage, babies interacting with adults regulate interactions by increasing or decreasing their activities and gestures.

Turn-taking in vocalizing between adult and baby was explored by Lewis and Freedle (1973) and Bateson (1975). It was shown that by the age of 7 weeks mothers and their infants took turns in vocalization, one at a time, sequencing vocalization carefully, without interrupting each other, and giving each other a chance to respond, comment, and initiate conversation. In such an interaction the infant both 'speaks' and listens, and learns that he or she must give the other participant the same chance if mutual communication is to be successfully maintained. Schaffer *et al.* (1977) explored the integration of visual and vocal channels of communication between 1 and 2 year olds and their mothers. It was found that with both age groups communications proceeded smoothly, showing that very young children have the ability to take vocal turns and to avoid overlapping responses. Where overlaps occurred they were short and did not appear to disturb the smoothness of a preverbal dialogue. Such ability to take vocal turns is essential for later verbal conversation.

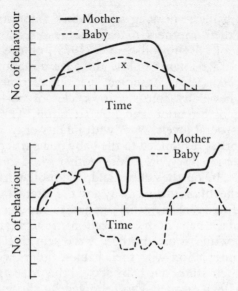

Figure 3 Two cases of mother–baby interaction
Source: Brazelton, T. B., Koslowski, B. and Main, M. (1974), in Lewis and Rosenblum (eds), *The Effect of the Infant on its Caregiver.*

A number of studies have shown that the speaker and listener are co-ordinated both verbally and non-verbally, and that a great deal of this co-ordination is below the level of awareness (Key, 1980; Leonard-Dolan, 1980). In fact, when it is brought to awareness the co-ordination can break down. Leonard-Dolan (1980), in her analysis of films of linguistic–kinesic behaviour, discovered complex co-ordination of communication below the level of awareness. Frame-analysis of films showed patterns that were either interpersonally symmetric and comfortable to speakers, or were asymmetric, in which case the interaction was felt to be uncomfortable or even at times broke down. She produced evidence indicating that persons from the same ethnic culture, even if they have never met before, produce symmetrical linguistic–kinesic patterns, while interactions between people of different ethnic groups are likely to produce asymmetrical patterns. Evidence showed that such symmetrical and asymmetrical patterns occurred below the level of awareness but were related to success in dyadic conversation.

That asymmetry is experienced as uncomfortable was also established in a study by Erickson and Shultz (1982). The study was concerned with inter-ethnic counselling sessions that were filmed and subsequently analysed. The authors suggest that asymmetry, or arhythmia, as they call it, is experienced as uncomfortable because its unpredictable nature makes it difficult for the other participant to co-ordinate in joint action (Erickson and Shultz, 1982, p. 114). Arhythmia occurs, in particular, between counsellors and students of different cultural backgounds. The authors found that while in rhythmic interaction participants regulate each other, in arhythmical interaction this is not so because the listener fails to act at the right time. For example, arhythmical interaction prevents the speaker from making the next move, or leads him or her to make an inappropriate move, e.g. provide more explanation than is necessary.

Regulation of a dialogue through turn-taking

We have demonstrated that interpersonal communication between young children and their caretakers is synchronized at various levels of interaction and that the gestures of participants follow patterns of turn-taking, although there is no evidence that early turn-taking is consciously monitored. Turn-taking is also a basic characteristic of Mead's conversation of gestures discussed earlier. Evolutionally, a conversation of non-verbal gestures precedes verbal conversation, and it is from a non-verbal conversation of gestures that verbal conversation, or dialogue, develops (Wundt, 1916; Mead, 1934; Farr, 1980b). We have seen that preverbal dialogues are characterized by a synchrony and reciprocity of gestures of which participants are largely unaware. This does not mean, though, that as the child acquires speech he or she automatically copes with turn-taking in verbal language. Early students of child communication noted the difficulty for a child of waiting for his or her turn. For example, Isaacs (1933) claimed that children under 5 years of age could hardly believe that their turn would eventually come if they had to wait a few minutes, and we shall discuss this problem in some detail in the next section.

Taking turn in a dialogue does not mean, though, that each participant has to produce the same number of words or talk for the same amount of time as the other. A participant can take a turn without saying a word. The importance of non-

145

verbal communication and of 'silent language' has been highlighted by various researchers. Among them, Hall (1959) and
Birdwhistell (1970) have drawn particularly imaginative and
pertinent pictures of the power of silence. Discussing the
embeddedness of interpersonal communication in a cultural
setting, Hall (1959), presents the following example to bring
this point home:

When a husband comes home from the office, takes off his hat,
hangs up his coat, and says 'Hi' to his wife, the way in which he
says 'Hi' reinforced by the manner in which he sheds his overcoat,
summarizes his feelings about the way things went at the office.
If his wife wants the details she may have to listen for a while, yet
she grasps in an instant the significant message for her: namely, what
kind of evening they are going to spend and how she is going to
have to cope with it (Hall, 1959, pp. 120–1).

Birdwhistell (1970) described patterns of non-verbal communication in his own family. Thus, his mother was an expert in
'untalk' and her silences were louder than his father's
machinery. Moreover, her

thin-lipped smile, which could be confined to her mouth, when
accompanied by an audible input of air through her tightened
nostrils required no words – Christian or otherwise – to reveal her
attitude (Birdwhistell, 1970, p. 52).

Birdwhistell refers to equally detectable non-verbal codes used
by other members of the family, including his own 'talk-talk-
talk'. However, none of the family members were aware of
the pervading force of their messages. The author himself
learned only twenty years later that his own 'talk-talk-talk' was
well understood by his parents:

It was to be 20 years before I was to learn that I had had the
technique of telling a story which formed an audible camouflage
under which to escape – timing it to end as I went out the door.
Uninterruptible, the story could preclude the intrusion of
prohibition to go out that night or to use the car. And such stories
avoided discussion of torn pants or of inadequate report cards.
They used words to drown out relevant information or as a place
to store messages full of trivial information (Birdwhistell, 1970,
p. 53).

These examples are, thus, instances of perfect understanding of messages, whether expressed by silences or by extravagance of words, at different levels of awareness by the participants. Birdwhistell's examples point to the fact that the family members were unaware of the impact of their turns while, at the same time, perfectly understanding each other's intentions and attitudes. The kind and quality of interpersonal interaction thus depends on sensitivity to subtle cues and changes in the other person's non-verbal messages, and on his or her responses to those of the speaker him- or herself. As Hall (1966) points out, people unconsciously and then consciously avoid escalation of annoyance or hostility by being able to control barely perceptible signs of such attitudes in their non-verbal messages. If a break-down of communication occurs, in particular in the international and intercultural spheres, much of the problem lies in people's failure to respond early enough to the 'adumbrative or foreshadowing part of a communication'. When people eventually become fully aware of what is going on, it is usually too late to back out (Hall, 1966). In *Silent Language*, Hall (1959) discusses problems of communication resulting from the fact that participants do not share the same culture or social background. Such cases of misunderstanding highlight the embeddedness of interpersonal communication in cultural settings at large. For example, Hall shows that a misunderstanding can result from the varying attitudes that different cultures have towards time. Thus, while the American is future orientated, handles time like a material, earns it, spends it, saves it, and wastes it, a person from the Middle East does not organize his or her life with the intention of planning for the future. Such differences, Hall demonstrates, can result in a total failure to see each other's point of view.

In conclusion, a dialogue is a genuinely developmental process in which nothing is determined beforehand: the order of turns varies, the size of turns is not fixed, the length of conversation as such is not specified in advance, what the participants say is not predetermined, and so on (Sacks *et al.*, 1974). The quality and kind of dialogue depends primarily on the *communicative awareness* of the participants. Their communicative awareness involves their ability to judge what should be said and when to say it, their awareness of each other's feelings, thoughts and communicative intentions, and their awareness of themselves as participants in a dialogue. It also, and equally importantly, involves their ability to decode in the other person, and to control in themselves, the emission of those barely perceptible messages that might later escalate into a full expression of conflict and a break-down in communication. These messages, while manageable at the level of semi-awareness, might become uncontrollable once they reached the full awareness of the participants. Then, because of their fear of losing face, the participants would find it impossible to back out (cf. Chapter 6).

In the remainder of this chapter we shall examine turn-taking as a means of regulating a dialogue. Our main purpose will be to study the development of the child's awareness of turn-taking as a regulating factor in conversation, followed by a discussion of various theories of turn-taking.

Turn-taking in children's dialogues

Turn-taking in conversation represents giving both oneself and the other participant a chance of self-expression. In adult conversation, as Sacks *et al.* (1974) made clear, there are a number of factors that influence changes of turns. For example, speakers can select each other as next turn-taker by giving appropriate cues, such as asking questions, making eye contact, and so on. They are usually aware of proper timing with respect to pauses between turns, of possibilities of filling uncomfortable pauses, of when to start talking and when to stop. Of course, adult conversation does not always proceed smoothly, due to a variety of personal, interpersonal and situational factors. Errors are often made, leading to overlap or simultaneous talking of two or more participants, and other types of disruptions occur. However, if disruptions in conversation do occur, the participants are usually aware of them, and given good will they can bring the conversation back on to the rails.

Caregivers start teaching their children very early to take turns in conversation. Snow (1977) points out that communication between mother and infant is conversational from the very beginning, and that changes in the mothers' speech style correspond to changes in the nature of the interaction with their babies. Mothers rarely use monologue when talking to their babies. When babies are too young to reciprocate in speech, the babies' activities, direction of attention, vocalization and cry evoke speech from their mothers.

Snow demonstrates the changes occurring in mother–infant conversation as the baby becomes more cognitively and socially competent. When the baby is about 3 months old the mother responds to all of his or her physiological reactions, such as cries, yawns, burps and coughs, and to social reactions such as smiles and vocalizing. Her utterances are short and baby-centred, the physiological or social reactions are referred to specifically by naming. The conversation between Ann and her mother went as follows (Snow, 1977, p. 12):

Mother	Ann
	(smile)
Oh what a nice little smile!	
Yes, isn't that nice?	
There.	
There's a nice little smile.	(burps)
What a nice wind as well!	
Yes, that's better isn't it?	
Yes.	(vocalizes)
Yes.	
Yes!	
There's a nice noise.	

Thus, the mother acts as if the behaviour of the child were intentional and communicative. Snow points out that the common characteristic of infant behaviour is its easy interpretability and that it signifies something about the state of a child. Infant behaviour which is not easily interpretable, such as arm- or leg-waving, does not enter into maternal utterances unless it is part of some interpretable behaviour. The important aspect of these early conversations is that mothers attempt to maintain a conversation despite the inadequacies of their conversational partners: they do it by being repetitive, asking many questions which they answer for the baby, filling in for the baby, and taking turn for him or her.

At the age of 7 months babies become more active partners in conversation and mothers no longer respond to all vocalizations but only to 'high quality' vocalizations, such as particularly long babbles, elaborated consonantal babbles, and so on. Such 'high quality' babbles are imitated by the mother and become turns in a conversation, although these imitations may be mutual failures (Snow, 1977, p. 16).

Mother	Ann
Ghhhhh ghhhhh ghhhhh ghhhhh	(protest cry)
Grrrr grrrr grrrr grrrr	
Oh, you don't feel like it, do you.	aaaa aaaa aaaa

No, I wasn't making that noise.
I wasn't going aaaa aaaa   aaaa aaaa
Yes, that's right.

At this stage the mother still has to answer the questions she askes Ann, but at the age of 18 months Ann was successfully taking her turn. Her mother expected her not only to take turn but also to provide appropriate responses (Snow, 1977, p. 18):

Mother	Ann
Who's that?	Daddy
That's not daddy, that's Dougall	
Say Dougall.	

Sequences of responses, corrections, and corrected responses became an important part of the turn-taking at this stage. Although the mother still had to fill in for the child and Ann still violated the rules of conversation, on the whole it was becoming more effective and really reciprocal.

Garvey (1984) also points out that mothers give a great deal of assistance to their children in taking and formulating their turns. Perhaps as a result of such encouragement, children learn very early that questions require answers, although they may still be unable to provide appropriate answers. Garvey argues and gives evidence that before the age of 3 years many children attain the means of taking their turns even if they do not know what to say. For example, they may say 'hmmm' or repeat the mother's question, thus passing the turn back to her. Garvey (1984, p. 59) gives the following example of such an exchange of turns, when Jack was 30 months of age:

Jack	Mother
	What is that called?
(No response)	
	What is his home called?(Points at a picture of a nest.)
Mmmmm.	
	Do you remember?
Mmmm.	
	Do we call a baby bird's home a nest?
Yeah!	
	That's right. It's a nest.

One can see in this example that, just as in the above examples from Snow, the mother gives a great deal of help to the child in taking a turn and then expands the child's reply as the child might have done if he or she had been able to do so.

Ervin-Tripp (1979) explored children's turn-taking empirically. She recorded a set of telephone conversations between children, and between children and adults, the youngest children being 2 years of age. She also made videotapes of siblings, child–friend, child–adult, and child–parent dyads, the children's ages being between 1 year 3 months and 9 years. With respect to turn-taking she found that there were considerably longer gaps in children's talk than in adults' conversations, especially on the phone. The children also overlapped more than adults. The longer gaps with the younger children are partly due to their inability to process fast enough what the other said. Thus, the 2 year olds had from 27–55 per cent delayed responses, while 4 year olds had 9–20 per cent delayed responses when compared with the adult standard.

Children's interruptions in speech also undergo development. By the age of 2½ years children know that questions require replies, and analysis of dialogues of under 4 year olds show that if the child violates the norms of conversation, for example, by not answering questions, the other may use interruptions in order to re-establish those norms. In Ervin-Tripp's (1979) study, both Marko and Sonya were younger than 4 years. Marko asked questions and did not give Sonia time to reply, did not listen to what Sonia said, never replied to the questions Sonia asked him, in telling his narrative never tuned into the cues she gave him, so that she became bored. Sonia's interruptions at this stage were attempts to put the conversation back on to the rails. A year later when she was 4½ years old she asked him explicitly *to talk straight* when he did not conform to her expectations as a listener.

Another interesting topic in early regulation of interpersonal interaction is that of jokes. The same study by Ervin-Tripp showed that at about 4½ years the child realizes that if a joke is to be understood fully it is necessary to clear the field for it. At this age the child starts using deliberate strategies to attract attention so that the joke comes off. The child becomes aware that different kinds of communication require different styles in turn-taking for a particular point to be made.

It is clear from Ervin-Tripp's study that some children cope with norms concerning turn-taking by the age of 4½.

However, many children find it difficult not to interrupt when they want attention, they have an urgent desire to break into ongoing speech, they are also less able to cope with situations of competition, and are less able to anticipate the responses of others.

Umiker-Sebeok (1980) explored the ways children start taking their turns, and in particular their utilization of prestarters such as *well, uhuhh, hm, yes, oh*, and so on. Prestarters are conversational devices used a lot in adult conversation in order to indicate that one is about to start talking, or to fill in gaps, or to give oneself time to collect one's thoughts. Umiker-Sebeok found that such prestarters become more prominent in the conversations of 5 year olds in comparison to 3 or even 4 year olds. Thus, between 4 and 5 years of age the use of the word *well* dramatically increases as children start using it to indicate their hesitation. Its use reflects the growing awareness of the child that devices such as *well, uh-huh* and *yes* have a subtle function in transforming the meaning of an utterance, and the child's sensitivity to the conversational turn-taking rule not to leave gaps so that conversation can proceed smoothly.

In conclusion, preschool children develop a sufficient degree of communicative awareness to enable them to cope with turn-taking norms in everyday conversations. However, just as there are tremendous differences among people with respect to self- and other-awareness in general, there are also tremendous differences among people in their ability to master the art of conversation, whether as speakers, or listeners, or both.

Theories of turn-taking

Turn-taking in conversation has been the subject of considerable research effort for some time and the purpose of this section is to bring this point to the student's awareness. Since this research effort, however, explores turn-taking in conversation from the *structural* point of view rather than as a socio-developmental *process*, its relevance to the subject of this book is only marginal: for this reason, we shall not discuss this research in any detail.

Several studies (e.g. Wilson *et al.*, 1984; Wiemann, 1985) have attempted to identify the main approaches in the study of the structure of turn-taking in conversation. Wilson *et al.* (1984) examined the prominent approaches and categorized them under three headings: *stochastic modelling*, *signalling*, and *sequential production*.

Stochastic modelling (Jaffe and Feldstein, 1970; Capella, 1979, 1980) is based on the assumption that turn-taking is a probabilistic process in which various linguistic characteristics, such as lengths of silences of and between speakers, bursts of speech, simultaneous speech and so on, produce patterns which can be statistically modelled. This approach is concerned with a statistical, rather than with a social psychological analysis of turn-taking.

The *signalling approach* (Duncan, 1972; Duncan and Fiske, 1977; Duncan, 1983), on the other hand, assumes that the participants monitor each other's turns by displaying non-verbal signals to which the other responds. For example, the participants indicate by pitch, by gaze, or by other gesture that they are prepared to let the other party take the floor; alternatively, the listener may indicate that he or she wishes to have a turn. The non-verbal signals are discrete cues of a conventional nature, shared by all members of a particular culture, to which participants respond according to learned rules. The rules identify the point at which a participant is supposed to start or finish his or her turn, or inhibit or encourage a particular kind of behaviour. The main task in the signalling approach is to identify how the actions of one participant relate to the actions of the other, and thus how interactional sequences occur. The signalling approach distinguishes between two types of rule-governed interactional sequences: obligatory and optional. Obligatory sequences are those in which a participant must take some action if the other person signals; just as a person must stop when the light is red, so the listener must not take his or her turn while the speaker is gesticulating (Duncan, 1983, p. 155). In optional sequences, in contrast, a participant may or may not take a particular action in response to the other's signal. The criteria as to what counts as an obligatory and what as an optional signal, leading to the action sequence in question, is determined probabilistically.

The *sequential approach* (Sacks *et al.*, 1974), in contrast to the signalling approach, pays attention to the participants' knowledge of language, rather than to non-verbal cues. Interaction between participants is sequentially carried out and determined on a moment-by-moment basis. Allocation of turns comes about in a variety of ways. The present speaker may select the next one, the next participant may self-select him- or herself, or the present speaker may take two or more turns. The allocation of turns depends on the participants' sensitivity, by means of their knowledge of language in general and through intonation, to the completion of linguistic units. An important aspect of the sequential approach is that the participants are jointly responsible for the allocation of turns. However, the sequential approach has been criticized for not clearly specifying how participants recognize when their turn has arrived, or what kind of behaviour is appropriate at each moment with respect to turn-taking. Recently, Wilson *et al.* (1984) have proposed a *resource model of turn-taking*, which claims to combine various aspects of the signalling and sequential approaches. The resource model, rather than relying on non-verbal cues and knowledge of language only, sets interpersonal interaction into its social and cultural context. Thus, changes in intonation, grammatical completion, and non-verbal cues are only *resources* on which the participants draw when needed, rather than determinants of turn-taking. They may mean different things to interactants depending on the relationship between them, the reasons for the current conversation, the situation in which the conversation takes place, and so on.

All the above models are primarily concerned with the structural aspects of conversation, such as turn-construction, turn-allocation, gaps and overlaps in conversation. Although it is important to study the structural characteristics, real progress in the study of conversation can only be made by studying the *structure* of a conversation alongside the *process* of conversation as a *meaningful* socio-developmental phenomenon (Markova, in press).

Modification of speech due to the speaker's other-awareness

Motherese

It is fairly well known that when adults talk to young children they modify and simplify their speech in a number of ways. This simplified language of adults when talking to children is called *motherese* or *baby-talk*, although some researchers distinguish between these terms (cf. Elliot, 1981). Research has shown that motherese is characterized by simple syntactic structures, e.g. short utterances, fewer verbs, fewer utterances with subordinate clauses, and its semantics modified, e.g. semantically simple words are used. In addition, motherese has exaggerated intonation, many repetitions, higher pitch, there are more questions and commands and a number of other modifications simplifying speech (for reviews of motherese see Elliot, 1981; Fernald, 1984; Bohannon and Hirsh-Pasek, 1984).

Garnica (1977) found that the speech of adults to 2 year olds was not only different from the speech directed to adult listeners but also from that directed to 5 year olds. Thus, the speech to 2 year olds had higher pitch, included whispered parts of sentences, and contained more instances of primary stress in sentences. In the speech both to 2 year olds and to 5 year olds there was prolonged duration of certain words, and so on.

It has been noted that modification of speech to young children probably exists in all languages, and a number of studies have demonstrated such modifications cross-culturally (Ferguson, 1977; Harkness, 1977; Jocić, 1978).

Young children vary to a considerable degree with respect to the age at which they produce their first words, master grammar, develop vocabulary and acquire a general ability to express what they mean. Researchers have set for themselves the task of discovering the extent to which the ways mothers communicate with their children might influence the child's development of language and communication. Some studies have concentrated on attempts to discover correlations between various indices of maternal speech and various indices of the child's speech, for example on whether the content of speech, length of utterances, intelligibility, the number of questions and commands and the general complexity of maternal utterances is related to the child's level of language (e.g. Newport *et al.*, 1977; Furrow *et al.*, 1979). However, studies of this kind, focusing on linguistic and cognitive aspects of speech, appear to be generally inconclusive since it is difficult to control for the variables of the complex phenomenon of human speech and to control precisely for the linguistic level of the child.

A social psychological approach, focusing on the mother's awareness of the child as a participant in communication, has been more successful. Cross (1978) set out to test the relationship between maternal and child language measuring sixty features of maternal speech. Her principal finding is that it is the level of the mother's competence to assess what the child intends to communicate that is decisive as to whether the development of the child's language is accelerated or delayed. Cross found that those mothers who were more sensitive to their children's communicative intentions produced more expanded utterances, e.g. elaborated on the child's utterances, and used more semantic extensions in which they expressed the child's meaning using different words. In addition, there were more repetitions and sequences related to the children's preceding utterances in the speech of mothers of children with more developed speech. These mothers also produced fewer utterances that were new to the discourse and fewer utterances unintelligible to the child. Cross's study has also shown that syntax is not as important for the child's development of language as the mother's awareness of the child's communicative intentions.

The idea that it is the social sensitivity of parents rather than just their response to the lack of linguistic and cognitive development in the child that leads parents to modify their language, has been corroborated by other researchers (Nelson, 1973; Snow, 1972; Berko-Gleason and Weintraub, 1978; Retherford, Schwartz, and Chapman, 1981). Thus, Snow (1972) found that the actual presence of the child while the adult was talking, rather than just imagining his or her presence, was an essential condition for eliciting motherese. Parents do not react to their *knowledge* of what a child of a particular age is capable of, but to the cues given to them by children in the process of interaction. A number of researchers emphasize the active role that children play in monitoring adult speech (Bohannon and Marquis, 1977; Bohannon and Warren-Leubecker, 1982; Retherford, Schwartz, and Chapman, 1981).

Adults' modification of their speech to children is only one example of speech adjustment due to the particular characteristics of the listener. Research in the social psychology of language and in sociolinguistics has provided evidence that speakers talk differently to familiar and unfamiliar listeners (Fielding and Fraser, 1978), and to people of different status and different ethnicity (Scherer and Giles, 1979). Such differences in speech are expressions of two basic factors: first, of *the speaker's awareness of the listener's particular individual and social characteristics*, e.g. his or her personality characteristics, social power, knowledge shared with the speaker and relationship to the speaker; and second, of *the conventional aspects of language*, many of which are intuitive and normally below the level of the speaker's awareness. We shall deal with these factors in the following two sections.

The speaker's awareness of the listener as an individual

As in the case of the child's acquisition of empathy, it is hard to say just when the child starts talking differently to different kinds of people, because such a process is very gradual and there are considerable individual differences. Thus, Berko-Gleason (1973) found that 4 year olds did not change their speech when talking to other children of different age groups, while there were clear differences in the speech of 8 year olds when talking to younger and older children. In contrast, Shatz and Gelman (1973) found that 4 year olds spoke differently when talking to 2 year olds rather than to adults. In this study the 4 year olds were given the task of explaining the functioning of a toy to both an adult and a 2 year old. Substantial differences appeared between the two. When explaining the toy to the 2 year olds, the 4 year olds focused on demonstrating the toy, and telling the younger ones how to use it. They made no reference to mental states such as the speaker's thoughts, wishes or memories, made no suggestions about possible actions to be taken, but gave the young ones simple orders, such as 'do this', or 'do that'. Since they probably did not expect the young children to question the veracity of their statements, no modulators (phrases such as 'I am sure', 'I think', 'surely', and so on expressing degrees of certainty) were used. The children made clear, simple, and short statements about the topic. They used a great number of repetitive utterances with a variety of demonstrative and attention-increasing devices. Explanations given to adults were very different. Generally, the range of topics introduced in the speech was much wider. There was no need to call for the adult's attention. The children sought information from the adult, used modulators, and made affirmative comments on the speech of the adult.

It is important that in both cases the children sought to adjust to the listener, and to make themselves understood so that the listener could respond appropriately. Thus, communicative awareness, even in very young children, involves not only knowledge of linguistic rules but also the ability to take the role of the other, although in a primitive way, and to reflect upon one's own activity.

A study of 4–6 year olds communicating with mentally handicapped children was carried out by Guralnik and Paul-Brown (1977). The children were enrolled in a preschool programme to integrate non-handicapped and handicapped children. It was found that the non-handicapped children spoke differently to the non-handicapped and mildly handicapped on the one hand, and the moderately and severely mentally handicapped children on the other. Their speech, with respect to both its quantity and its quality, was more sophisticated when talking to non-handicapped and mildly handicapped children in terms of the number of nouns used, the number of questions asked and the general complexity of the language.

Conventionalized aspects of conversation

The kind and quality of a dialogue depends not only on the participants' awareness of each other but also on the degree to which they have internalized the conventional aspects of communication, the so called *regulative* and *constitutive rules* (Searle, 1969; Dittmar, 1984).

Regulative rules prescribe how social activities should be carried out. Such rules standardize or normalize procedures concerning interpersonal interaction situations, ceremonies such as weddings, meetings with a friend or a stranger, and so on. In language and communication they prescribe what one should and should not say, to whom, and under what circumstances. Such rules also include grammatical rules and conventions and the use of a lexicon. A great deal of research exploring regulative rules has been concerned with the analysis of conversations, for example with rules in turn-taking (e.g. Sacks, Schegloff and Jefferson, 1974; Duncan, 1972, 1974; Beattie, 1983), and starting and finishing a conversation (Schegloff and Sacks, 1973), with rules of coherence (Tracy, 1985; Craig and Tracy, 1983), and sequencing (Street and Cappella, 1985). Regulative rules develop in interactive processes and make discourse predictable. In the process of mutual co-operation, in which they consider each other's expectations and signal their own expectations to each other, participants develop *contextualization conventions* (Gumperz and Cook-Gumberz, 1982). Such conventions in discourse become guiding posts for monitoring the progress of conversational interaction and, together with the knowledge of grammar and lexicon, are used in decision-making with respect to the discourse tasks to be performed. It is important that, once properly learned, contextualization conventions, like grammatical knowledge, do not have to be consciously chosen by the individual (Gumperz and Cook-Gumperz, 1982, p. 18). Their meanings are implicit and not mentioned out of context because they make sense only with respect to a particular message. If participants produce relevant *contextualization cues* (Gumperz, 1982) and interpret them habitually, the cues pass unnoticed. However, if a participant does not react to a cue or reacts differently than expected, the others become aware of them, misunderstandings may occur and communication may break down. Contextualization conventions are routinized interactive exchanges which children learn from a very early age. Children's awareness of discourse rituals is learned, for example, in pretend play (cf. Chapter 3). Garvey gives many examples that demonstrate that very young children master such routines. For example, when Anne, 35 months old, speaks on the toy telephone, she starts with Hello and ends with Bye (Garvey, 1984, p. 155).

In non-verbal communication, too, regulative rules determine what kinds of messages are appropriate for specific situations, and to whom particular messages can be addressed. *Kinesics* (Birdwhistell, 1970), or body language, refers to gestures, movements of various parts of the body, posture and eye-gaze. Shaking hands, touching the other person, staring and gazing, are all regulated by rules specific to different cultures. Lack of knowledge of such rules may lead to misunderstanding among people belonging to different cultures, and violation of such rules within a culture may signify changes in interpersonal interaction and relationships. Body language is an organic part of interpersonal communication, and if it is performed in accordance with the participants' habits and conventions a great part of it goes unnoticed. We have already discussed the rhythmic and symmetrical nature of non-verbal and verbal communication (see pp. 138–45). It is only when the rhythm and symmetry become distorted in the flow of a discourse that one notices its non-existence. Birdwhistell (1970) explored kinesics in a variety of contexts and with a variety of people. He noted that it is not the existence of a different repertoire of expressions in the body language of people with various kinds of mental illness and emotional disturbance that makes their communication disorganized and incomprehensible to others. Rather, they display the same kinds of behaviour as people without mental illness or emotional disturbance, but their behaviour is inappropriate for given situations, and its duration and intensity are different from those expected by convention. Such people also seem to have less ability to comprehend the behaviour of others, and they misinterpret much of what others express through their body language. Moreover, emotionally disturbed people appear to have less ability to modify their behaviour when it offends, or is incomprehensible to others.

Hall (1966) has made an important contribution to the study of the rules of *proxemics*, i.e. the use of space as a specialized elaboration of a culture. Different cultures have different rules as to the distance one should keep in various social encounters. The rules concerning the distance to be kept in interpersonal interaction can be properly comprehended only as a part of the life of a particular culture. Thus, in the background of such rules are people's attitudes to what should and should not be kept private, attitudes towards personal space, and the role the different senses play in cultural life in general. For example, Hall refers to olfaction as playing a more important role in Arab life than in the life of the Americans. Because of the importance to them of olfaction, the Arabs try to enhance body odours to make them pleasing to others, and breathing into the other person's face is a sign of being involved with the other person. To deny one's breath to a friend is to act ashamed (Hall, 1966, p. 149). Hall's classic book on *The Hidden Dimension* (1966) thus combines scientifically important observations of proxemics in different cultures with entertaining reading.

The second kind of rules is *constitutive*. In contrast to regulative rules, constitutive rules define an activity, and without them the particular activity would cease to exist. The usual examples given to illustrate constitutive rules are those of games. Thus, a game of chess or a game of football would not make sense apart from the rules that specify them.

In interpersonal interaction, constitutive rules make it possible to identify *situations* by recognizing the rules of the particular game. Fishman (1972) defines a *situation* as the co-occurrence of two or more participants who are related to each other in a particular way, talking about a particular subject matter in a particular setting. An example of a situation would be a group of students with their tutor in a pub. A different situation would involve the same people in the context of a tutorial at the university. Differences between situations would be marked by differences between the subjects discussed and also by differences in language styles, grammar and lexicon. Participants know the rules belonging to different situations, and they also know when to shift from one language style to another. Fishman talks in this sense about *situational shifts*. Shifts in situations may also necessitate shifts in language styles, and consequently may also signal changes in interpersonal relationships. Fishman also points out that a switch in language variety may occur without actual changes in settings, and can be *metaphorical*. For example, participants may switch from the received pronounciation to a dialect, with the intention of making a contrast or to emphasize a point. However, Fishman remarks that metaphorical switching can be dangerous in interaction if participants are not aware of the meaning of such switching. Thus, metaphorical switching is a luxury and can be used only if all participants share the same situational norms and have 'the same view as to their inviolability'. However, in most cases the participants are members of different social networks that have their own situational norms, and metaphorical switching can therefore be easily misunderstood and can create communication break-down.

In his analysis of proxemics to which we have just referred, Hall (1966) described four distance zones for interpersonal interaction: intimate, personal, social, and public. The *intimate distance zone* is used by interactants to express loving, comforting and protecting relationships: physical contact plays an important part in such interaction. The *personal distance zone* is used by close acquaintances and friends and it enables interactants either to touch each other or to keep each other 'at arm's length'. People conduct business or work together at the *social distance zone*, or they use it when attending casual social gatherings. Finally, the *public distance zone* may be adopted by people if they feel threatened, uninvolved with each other; or it is the distance set around important public figures. One must understand that distance zones are concepts defining particular kinds of interpersonal relationships as seen from the point of view of the participants involved in such relationships, rather than properties that can be defined by actual physical measurements. Although Hall, on the basis of his observations, actually attached physical measurements in feet to particular distance zones, I prefer not to confuse the issue by quoting his numbers. These numbers were based on observations of a particular kind of American subculture some twenty years ago. What is an appropriate physical distance for a particular distance zone in one subculture, at a particular time, and in particular situations, may be totally inappropriate for other subcultures, at other times, and in other circumstances. However, Hall's classification of distance zones, as long as it is understood in terms of human awareness of social relationships, represents constitutive rules for particular social relationship 'games'. As long as such rules are understood by the participants, these games may be played smoothly. Changes with respect to distance zones during the course of a communication may signify changes in the interpersonal relationships. Thus, a shift from one zone to another by one participant can be accepted or rejected by the other, depending on the willingness to move from one kind of relationship to another one. Hall made it quite clear, though, that physical distances are only one aspect of distance zones. Fundamental to distance zones is the involvement of the different senses, depending to a considerable extent on the physical distance between people. For example, the sensation of warmth from a person may delineate the boundary between intimacy and non-intimacy, standing and looking down on the other person may have a domineering effect, and so on (Hall, 1966).

Various researchers have proposed theories to account for the regulation of non-verbal interaction. The best known of these is the approach-avoidance theory of proximity by Argyle and Dean (1965). The theory assumes that people are both attracted and repelled by each other, and that in the process of interaction they establish an equilibrium position with respect to each other. For example, those people in laboratory experiments who were seated 2 feet apart leant backwards, while those seated 10 feet apart leant forward as if trying to achieve a comfortable distance with respect to each other. Proximity is only one of the ways by which people can achieve intimacy. Other means of achieving intimacy are eye-contact, smiling, saying certain kinds of things, and so on. The Argyle and Dean theory predicts that if people are prevented from using a certain kind of behaviour, natural to them in their particular situation, they will adopt some other behaviour to compensate for the change in level of intimacy. Recently, Patterson (1985) has proposed a sequential functional model of non-verbal exchange. This model, in contrast to that of Argyle and Dean, attempts to take account of the complexity of the cultural and interpersonal background of the participants in interaction. It describes and analyses interaction with respect to the personal, experiential and relational-situational antecedents of interaction, and considers changes in the arousal, cognition and behaviour of both participants.

Contextualization and decontextualization

Whatever people say to each other, it is always embedded in a social context. The *more* the participants understand the context in which something is said, the *less* that needs to be said, and vice versa. Young children are usually well understood by parents long before they can express their intentions in speech because the context in which the child expresses him- or herself is well understood by parents. An important factor in the development of communicative intentions is related to the emergence of the child's ability to single out objects in his or her environment and to reach out for them. Vygotsky (1962), like Mead (1934), argued that non-verbal gestures are an important precursor of the child's development of symbolic speech. Vygotsky points out that the child's development of symbolic speech from non-verbal gestures proceeds in three basic stages. Originally, in the first stage, a pointing gesture is simply an unfinished grasping movement, directed towards an *object* and only foreshadowing future action. The child tries to grasp an object out of reach, his or her hand just hanging in the air. At this stage, it is just a gesture on its own. At the next stage, the *other person*, the mother, gives a new meaning to this gesture, because she responds to it. It becomes a *gesture for the other*. Finally, as a result of the mother's responding to the gesture the child becomes aware of it him- or herself. It now becomes, in the last stage, a *gesture for the self*. At this stage the child no longer attempts to grasp the object. He or she just *points* and makes a *sign* (Vygotsky, 1978, p. 56). In Vygotsky's description of the development of gestures we notice a close similarity to Mead's account of the conversation of gestures and the development of self-consciousness or self-awareness. Just like Mead, Vygotsky points out that every mental function is *social*, i.e. outer, before it becomes conscious, i.e. inner. The development of a gesture from a grasp to a pointing sign represents a process of singling out an object from its context.

The first words of a child, too, are *context*-dependent

(Nelson, 1973; Braunwald, 1978; Bruner, 1978) and are embedded in social interaction between child and parent. As Braunwald (1978) points out some of these words are not, in fact, words of an adult vocabulary, and the mother is able to understand the meanings of these utterances only because she is aware of the development of the contexts in which these first words occur. Braunwald studied the production of the first fifty words of Laura and found that although twenty-one of the fifty words were plainly recognizable words in the English language, only eight were used with essentially the same range of reference, and hence had the same meaning as the standard adult words. The rest of the words either had meanings that were idiosyncratically extended, or the words were used briefly and then disappeared, or they were unmatched to adult meanings.

The child's first words are fully embedded in the social context, they accompany actions and interactions. Rommetveit (1968) has examined the way a simple noun like 'cup' is acquired by a child: it is through events involving such activities as drinking from a cup, washing up a cup, pouring from a cup, requests for a particular cup, pointing to a cup, finding a cup, and so on (Rommetveit, 1968, pp. 124–7). This is a stage in which the child does not have a precise, i.e. adult, definition of a cup, but has what can perhaps be called a 'pseudo-concept' of a cup. He or she has mastered a chain-complex of activities (Vygotsky, 1962) in which a cup plays a role but the object 'cup' is not as yet singled out from these activities. The singling out of an object, i.e. the distinguishing of it from glasses, bowls, pots, pans, and other kinds of container, is a later part of the process of word acquisition. It is the stage of *decontextualization* (Werner and Kaplan, 1963; Rommerveit, 1968; Bruner, 1978) during which an object is gradually separated from the set of activities in which it was originally embedded. As the child acquires language he or she becomes able to talk about physical and social objects outside their immediate context, that is, the presence of these objects is not required for the child to be able to communicate about them. Studies in child language have been concerned to establish when the child starts using sentences rather than individual words, which abilities underlie the acquisition of subordinating constructions, how the process of semantic disambiguation proceeds, and so on. The use of decontextualized language and explicitness in communication has in general become a criterion of language accomplishment and of the child's advance from *egocentrism* to *decentration* (cf. also Chapter 2).

Socialization and decontextualized language

An interest, in psychological studies of language, in the child's ability to use fully-fledged sentences has become prominent in the assessment of linguistic competence. Support for the claimed superiority of decontextualized language, i.e. language consisting of well-formed and fully-fledged sentences, over language embedded in context also comes from the studies of Bernstein (1971) who has been concerned to discover the relationship between the development of language and a child's socialization in a family. According to Bernstein, various forms of socialization orientate the child, either towards a language in which the meanings of messages are expressed explicitly and independently of context, using *elaborated speech codes*, or towards one in which the meanings of messages are dependent on context, using *restricted speech codes*. Elaborated codes, which are linguistically explicit, are less tied to a particular social context and require less sharing of knowledge with the listener. Characteristic of speech using elaborated speech codes are sentences with accurate grammatical structures, complex sentences, prepositions indicating logical relationships between parts of a sentence, nouns rather than pronouns, and a range of adjectives and adverbs discriminating among subtle properties of referents and encouraging the conceptual organization of life experience. In other words, the speech is carefully edited both grammatically and lexically since a speaker who uses elaborated speech codes does not take much for granted on the part of the listener. Bernstein points out that the use of elaborated speech codes involves speakers in particular role relationships with respect to listeners: since they do not assume shared knowledge, their individual I's stand over the We (Bernstein, 1971, p. 166).

Restricted codes, on the other hand, are tied to particular social contexts and the listener can understand such speech only if he or she shares a great deal of knowledge with the speaker. Speech using restricted codes is short, grammatically simple, with unfinished sentences and its grammatical structure poor. It is repetitive, using a limited range of adjectives and adverbs, together with what Bernstein (1971) has called 'sympathetic circularity', in which previous statements are reinforced by phrases like 'wouldn't it'?, 'you see?', 'you know?', and so on. The underlying social relationship between the participants assumes common history, knowledge and experience, and affective closeness. The speech is likely to be metaphorical, concerned with *how* and *when* something is said, with silences taking a variety of meanings. It is for these reasons that such speech cannot be understood properly outside the context in which it appears.

In order to highlight the difference between restricted and elaborated codes Bernstein (1970) refers to the following experiment by Hawkins analysing the speech of middle-class and working-class children. In this experiment, 5-year-old children from both social classes were presented with a series of four pictures that represented a story. The first picture showed boys playing football, the second showed the ball breaking the window of a house, the third depicted a woman looking out from the window while a man gesticulated, and in the fourth picture the children were running away. The children were asked to tell a story about the events in the four pictures and Bernstein (1970, p. 167) presents two of the stories they told:

1. Three boys are playing football and one boy kicks the ball and it goes through the window the ball breaks the window and the boys are looking at it and a man comes out and shouts at them because they've broken the window so they run away and then that lady looks out of her window and she tells the boys off.

2. They're playing football and he kicks it and it goes through there it breaks the window and they're looking at it and he comes out and shouts at them because they've broken it so they run away and then she looks out and she tells them off.

The first story, Bernstein points out, is free of the context of the four pictures while the second story cannot be understood independently of the pictures. In other words, the first story is context-free and relies upon elaborated codes while the second story is context-tied and relies upon restricted codes. The first story is characteristic of middle-class language, while the second story represents the language of a child from a lower working-class family.

The supposed connection between speech code and class, of the superior code of the middle class and inferior code of the working class, has become the subject of severe criticism on methodological, political and ideological grounds (Labov,

1969; Elliot, 1981; Osser, 1984). Bernstein points out, though, that the differences between the two kinds of code are not due to lack of vocabulary or grammar in working-class children. They are more due to the fact that a middle-class child takes very little for granted and sees the task as a requirement for explicitness. The working-class child, on the other hand, takes for granted a great deal of shared knowledge between the speaker and the listener and does not interpret the task as a requirement for explicitness. According to Bernstein, these two different kinds of interpretation of the instruction, the one calling for explicitness and the other calling for implicitness, are functions of different family structures and interpersonal relationships. One could add that the elaborated code, which is linguistically explicit, is favoured by the educational system: a pupil is expected to make him- or herself understood by people outside his or her own social group, and is encouraged to use language free of local restrictions. In other words, the pupil is encouraged to use decontextualized speech consisting of well-formed and fully-fledged sentences. Although Bernstein has often been misunderstood and severely criticized on the grounds that there is insufficient evidence for his claims associating speech codes and social class, his work has led to close attention being paid to the very important issue of the embeddedness of speech in its social context.

Communicative awareness and social context

Speech and communication, just like any other human activity, always take place in some social context, and therefore their decontextualization, i.e. their explicitness, is always only partial. The degree of decontextualization depends on various factors such as the social setting, shared knowledge, and inter-personal relationships of the participants. Moreover, explicitness or implicitness in speech may reflect the speaker's and listener's communicative awareness or lack of it with respect to such factors. Two examples will make this point quite clear. The first example is from Rommetveit (1974, p. 112).

He was bigger when he was smaller, and he will become bigger when he gets big, because his father was also small when he was smaller.

This seemingly incomprehensible sentence becomes completely

comprehensible when uttered in the particular setting of the anecdote: a mother, walking with her 4–year-old son meets her neighbour who knows the boy's age and says: 'Your son is small for his age.' The sentence, originally unintelligible, is now understood in the particular social context of the mother's response to the neighbour's remark.

Another illustration comes from Labov and Fanshel (1977). During the discussion of the importance of social context at a student seminar, the following episode was presented:

At one point in the conversation, a wife said to her husband, *You don't say that blood is thicker than water!* The husband then turned his head away from his wife and the group as a whole.

The common interpretation of the episode by the students was that the husband's gesture expressed hidden anger at the wife's insult. The truth, however, was that the wife's claim was not an insult but a compliment to her husband for showing his concern for her family, and the husband's gesture expressed a modest turning away in embarrassment at his wife's compliment (Labov and Fanshel, 1977, p. 351).

The embeddedness of speech in its social context has been highlighted even more in Labov and Fanshel's (1977) analysis of a therapeutic interview between a therapist and her anorexic patient. As part of this analysis the authors carried out an *expansion* of what the participants actually said by making their verbal utterances absolutely explicit and filling in the gaps in what had been said. Thus, the text was expanded into full sentences, pronouns were substituted by the names of people, by things and by events. In order to do this it was necessary to use the knowledge the experimenters had of the interview participants. The meanings conveyed by cues were expanded to their nearest equivalents in textual terms according to the researchers' best understanding. The following were all made explicit: first, the referents of pronouns, second, factual material that was presented before and after an utterance, sometimes from different parts of the interview, and third, knowledge shared by the participants, derived from recordings of other interviews and the playback with the therapist. For example, the following utterance of a patient

An-nd so – when – I called her t'day, I said, 'Well, when do you plan t' come home?'

was expanded as follows:

When I called my mother today [Thursday], I actually said, 'Well, in regard to the subject which we both know is important and is worrying me, when are you leaving my sister's house where your obligations have already been fulfilled and returning as I am asking you to a home where your primary obligations are being neglected, since you should do this as head of our household?' (Labov and Fanshel, 1977, p. 50).

When one compares the patient's actual utterance and the expansion one realizes how much of what one says remains unexpressed, simply because one knows that the listener knows what one is talking about. As the authors point out, this kind of exercise is open-ended, and one can bring in an unlimited number of explanatory facts that are an implicit part of an interaction. Such over-explicitness is important in order 'to gain some understanding of this process, and those who are already skilled are aware of how much they can gain from each advance in self-awareness' (Labov and Fanshel, 1977, p. 349). Such over-explicitness also reveals implicit assumptions and beliefs which may become particularly important in the context of therapeutic sessions in which patients or clients may try to hide their emotional problems.

When conversing, people do not just produce words but also non-verbal cues – the bodily positions, movements, facial expressions and tone of voice that complement verbal messages. The degree of explicitness of speech is to some degree determined by the speaker's awareness of the listener's access to such non-verbal cues which can assist him or her in decoding the message, and partly by the familiarity of the communication channel. By 'communication channel' in this context we mean the bodily position of one person with respect to the other. A classical experiment by Moscovici and Plon (1966) demonstrates this point well. In this experiment pairs of high school girls were asked to discuss a film for twenty minutes while sitting in different positions in relationship to each other. In a *face-to-face* situation participants were seated opposite and facing each other. In a *back-to-back* situation they were prevented from using non-linguistic cues. In addition, the situation itself was unfamiliar because, although people often talk to each other without seeing one another, it rarely happens in a back-to-back situation. In a third situation the participants were seated *side-by-side* as in a classroom. They were reminded, however, that in a classroom students are not supposed to turn towards their neighbours while talking, but to look forward. The situation itself, however, was familiar. Finally, participants were seated facing each other but with a screen between them so that they could not see each other. Thus, this situation was similar to the face-to-face situation but non-linguistic cues were not visible.

The study showed that back-to-back and side-by-side situations encouraged the use of a more elaborated speech. The participants used syntactically complex, nominative and properly structured grammatical sentences so that speech was more like written language. In both face-to-face situations participants used speech that was both stylistically and syntactically simple and which had implicit meanings. It thus appears that the elimination of non-verbal cues from a familiar channel of communication is not enough to force speakers to modify their speech. It is the unfamiliarity of the communication channel that encourages the use of elaborated speech. Commenting on this experiment Rommetveit (1974) has drawn attention to the use of explicit and implicit language in yet other communication contexts: in the poet-to-reader-of-poetry setting and the reporter-to-reader-of-newspaper setting. The poet addresses the reader intimately, using a cryptic and implicit language of emotional closeness. In this sense he or she resembles the speaker in a face-to-face situation with a screen between him- or herself and the reader. The poet assumes that the reader, being addressed intimately, will actively elaborate the poet's implicit meanings in an attempt to decode the poet's perspective, to share and endorse it. The newspaper reporter, on the other hand, presents the reader with fully-fledged facts of which the reader may have little or no knowledge. Thus, the reporter's language is more like that of side-by-side or back-to-back settings, taking little for granted, being elaborated and leaving little to the reader's imagination. If, however, such newspaper 'facts' are, for some reason, presented to the reader like a verse in a poem, the reader's perception of the whole situation alters: newspaper 'facts' are no longer perceived as sheer facts but, 'when read *qua* poetry' are 'assumed to convey some more profound meaning' (Rommetveit, 1974, p. 61) and the reader starts searching for underlying meanings that otherwise would not be expected. Moscovici and Plon's (1966) experiment and Rommetveit's (1974) analysis thus clearly demonstrate that in different social contexts both speakers and listeners contextualize and decontextualize language on the basis of their communicative awareness. The speaker does so bearing in mind the situational demands and his or her awareness of the listener's expectations, while the listener does so according to his or her understanding of the situation and the speaker's intentions. As Rommetveit puts it:

We are writing on the premises of the reader, reading on the premises of the writer, speaking on the premises of the listener, and listening on the premises of the speaker (Rommetveit, 1974, p. 63).

Rommetveit calls such close interdependence of the actions of speaker and listener *complementarity*. The speaker anticipates the listener's response and the listener anticipates the speaker's next move. Erickson and Shultz (1982), in their analysis of counselling interviews, provided evidence of this interrelationship between the counsellor and client, showing how listeners regulate speakers' ways of speaking. Any mismatch between cultural styles in speaking and listening leads to arhythmia, the inability to co-ordinate speech (cf. pp. 144–5). 'Retrospective-prospective awareness' (Erickson and Shultz, 1982, p. 97), or '*encoding* . . . tacitly assumed to involve anticipatory decoding' (Rommetveit, 1974, p. 55), requires precise timing in the process of interaction.

Shared knowledge and communicative awareness

Kreckel (1981) explored the effect of shared knowledge on the understanding of interaction in natural discourse using part of a real-life television documentary. This documentary, called 'The Family', was shown on BBC television in the United Kingdom in 1974, and it presented the daily life of a family in full detail apart from the most intimate personal situations. In order to achieve realism of interpersonal interactions, the film team of three people lived with the family for two months before the documentary was filmed so that the family members got used to their presence. Kreckel obtained permission from the family some time later to use the filmed material for research purposes and the family members actually helped with the research by coding and interpreting their filmed interactions. The codings and interpretations by the family members were compared and contrasted with those of outside observers who helped with the research as volunteers.

Kreckel distinguishes between *private, shared* and *common knowledge*. By private knowledge she means individuals' idiosyncratic experiences and life histories. Shared knowledge is knowledge based on shared history, experience and mutual influence among the members of the family, which is not, therefore, available to outsiders. Common knowledge, on the other hand, is knowledge obtained from books, educational institutions, the mass media and casual acquaintances. In other words, it is knowledge common to people who do not know each other as persons but are members of the same culture. Kreckel expected that there would be differences in the interpretations of filmed family interactions between family members and outside observers due to the differences between shared and common knowledge. The main findings of the study were the following. First, the agreement among the outside observers with respect to the way they coded and interpreted interactions in the film was considerably lower than that of family members. Second, the outside observers had lower inter-observer agreement not only when interpreting private conversations among the family members, but also in their interpretations of public discussions of family members with the film director. Third, agreement among the family members was considerably higher when interpreting public rather than private interactions. This showed that the family members agreed among themselves about the ways individual members presented themselves in public rather than about the ways they interacted at home as they really were. Whatever the reason for this finding, it makes one aware of the complexity of informal interactions and of their contextual dependence. Fourth, it was found that shared knowledge also affects the ways family members organize experience and form interpersonal concepts. For example, Kreckel also shows that members of one family had their idiosyncratic ways of organizing knowledge and experience and differed in some ways from another family when interpreting what constitutes the concept of 'warning'. While one family focused on making a person aware of a possible dangerous outcome of an existing situation, the other family focused on an attempt to prevent the person from performing an act with dangerous consequences.

It is clear that the more people share their knowledge and

experience the less they need to say to each other in order to convey what they mean. Rommetveit (1974) pointed out that full sentences are used when personal relationships are rather distant, as, for example, in the case of a headmaster and a pupil. On the other hand, incomplete speech, i.e. unfinished sentences, ellipsis, phrases with implicit and metaphoric meanings are used under conditions of more or less perfect understanding. Thus, Vygotsky (1962) gave a number of examples of speech condensed to its very limits, referring to Tolstoy's *Anna Karenina*, in which Kitty and Levin declared their love for each other using just the beginnings of words. Berger and Bradac (1982) also point out and give evidence to show that as people become more certain of their partners and the way they think, they become increasingly likely to abbreviate their messages. Zipf (1935) and Miller and Steinberg (1975) argue that because an abbreviated message requires less expenditure of energy, it would seem reasonable that people should abbreviate speech under such circumstances. One can thus see that speech and its social context are mutually interdependent. Communicative awareness is just as much concerned with the participants' ability to know what to say to whom and under what conditions, as with their ability to use *contextualized language*.

Summary

Communicative awareness is awareness of, and response to, the feelings, thoughts and communicative intentions of participants in the process of their interpersonal interaction. Because they are able to assess each others' feelings, thoughts, and intentions, participants can respond to each other idiosyncratically and effectively. An elementary act of interpersonal interaction consists of a minimum of three steps, and more complex communicative processes are derived from such three step units. Although communicative awareness is an expression of self- and other-awareness, people are unaware of much they convey to each other.

Communicative awareness develops in human beings from early childhood. Research studies have demonstrated the existence of synchrony in turn-taking of participants both at micro- and macro-levels. As children grow older they gradually become aware of turn-taking as a means to regulate verbal dialogue, although, just like other aspects of self- and other-awareness, communicative awareness continues to develop throughout the course of one's life. Speakers modify their speech both because they are aware of particular individual and social characteristics of listeners, and because they have adopted conventional aspects of speech expressed in regulative and constitutive rules.

Speech and its social context are mutually interrelated. Early child speech is highly context-dependent, and an adult can understand what the child expresses only as part of the whole social situation. As the child acquires language his or her speech becomes decontextualized, i.e. the message is no longer intimately embedded in social situations, but can be understood by others in isolation from the particular context. However, decontextualization is invariably only partial because the use of verbal language always assumes some commonalities with respect to knowledge and feelings that are shared among participants. Appropriate use of contextualized language is an expression of communicative awareness.

6 The manipulative and aggressive self

So far we have discussed the self's awareness of the other person's feelings, thoughts and actions, arguing that this is a fundamental requirement for the development of effective interpersonal interaction. We have implicitly assumed, and often explicitly suggested, that in taking each other's point of view the interactants adopt an active interest in each other, empathize with each other, and negotiate their mutual positions. Moreover, we have demonstrated that as children grow older, they become more communicatively aware. For example, they learn to take turns, to modify their speech with respect to who is the listener, and, in general, they adapt to their social counterparts so that communication proceeds more smoothly and effectively.

Yet, it is one's common experience that although people have the capacity for self- and other-awareness, a great deal of their interpersonal communication proceeds without taking any consideration for each other. Thus, in spite of having a capacity for empathy, people often pursue their own interests rather than helping someone in need. Governments sell weapons to countries in conflict to increase their profits, although they know perfectly well that their actions will result in much human suffering. The ability to take the listener's point of view does not prevent insensitive remarks, rudeness, and a breakdown in communication. Part of the problem surely is that people are in control of only a small part of the message they convey to the other person. As we have already pointed out, what is said represents only the tip of the iceberg, while the non-verbal components of a message, and its cultural and situational context, remain below the level of awareness.

It was mentioned in Chapter 2 that people often do not empathize with each other because their own self-interests clash with interests of the other person. In other words, one is often faced with a dilemma as to whether to help oneself or the other person. The other person may want something that one would like to have oneself. Under such circumstances, it is precisely one's awareness of the other person's feelings, thoughts, intentions and actions that enables one to manipulate the other person to one's own advantage.

The aim of this chapter is to discuss the means the self uses to manipulate the other person because he or she is aware of the other's feelings, thoughts, and intentions. The chapter has two main parts, although they are closely related. In the first part we shall be concerned with the self's search for social recognition and with the self's strategies for achieving this. The second, shorter, part will discuss the various manipulative strategies one uses to enhance one's social position.

The search for social recognition

In Chapter 3 we made reference to two fundamental characteristics of human awareness. First, one is able to confirm the other person as a self-aware being. This means that one recognizes the other, both as an agent, as the I, and as someone who evaluates oneself and others, as the Me. To put it in yet another way, one can recognize the other person as having the same kinds of powers, namely agency and reflexion, as one has oneself. The second fundamental characteristic of human awareness follows from the first. Since one recognizes others as agents and reflexive beings, one, oneself, desires to be recognized or confirmed by others as an agent and a reflexive being. So far in this book we have discussed the former characteristic of human awareness, that is, the self's ability to recognize the other's self- and other-awareness. In contrast, in this chapter we shall focus on the latter fundamental characteristic of human awareness, that is, on one's desire for confirmation and recognition by others. That the individual should be treated by others in this way is essential for the development of his or her self-concept. In Chapter 3 we discussed the ways in which the individual can be treated as non-human and as invisible. The use of stigma, the adoption of racist attitudes toward others, treating adult people with a mental handicap as 'boys and girls', are all examples of degrading other people to inferior positions in society.

The question is the following: what do people do if they believe that their social recognition is threatened or if they believe that they are not receiving sufficient social recognition? We shall not address the issue as to whether people's beliefs that they are not receiving social recognition are justified. We shall only focus on their strategies of obtaining what they think they deserve.

There are two essential kinds of strategy in the person's search for social recognition, corresponding to the two components of the self, the Me and the I. The first kind of strategy for social recognition focuses on one's awareness of oneself as an *object*, as the Me, and we shall call it the *Me-strategy*. One may seek to increase one's recognition by others by displaying characteristics that one believes will enhance one's desirability in the eyes of others. The second kind of strategy for social recognition focuses on one's awareness of oneself as a *subject*, as the I, and we shall call it the *I-strategy*. One may seek to increase one's recognition by others through the exercise of power over one's social environment.

Several points of caution must be borne in mind concerning our examination of strategies for recognition. First, 'the other' in relationship to 'the self' can include not only significant others such as a parent, friend, lover or employer and various groups of which the self is a member, but also various forms of the 'generalized other', such as the self's conscience and his or her own sense of duty. Second, just like all human activities, strategies for recognition may range from those clearly defined and performed according to the individual's intention, to those of which the individual is only partly aware. Third, there are tremendous individual and cultural differences in people's needs for social recognition. Finally, strategies for recognition vary considerably according to the individual's goals, the persons at whom they are directed, the individual's motives, and the strength with which they are pursued.

The subject of the search for social recognition cuts across a wide variety of social psychological issues that traditionally have been explored under a range of headings and within the framework of different theoretical approaches and terminologies. Such issues cover anything from attitude formation and change, social power, attribution processes, social influence, self-presentation and impression management, to deviance, aggression and violence. It is important to remember that the purpose of this chapter is not to discuss these social psychological issues in their own right. Instead, these issues will become part of our discussion only to the extent that they provide material for our exploration of the strategies for social recognition within the subject of self- and other-awareness. For example, with respect to the subject of *conformity*, one can *conform* to the demands of others for various reasons; thus, one may conform because one may not consider the issue for which conformity is sought particularly important and may wish to cut any further discussion short; or one may conform because one wishes to help the others, or one may conform in order to be evaluated positively and therefore because one seeks recognition. Of all these reasons, it is only conformity in order to be evaluated positively that is relevant to our discussion in this chapter.

The Me-strategies for recognition

We have already remarked in Chapter 3 that, in his or her role of the *perceived*, a person is the object of the others' perception and cognition. Being a self-aware agent, a person is someone who is conscious of the evaluative nature of perception, and who may therefore attempt to modify the others' perceptions of him- or herself and thus to retain some control over their evaluation. Heider (1958), in his excellent analysis of the other person as perceiver, draws attention to the awareness of the perceived that being perceived means being evaluated, with the possibility of having one's self-esteem threatened. In order to avoid a negative evaluation by others, the perceived may try to control his or her perception by camouflage, by altering him- or herself on the surface in order to disguise the underlying reality:

We force a laugh in order to show that we understand a joke; we pretend agreement by nodding; we feign happiness by exaggerated good cheer, we conceal contempt by silence; we pretend to be brave when we are frightened (Heider, 1958, p. 64).

The awareness that one can indulge in self-camouflage plays an important role in manipulating the other's perceptions of oneself. As an agent, a person can disclose some information about him- or herself while concealing other, or be selective in displaying some characteristics while suppressing others. By means of dress, tone of voice, non-verbal gestures and through other means, one can create a gulf between how one is for oneself and how one is for others: one makes a distinction between *reality* and *appearance* and this distinction plays a major role in the Me-strategies for recognition.

The reality–appearance distinction in child development

The process in which the child learns to distinguish between *real* private feelings and thoughts on the one hand, and public *appearances* on the other, is a complex one. Our physical and social environments are replete with objects and situations where appearances differ from underlying realities. However, the nature of the relationship between the conceptual abilities and social understanding that are necessary for the child to become aware of differences between reality and appearance in physical objects, other people, and the self has not as yet been fully explored. Concerning the reality–appearance distinction in physical objects, Flavell and his co-workers (Flavell *et al.*, 1983a; Flavell *et al.*, 1983b; Taylor and Flavell, 1984) have carried out a series of experiments exploring the child's conceptual difficulties in making such a distinction. In one of the studies (Flavell *et al.*, 1983a) 3–5 year olds were presented with highly realistic imitations of objects such as a piece of rock and a pencil; in another version of the experiment another group of 3–5 year olds were presented with highly realistic imitations of objects such as a candle that looked like an apple and a sponge that looked like a piece of rock. The experiments investigated the children's ability to identify objects and their real and apparent properties. It was found that 3 year olds have some ability to distinguish between what the object is and what it appears to be, and that this ability increases with age. However, even older preschool children continue to make errors with respect to what something looks like and what it really is. Awareness of the distinction between reality and appearance in physical objects emerges at approximately the same age as the role-taking pretend play and play with language discussed in Chapter 4. We still have to explore whether the conceptual and social knowledge underlying awareness of the reality–appearance distinction in physical objects is the same as that required for pretend role-play.

For pretend role-play to be successful it is essential that all participants know that the real world has been temporarily suspended and a pretend world has taken its place instead. However, this kind of role-play is different from one in which a child pretends without telling the other participant that he or she is pretending, or in which the child is, indeed, practising deliberate deceit. For example, the child may deliberately put on a facial expression that does not correspond to his or her real feelings. Just as the distinction between reality and appearance develops gradually, so the skill to monitor and control facial expression grows with cognitive abilities, control of facial muscles and the individual's personal and social experience. In discussing Selman's (1980) work it was made clear that only at the stage of reflexive understanding at about 7–12 years did children discriminate between inner experience and outer appearance.

In a series of studies Saarni (1979, 1982, 1984) explored the child's application of the socially accepted facial expressions, the so-called *display rules*. The concept of display rules (see Chapter 2) comes from Ekman (1971). *Display* refers to the actual outer expressive activity and the *rule* refers to the prescriptive and regulatory nature of the display. As Saarni (1984) pointed out, one generally accepted display rule in western culture is 'to look pleased and smile when someone gives you something which they expect you to like – even if you don't'. She carried out a study with 6–10-year-old American children over two sessions. In the first session the children were asked to help the experimenter with a task of evaluating children's books and in return for their help the children would receive a gift. At the end of the session the participants actually received an attractive package containing a can of juice, a sweet bar and 50 cents. They were told that if they helped again in the future, they would receive another gift. In the second session, however, the gift was an unattractive baby toy unsuitable for the children's ages. In both sessions the children were videotaped while receiving and opening their gifts.

The analysis of the children's facial expressions while unwrapping their gifts demonstrated that older children, more frequently than younger children, put on positive facial expressions when receiving an inappropriate baby toy, such as a broad smile with teeth showing accompanied by an enthusiastic 'thank you'. The youngest children, more frequently than older ones, showed negative facial expressions such as a puckered or pursed mouth and a wrinkled nose, and they omitted the 'thank you', abruptly leaving the room. The middle group of 8 year olds appeared to be in a transitional stage. These children showed hesitation as to how to respond, and their initial expressions of disappointment quickly changed into socially acceptable ones. During the debriefing session the oldest children said that their baby toy gifts were disappointing but they did not want 'to make a fuss over it'. Saarni suggests that it was the children's awareness of social conventions, their ability to produce conventional expressions, and their motivation to put on conventional expressions that determined the behaviour of the 8 and 10 year olds. On the whole, boys were more likely to show negative facial expressions than girls, which Saarni explains by differences in societal expectations for boys and girls. While in North America boys' nonconformity to social conventions is tolerated, girls are expected to appear pleased and contented despite their actual feelings.

In another study (Saarni, 1982) children were asked to discuss their personal experiences as to when and why they would *not* reveal their feelings and when they would do so. The most common reason cited across all age groups of children 6–10 years old for the substitution of one's real feelings by a socially acceptable facial expression was for pretend purposes and for play. Children of all age groups also said that the substitution of facial expressions was used in order to get attention and help. Children also provided a variety of reasons as to when it is appropriate to show one's emotions. Examples of such reasons were the following: if one's feelings were very intense, or one was sick, injured or bleeding, if one was with parents or friends, or if particular misfortunes happened such as being in a fire. In contrast, the children were aware of controlling their emotions if disapproval from others was to be expected.

Additional evidence concerning children's awareness of the dissociation of emotions and overt activities comes from a study by Harris *et al.* (1981) in which children, 6–15 years old, were asked whether they could pretend to be happy, angry and afraid. Children from all age groups thought that they could deliberately display an emotion verbally or by means of actions or facial expressions. Younger children, however, discussed pretending almost exclusively as an outer behavioural display. For example, they were aware that they could conceal their true emotion by a different behavioural, verbal or facial expression such as laughing or being friendly. Older children, on the other hand, in addition to the availability of outer display also expressed their awareness of the conflict between pretend and real emotions, and of the possibility of inner re-direction and masking of their emotions and possible failure to achieve this. For example, they pointed to the possibility of controlling one's emotions, such as 'you mustn't think of it any more, otherwise you'll get sad again', or 'I think that I can try to hide it but I think that I'll show it anyway'. As children grow older, they are able to produce a variety of reasons for the separation of emotion from expression and are aware of the subtleties of such a separation (Harris, 1983; Harris and Olthof, 1982; Harris *et al.*, 1985). De Paulo *et al.* (1982) studied the detection of deception in 11–18 year olds. Participants in every age group were able to identify deception, although the oldest age groups were more sophisticated in their detection of subtle expressions of pretence.

According to Saarni there are several reasons for children's modification of their expressive behaviour. There are cultural display rules or conventions which prescribe how one should behave, what one should wear and what one should say on particular occasions. Second, there are personal display rules which serve as coping strategies protecting the self from embarrassment and from the loss of face. Third, a person may engage in a deliberate deception to mislead others in order to gain some advantage or avoid disadvantage. All of these reasons point to the fact that as children grow older they become aware that their appearance and performance is the subject of evaluation by others, and that they desire to be evaluated positively.

In conclusion, as children grow older they acquire more ability to control and regulate their self-presentation, and to use it as a strategy for recognition of the self by others. In other words, the distinction between reality and appearance becomes an essential means for making Me-strategies for recognition effective.

Self-presentation

The purpose of self-presentation is to make *others*, first, perceive oneself in a particular way, and second, adopt certain desired attitudes to or beliefs about oneself. Self-presentation may be either conscious and intentional, or unconscious, when it becomes part of the societal norms that the individual has adopted. One may engage in self-presentation for various reasons, for example, in order to embarrass, to please, or to exploit the other person. In any case it means that the self is aware of others as agents, and acknowledges their power to perceive, evaluate, understand and 'punish' him- or herself. In order to minimize the others' chance of 'punishing' oneself and to maximize one's chances of being evaluated positively as a self-aware agent, one engages in positive self-presentation.

Self-presentation is a common human phenomenon, and its precursors have been identified even in animals (cf. Chapter 1). Great literature has provided remarkable insight into the psychological aspects of the human ability to display totally different sides of oneself to different people and in different situations. For example, in his *Moral Essays* Alexander Pope (1734) gave a portrait of the same man, drunk and civil, cornered and wise, 'friendly at Hackney, faithless at Whitehall'; and Shakespeare's plays are replete with examples of the deception and disguise that are due to the self's ability to manipulate others' perceptions and actions.

Although people's ability to disguise their true emotions, attitudes and thoughts has been known for a long time, it came under the scrutiny of social scientists not so long ago. Ichheiser (1949) made a distinction between the terms 'expression' and 'impression' in social perception. By 'expression' he meant the relationship between a person's actual emotions, tendencies, impulses and attitudes on the one hand, and the outward manifestation of these on his or her face and in his or her behaviour on the other. While, biologically, certain emotions correspond to certain expressions, such as sadness to crying and anger to clenched fists, socio-psychologically people can camouflage their emotions. They can repress an outward expression and replace it with the manifestations of pseudo-emotions, that is, create a suitable *impression* on the other person. Interest in self-presentation in social psychology has gained popularity through Goffman's analyses of the public and private self, and in particular through his *The Presentation of Self in Everyday Life* (1959). Goffman describes the various roles that enable people to adapt their self-presentation to different situations in such a way as to satisfy the existing norms and the desire for recognition. Following Goffman's work social psychologists have explored self-presentation in laboratory situations (Jones, 1964; Jones and Pittman, 1982), and recently they have re-interpreted most of the post-war social psychological research in terms of self-presentation (Baumeister, 1982; Tetlock and Manstead, 1985). From the point of view of Me-strategies for recognition, we shall discuss self-presentation, first, in interpersonal situations with respect to the particular other person, and, second, with respect to the other in public situations.

Self-presentation in interpersonal interaction

Laboratory studies into self-presentation in interpersonal interaction were initiated by Jones and his co-workers in their investigations of *ingratiation*. Jones defined ingratiation as 'a class of
strategic behaviors illicitly designed to influence a particular
other person concerning the attractiveness of one's personal
qualities' (Jones and Wortman, 1973, p. 2). Ingratiation, as a
form of self-presentation by which the ingratiator seeks to be
liked, has been explored by Jones and his co-workers in interview situations in which the experimental subject was given
the instruction 'to give a good impression' to the interviewer.
Several strategies of ingratiation have been discerned (Jones,
1964; Jones and Wortman, 1973; Jones and Pittman, 1982).
First, using a *self-enhancing* strategy, ingratiators present themselves more favourably than in situations in which they are not
motivated to ingratiate. The second strategy is to *enhance the
target person*. Ingratiators present themselves as modest and thus
less favourably than in authentic situations, and they attempt
to impress the other person by modesty, innocence and flattery
emphasizing the qualities and strengths of the other. The third
strategy, *opinion conformity*, is based on imitation of the other
person's point of view, making oneself similar to the other
person and expecting that conformity will increase one's
attractiveness to the other. The fourth strategy is based on
rendering favours for the target person in order to increase his
or her liking for the ingratiator. In addition to these four strategies of ingratiation, the aim of which is to increase the target
person's liking for the ingratiator, Jones and Pittman (1982)
identified other strategies of self-presentation: the strategy of
self-promotion aims at the recognition of the self's competence,
often in particular areas such as knowledge, athletic ability or
intelligence. The strategy of *exemplification* is based on one's
desire to be respected for one's personal integrity and moral
worth. The strategy of *intimidation* is based on the effort to
present oneself as powerful or even dangerous so that the target
person complies with one's demands. Finally, those who lack
any resources may employ the strategy of dependency,
presenting themselves as weak and as such appealing to social
responsibility. Jones and Pittman calls this strategy *supplication*.
The supplicant uses moral blackmail, emphasizing his or her
weakness and dependence upon others. However, as Jones and

Pittman point out, to advertise one's helplessness and incompetence may eventually decrease one's self-esteem.

Which of the strategies of self-presentation is actually employed depends on the individual's personal characteristics, on the situation and societal context in which self-presentation takes place and on the individual's awareness of the personal characteristics of the target person. For example, Jones (1964) found that participants of low status in a naval training programme presented themselves less favourably when dealing with high status personnel, although the topic of discussion was also an important determinant of the strategy of the ingratiator. Jones also found that on the whole boys tend to impress by being aggressive and independent, while girls tend to impress others by being modest. This is just another example of presenting oneself in accordance with the traditional expectations of certain cultural roles.

Joking as a strategy of self-presentation

Humour, jokes, and wit are forms of self- and other-awareness that serve a variety of purposes of which one is self-presentational. Telling jokes is a social activity, and there are at least two ways in which telling jokes about oneself or about a category of people to which one belongs has the aim of enhancing oneself in the eyes of others. The first way is by emphasizing one's positive features, while the second is by ingratiating self-criticism; the two ways thus corresponding to Jones's (1964) strategies of enhancing the self and enhancing the target person.

Concerning the first, in his analysis of Jewish jokes Freud pointed out that jokes made and told by Jews themselves often served the purpose of an exhibitionistic self-display (Freud, 1905, p. 143) used to impress others with one's wit and cleverness. Following this line, Coser (1959) observed the use of self-aggrandizement in humour by hospital patients. The second kind of joking used as a strategy in self-presentation is that of self-ridicule. It is a way of coping with non-recognition by others, and therefore a form of ingratiation used particularly by various stigmatized minority groups and individuals in inferior social positions (Allport, 1954; Wilson, 1979). Self-criticism used in such jokes is based on the common knowledge that every human characteristic can be evaluated both positively and negatively depending on the criteria used. Thus, English politeness can be perceived as tact, although, using different criteria, it can be referred to as coldness (Wilson, 1979, p. 146); or, one's tendency to conform can be seen either as a weakness of being easily influenced by others, or it can be interpreted as trust with respect to others, and so on. Again, Freud's analysis of Jewish jokes exemplifies this point. Freud maintained that Jews are well aware of both their faults and their good characteristics, as well as the relationships between the two. They have made use of this self-awareness in joking about their own character more than any other ethnic group, expressing their self-awareness as 'I know my faults but I also know my virtues' (cf. Wilson, 1979). Moreover, Reik (1962, p. 220) maintained that making a joke pre-empts possible criticism and hostility on the part of the other participants in interaction, in particular of possible persecutors, towards the joker. Humour and jokes reduce hostility and calm the feelings of both parties, and it is in this sense that jokes are a form of apologetic ingratiation (Wilson, 1979, p. 147). In support of this claim, Coser (1960), in the above study of humour used in hospitals, found that jokes in which junior staff ingratiated by acknowledging their inferior position with respect to senior staff, actually helped to smooth interpersonal interaction between the two parties, making it more relaxed and thus contributing to a reduction of the social distance between the two parties.

Self-presentation in group interaction

Just as in interpersonal so in group interaction there are a variety of strategies aimed at increasing the evaluation of the self by others. In social psychology, mainly two such strategies have attracted the attention of psychologists: that of *public compliance*, on the one hand, and *uniqueness*, sometimes called *individuation*, on the other. In the 1950s and 1960s psychologists extensively studied public compliance, in particular within the context of persuasive communication. In contrast, in the 1970s and 1980s, with the growing interest in the study of the self, the focus has been more on uniqueness and individuation.

Public compliance as a strategy for recognition is a conscious or unconscious process of yielding to the real or imagined pressure of others. A long tradition of laboratory experiments into public compliance goes back to Asch's (1952, 1956) classic studies based on 'visual discrimination' in which the task for the experimental subjects was to compare the length of one of three lines with a given standard. All the participants, except for one, were the experimenter's confederates and the experiment was set up in such a way that naive subjects gave judgements after the confederates had announced theirs. The confederates were instructed to give incorrect answers in between correct ones, and a proportion of naive subjects complied with their judgements and also gave incorrect responses. In subsequent interviewing these subjects revealed that they were concerned with their public image, and felt that if they gave their own answers, different from those of the others, they would attract the attention of the experimenter, and would stand out and might be laughed at. Deutsch and Gerard (1955) employed Asch's method to explore compliance under three different conditions. First, just as in Asch's experiments, the subjects expressed their judgements in face-to-face situations. Second, they gave their results in anonymous situations in which they were separated from each other by partitions that prevented them from seeing and talking to each other. Moreover, they had to announce their judgements by pressing buttons. Third, subjects expressed their results in a group situation. This condition was the same as the anonymous one but the subjects were led to believe that they were members of one of five groups that competed with each other. It was found that most compliance occurred in the last condition, followed by the face-to-face condition in which the subjects were publicly identified by their judgements. The smallest amount of compliance occurred in the anonymous situation. Numerous subsequent studies on conformity have led to further understanding of this phenomenon. It has been shown, for example, that similarity of attitude to those of others (e.g. Simons *et al.*, 1970), the attractiveness of the others (Byrne, 1971) and fear of rejection by the others (Darley and Darley, 1976; Freedman and Doob, 1968) lead to greater compliance. In addition, people differ considerably with respect to their need for positive evaluation by others. Maslach *et al.* (1985) have found that those with a high need for positive social evaluation also scored high on social anxiety (see the next section, pp. 188–9), and low on dissent from the opinions of others (Santee and Maslach, 1982).

However, while some studies have explored compliance to public opinion, so have other investigations focused on non-conformity, uniqueness, or individuation as strategies for recognition by others. To be seen by others as a conformist or yielding to others' influence can lead, not to increased evaluation by others, but to their contempt. Cialdini *et al.* (1974)

have shown that a non-conformist is evaluated as more intelligent than a conformist, and difference from others in a group is clearly seen as more influential than similarity (Taylor *et al.*, 1979). In addition, the distinctness of oneself and one's own identity is evaluated as a desirable aim in present western culture (Erikson, 1959; Maslow, 1962; Tyler, 1965; Snyder and Fromkin, 1980). In their conceptual analysis of public individuation, a process of personal differentiation that can be seen and evaluated publically, Maslach *et al.* (1985) suggested that a different kind of social sensitivity is involved than in compliance. While the complier orientates others to view his or her similarity to them favourably, the non-complier orientates others to view his or her differentness favourably. Despite the fact that in choosing a particular manner of individuation a person is acting differently from others, he or she is still concerned to impress others and seek recognition, and this is just the particular way chosen for achieving it.

In conclusion, both public compliance and public individuation are Me-strategies for recognition by others, although they use different ways to achieve their aims. The public compliance strategy is based on seeking social recognition by presenting oneself as *similar* to others. Public individuation, on the other hand, is based on seeking social recognition through establishing one's *difference* from others. It is important that both strategies treat the others, whoever the others may be, as self-aware and other-aware agents, i.e. as equal partners in interaction with the self.

Spoilt self-presentation

The notion of 'self-consciousness' has at least two different, though related, meanings in social psychology. The first meaning of self-consciousness was introduced by Mead (1934) to refer to one's ability to conceive oneself as an *object*, as the Me. In this sense of the term, a self-conscious individual reflects upon his or her actions and experience, and evaluates these in terms of the perceptions and understanding of the other person, and, in the broadest sense, in terms of the 'generalized other'. The other meaning of 'self-consciousness' refers to *social anxiety*, i.e. one's exaggerated preoccupation with the fact that one is the object of others' observation and evaluation. One's awareness of being the object of another's scrutiny often leads to blushing (see pp. 19–20). Darwin (1872) drew attention to the fact that although the young blush more readily than the old, they do not blush during infancy, even though at that stage they 'redden from passion'. Darwin observed that children start blushing at about the age of 2 to 3 years. These observations, just like the observations of students of empathy (see Chapter 2), show that before the age of 3 years children are able to see themselves as social objects, i.e. in the same way that they think others see them.

In recent years there has been a considerable increase of interest in the study of the various forms of social anxiety that result in spoilt self-presentation. In this brief section we shall consider the most common forms of the individual's feelings of threat or of spoilt self-presentation, shyness, embarrassment and shame.

Shyness
Shyness can be defined as a state of social anxiety in contingent interactions in which one is motivated to present oneself positively but doubts one's ability to do so (Leary and Schlenker, 1981). In contrast to embarrassment (see below, pp. 190–1), shyness occurs despite the fact that no particular event actually threatens the Me aspect of the self. Following Leary and Schlenker, let us clarify the key notions in the above definition of shyness. Shyness, defined as a *state* of social anxiety, refers to particular situations, and is dependent on time and individual dispositions. Shyness as *social anxiety* points to the individual's apprehension of evaluation by others with a possible negative outcome such as rejection, or disconfirmation (see pp. 69–71). *Contingent interactions* are ones in which the individual's action is dependent on the responses of the other participants as we have discussed them with respect to Mead's conversation of gestures (cf. Chapter 5). In such interactions, although each participant has interactional intentions and aims, their fulfilment, nevertheless, depends also on the responses of the other participants in the interaction. Shyness, being anxiety about one's self-presentation, and a doubt about one's ability to respond satisfactorily to others, inhibits one's interactional activity. A shy person may use various means of avoiding communication, such as withdrawing eye contact, giving insufficient responses, or failing to speak up (Buss, 1984). Shyness is also manifested physiologically in sweating, blushing and neurotic movements. It is usually distinguished from *audience anxiety* (Leary and Schlenker, 1981; Schlenker and Leary, 1982;

Buss, 1980, 1984), which occurs if the individual has to perform in front of others. In sum, shyness is a behavioural, cognitive and emotional response leading to inhibition of interactional activity because of anxiety about one's self-presentation.

Embarrassment

Shyness occurs in social interaction in the absence of any actual event threatening the self's devaluation by others. In contrast, embarrassment results from a particular social event in which one becomes aware of a discrepancy between the way one attempts to present oneself, and the way one actually is perceived by others. In his analysis of the state of embarrassment, Goffman (1967) pointed out that in the process of interpersonal interaction the individual is expected to present him- or herself as possessing particular characteristics, and to act in a way that is appropriate for the situation in a unified manner. For example, the hostess is expected to be polite to guests, the teacher to have knowledge of the subject he or she teaches. If a person becomes discredited by being rude to a guest or by showing ignorance with respect to the subject of his or her speciality, a feeling of embarrassment can occur, both in the perceiver and the perceived, from their awareness of the perceiver's false presentation.

Goffman differentiated between two characteristics that help a person to avoid embarrassment. The first is 'poise', which refers to the individual's capacity to maintain his or her composure after a discrediting event has occurred. The second characteristic is 'tact', which is the capacity to avoid embarrassing other people. Moreover, Goffman pointed out that embarrassment is not to be understood just at an interpersonal level. The societal structure and the fact that every individual has to take on a number of different roles forces people to adopt self-presentations that are in mutual contradiction. For example, the self-presentation required in taking on the role of a friend is different from that of a lawyer, which again is different from that of a churchgoer. The roles that the individual takes on are usually performed in front of different audiences, so that the individual is not, on the whole, faced with the embarrassing dilemma of performing differently in front of the same audience. However, from time to time the individual may be caught when such a segregation of roles and audiences is not sustained, leaving the individual multiple-faced in the eyes of the others.

In addition to the already mentioned causes of embarrassment, Buss (1980) refers also to conspicuousness, i.e. awareness of being different with respect to one's behaviour, appearance or background. Conspicuousness may also explain embarrassment due to public overpraise and excessive compliments. Finally, breaches of privacy, such as seeing and touching parts of the body that are considered private, or seeing behaviour that one considers strictly private such as sexual contact or defecation, lead to embarrassment. These two cases of embarrassment, conspicuousness and breaches of privacy, are due to the perceived's awareness that he or she has become an object on which others can act without control.

Shame and guilt
Shame is a form of social anxiety which is in many ways similar to embarrassment. This means that some authors do not differentiate between the two (Goffman, 1967; Zimbardo, 1977). Buss (1980), on the other hand, thinks that the two should be distinguished because shame is more serious and more enduring than embarrassment, and its causes, too, are different: shame carries moral responsibility while embarrassment does not. It could be argued that the differences between shame and embarrassment are ones of severity rather than of kind. However, a convincing conceptual analysis differentiating the two has not yet been offered, and students will find that the two notions are usually used interchangeably in psychological literature. Shame and embarrassment can be felt by the individual at the same time. Shame arises from actions that a given society considers immoral, although its individual members differ considerably as to what and how deeply something is considered immoral. Shame is usually accompanied by a feeling of self-disgust and self-disappointment, and a fear of rejection and disconfirmation by others. While shame is a form of social anxiety, *guilt*, in contrast, is a *private feeling* of harmful-doing and of transgression of the code of the generalized other. While shame decreases when the individual escapes the presence of others, guilt can only be decreased by resolving one's personal conflict about the issue in question.

The I-strategies for recognition

It has been shown that Me-strategies for social recognition have two main features. First, the individual recognizes others as *agents*, and second, the individual is concerned about their evaluations of him- or herself. Thus, Me-strategies are based on one's striving to win recognition by others by constantly monitoring both one's own actions and the evaluations of one's actions by others.

I-strategies for social recognition stem from the self's agency, from the I, rather than from the Me. Just as the I, as agent, in its attempt to control the world in which it lives, acts upon it, so, in striving for the recognition of itself by others, the I imposes its own power upon others, it acts upon them. Let us elaborate on this feature of I-strategies. A person as an agent acts upon his or her physical and social environment. In moulding physical objects, e.g. painting pictures, or digging ditches, human agents aim to express themselves in their actions, and to control and predict their physical environment, or rather, their psychological environment, to use Lewin's term (cf. Chapter 4). A person as an agent can also act upon his or her social environment, i.e. upon other people. An agent can express him- or herself just as much in moulding other people as in moulding physical objects. *Acting upon others*, rather than *interacting with them*, however, means degrading them to the level of physical objects and denying them their agency.

There are thus both similarities and differences between I- and Me-strategies for social recognition. Both kinds of strategy are based on the recognition of the other person's agency. Using Me-strategies one negotiates with the other, and presents oneself as well as one can. In contrast, using I-strategies, one does not believe that one can, or at least does not try to, achieve one's recognition by negotiation with the other or by presenting oneself favourably. Using straightforward action upon the other, the self attempts to crush the agency of the other, or, at least, the self acts upon the other without considering how that action will affect the other. I-strategies, in this sense, are aggressive or even violent. They are the last resort that the self thinks are available to it to win social recognition. It is by using I-strategies that the self is convinced that it can achieve acknowledgement as an *agent*.

Aggression and violence are direct and deliberate acts of coercion, whether verbal, gestural or physical, aimed at the other person, in the self's attempt to win the acknowledgement of the self's power. The difference between aggression and violence as discussed here is understood to be a matter of degree, with violence being a more severe form of aggression.

In general terms, aggression is a biological and social phenomenon that arises from a variety of motives and for a variety of reasons. A person might be aggressive towards the other because of the malfunction of the nervous system, psychopathy or epilepsy. Aggression can be learned through imitation, and so on. Although the various motives and reasons for aggression and violence are important and interesting in their own right, they are not directly relevant to our discussion of self- and other-awareness. We shall be concerned with these phenomena only as they are I-strategies for recognition while, at the same time, being aware that on other occasions people are aggressive and violent for various other reasons and motives.

Verbal aggression

Verbal aggression is perhaps the most common kind of I-strategy. Verbal aggression and verbal abuse occur commonly not only in interpersonal communication. Satirists, cartoonists and reporters have been persecuted throughout history for the threats they have posed to rulers, autocrats, politicians and individuals in high social positions. The power of language has often been all that the powerless have left to assert themselves as human beings. Making a verbal evaluation of another person or passing a judgement on his or her deeds puts a speaker in a priviledged position. Just like photographs (see Chapter 4), words have a power of their own (see Chapter 7). Giving something a name or passing a judgement on it gives that thing an identity. Moreover, it is generally believed that 'there is no smoke without fire', and therefore, words, even without the substantiation of evidence, create uncertainty and incongruity in what until then appeared unproblematic. There is evidence provided by experimental social psychology that if a person of low standing makes an unfavourable statement about a person of high standing, then a listener tends to change his or her attitude towards both the high and the low standing person. The standing of the one in the low position will increase and the standing of the one in the high position will decrease. Experimental social psychology refers in this context to a tendency of people towards congruity (Osgood, Suci and Tannenbaum, 1957). Thus, hearing something negative about a high standing person creates an incongruent situation which the listener resolves by upgrading the low standing person and downgrading the high standing person. This, of course, is exactly what I-strategies aim at.

Forms of verbal abuse and aggression are infinite, and include direct reproach, humour, wit, satire, parody, irony, jeering, sneering, sarcasm, travesty and ridicule. Each of these forms can bring about the degradation and humiliation of the one who is perceived as powerful by the person searching for social recognition (they can, of course, bring about degradation of anybody, but that is not the focus of our interest here). Satire, in particular, has been the weapon used against the oppressor throughout history. Makking the oppressor look stupid and incompetent boosts the self of the satirist and thus the self of everybody whom he or she represents. The satirist's powers are endless. For example, Wilson (1979) refers to the case of Governor Pennypacker of Philadelphia, who awoke one morning in 1902 to discover that he was portrayed, in a newspaper cartoon, as a talking parrot. Having been offended by such a disgrace, the Governor persuaded his fellow politicians to introduce a bill to prohibit 'the depicting of men . . . as birds or animals'. The cartoonist responded quickly by portraying politicians as vegetables. Freud (1905), in his study of jokes and the unconscious, analysed examples of verbal aggression, that is, of what he called tendentious jokes. He pointed out that tendentious jokes are particularly favoured because they make possible direct aggression or criticism against those who claim to be in authority. Tendentious jokes humiliate and degrade such individuals, they represent a rebellion against authority and a liberation from its pressure. By degrading those in authority they make them human, just like you and me. Since tendentious jokes liberate one from the pressure of internal inhibitions and repressions, they also have a healthy function. They defuse the aggression against the oppressor and make it possible to laugh at one's misery (Freud, 1905).

Physical aggression

Among the many approaches to the study of physical aggression, Toch's (1969) field social psychological approach illustrates the point of view of human awareness. Toch's research on violent men is based on peer interviews of convicted offenders serving prison sentences, paroled prisoners, and assaulted police officers. Toch believed that a researcher can get insight into human violence only if the data are obtained by the persons actually involved in violent acts rather than by observers of such events. Thus, in his research the convicted offenders were given the roles of researchers and they themselves developed and administered the prison interview schedule. In addition, paroled prisoners interviewed the parolees in the study; and police professionals interviewed the assaulted police officers participating in the research. Interviews were tape-recorded and transcribed, and subsequently analysed. On the basis of his analysis of the data Toch argued that proneness to violence must be studied as an interactional, rather than as a personal phenomenon. He distinguished two basic types of interpersonal conditions that orientate the individual to committing a violent act. In one orientation the person sees others as tools designed to serve his or her needs, and their lack of compliance with the person's expectations may lead to violent action. In the other orientation the person perceives him- or herself as degraded by others and acts violently to obtain recognition. Both orientations stem from a focus on power-centredness in a human relationship in a particular social situation and the desire of one person to assert him- or herself as powerful. These orientations apply both to interpersonal and collective situations. Toch refers in this context to an investigation into rioting and other forms of collective violence in the USA in the 1960s. The President's Commission on Civil Disorders (1968) listed five catalysts of collective violence. Most of these catalysts can be interpreted directly in terms of the search for social recognition. They are as follows: first, frustrated hopes that developed in the course of civil rights struggles; second, a climate approving and encouraging violence; third, feelings of powerlessness to affect any changes in the system; fourth, a feeling of self-esteem and enhanced racial pride, especially among young people; and fifth, the view that the police represented the white oppressors. Toch's analysis of the Watts Riot that occurred in August 1965, and quotations from two of the participants of the riot, and from a black psychiatrist, support his claim that the search for recognition can lead to violence and rioting:

I don't believe in burning, stealing, or killing, but I can see why the boys did what they did. They just wanted to be noticed, to let the world know the seriousness of their state in life. . . . Negroes are ready to die for respect (Toch, 1969, p. 201).
They feel the whole world is watching now. And out of the

violence, no matter how wrong the acts were, they have developed a sense of pride (Toch, ibid., p. 202).

In her analysis of aggression, Siann (1985), too, explores aggression and violence in the framework of the self theory. She presents a great deal of evidence from a variety of studies showing that a denial of opportunities for self-affirmation in the process of socialization, and the subsequent sense of being treated as an unworthy and devalued being, often leads to violent actions. Her quotations from Jimmy Boyle, describing his life as a gang leader in a deprived Glasgow area in the 1960s, express this point particularly well:

Our activities on the gang scene became more intense. I was intent on making a name for myself, and the only way it could be achieved was by violence . . . when I was with my pals, there was the feeling that it was okay and that having attacked a gang single handed the previous night, I had in some way proved myself and gained enough confidence to fight alongside them. I had this hunger to be recognized, to establish a reputation for myself and it acted as an incentive being with the top guys in the district at sixteen. There was this inner compulsion for me to win recognition amongst them (Boyle, 1977, pp. 67 and 79).

It is clear from Boyle's account that violence for him was the only possibility of achieving some sort of recognition as an agent. Acting violently for Boyle meant acknowledgement, solely of his power, by those who had degraded and manipulated him into his present state. Moreover, it also meant acknowledgement of his agency by his own gang and by the Gorbal children who looked up to him as 'the same guy who could do anything and had done things which they saw as heroic' (Boyle, 1977, p. 239). Siann (1985) has suggested that most people, if devalued by other human beings, can be driven to aggressive behaviour to regain their human status. The use of violence as an I-strategy for social recognition was also acknowledged by Kropotkin, a Russian anarchist who advocated terror as a weapon against opponents. He argued that violence and terror are effective because they make the self visible. According to him, an aggressive act does much more propagandizing in a few days than thousands of pamphlets:

Indifference (following terrorist acts) is impossible. Those who originally did not even ask themselves what 'those lunatics' were after, are forced to take notice of them, to discuss their ideas, and to take a stand for or against. Through the deeds which attract general attention, the new idea insinuates itself into peoples' heads and makes converts (quoted by Thornton, 1964, pp. 82–3).

These examples clearly demonstrate that a person committing a violent act does so in order *to be recognized as an agent*. Aggression and violence as the I-strategy must be seen, of course, as part of a complex interpersonal and societal relationship. Thus, one might commit a violent act as an attempt to obtain self-recognition as an agent and, as such, act as the I. At the same time that person may be a member of a group the aim of which is to act violently in order to obtain particular goals. The person committing a violent act may thus, as a member of a group, be searching for recognition by other members of his or her group, and in so doing be assuming the role of an object, the Me. The researcher studying I- and Me-strategies must be aware of the different levels at which self- and other-awareness express themselves.

The I- and Me-strategies for recognition, just like the two components of the self, the I and the Me, are interdependent. As we have shown in Chapter 4, the I and Me constantly transform one into the other as the agent reflects upon his or her action, and acts on the basis of his or her reflexion. In a similar vein, one may use a combination of both strategies to win recognition, focusing now on one's own agency, and then on the other person's agency, switching from the I- to the Me-strategy and vice versa. Moreover, while in this chapter, in order to clarify the distinct features of the two kinds of strategies, the I- and Me-strategies have perhaps been presented as rather inhuman, in real life it is not always so. People manipulate those whom they love just as they do those whom they hate. There are tremendous differences in the quality of such activities as manipulating one's girlfriend to type one's essay, and blackmailing someone to peddle drugs in order to increase one's profits. I- and Me-strategies for social recognition are part of everyday life and one uses them, sometimes with full awareness, on other occasions without it. It is important, though, that readers realize the nature of the distinction between I- and Me-strategies made here, the full potential of these strategies, and their social psychological implications.

The machiavellian self

In addition to the search for recognition one may manipulate the other person for a variety of other reasons in order to enhance one's chances in life, and to improve one's social or economic position. The essential characteristic of these manipulating strategies is *acting upon*, rather than *interacting with*, the other person. In the remainder of this chapter we shall discuss two examples of such strategies, namely persuasion and machiavellianism.

Persuasion

Attempts to change people's *attitudes*, i.e. their likes and dislikes, their *beliefs*, i.e. what they think is right or wrong, and their *behaviour*, are, perhaps, as old as human speech. It is through speech and arguments that people exercise their power over others without resorting to physical force (Brown, 1963).

Most definitions agree that *persuasion* involves intention on the part of the persuader to manipulate or influence the other person (Miller and Burgoon, 1973). Persuasion is not directly coercive, but in order to change the other's thoughts, feelings and behaviour, the persuader may use indirect coercion, such as promises of reward, threats of punishment, and warnings. Using such means of indirect coercion, the *persuader*, in contrast to the *educator*, relies not only upon rational arguments and reliable information, but also upon emotionally loaded messages, uncertain information, and half-truths. While the educator aims at changing a person's beliefs and cognitions, the persuader aims, in addition, at changing the others' feelings and dispositions to actions. In general, while education aims at teaching truth, persuasion is often based on deception. In real life, however, the distinction between the two is frequently blurred and just as persuasion can involve elements of education so education can use means of persuasion.

The study of *persuasive communication* was one of the most prolific research areas in the USA after the Second World War. It was the period when behaviourism flourished in the USA, and studies of persuasion took as their starting point the exploration of the principles of the control and prediction of human behaviour: their focus was on the *effectiveness* of persuasive communication. The research on persuasive communication was based on a simple scheme involving the *source* of the message, the structure and content of the *message*, and the personality characteristics of the *recipient* (Hovland *et al.*, 1953).

The effectiveness of the source was studied in terms of its credibility, expertness and trustworthiness. It was shown that low credibility sources were perceived by the audience as more biased and unfair than those with high credibility, while high credibility sources had a substantially greater persuasive effect on the audience in terms of changing people's attitudes than low credibility sources. There was evidence that it was source credibility that influenced the audience's motivation to yield to the message, rather than attention to and comprehension of the message; and the persuasive effect of the high credibility sources tended to wane after a period of some weeks (Hovland and Weiss, 1951; Hovland and Mandell, 1952; Kelman and Hovland, 1953; Weiss, 1953). Moreover, sources perceived as attractive by the audience were found to have a greater persuasive power (Mills and Jellison, 1968).

With regard to *the effectiveness of the message*, two kinds of variables, the structure and content of the message, were explored. The structure of the message was concerned with the position of the arguments for and against, the effect of delivering the message explicitly or implicitly, and the effect of giving one or both sides of the case. With respect to the content of the message, questions explored included the kind of message that aroused the emotions, and that took into consideration existing group norms that might function as incentives for the acceptance or rejection of the message, and so on (Janis and Feshbach, 1953; Hovland and Mandell, 1952; Lumsdaine and Janis, 1953; Cook and Insko, 1968).

Concerning *the recipient*, differences in persuasability have been investigated in relation to self-esteem, intelligence, anxiety, depression and aggression (e.g. McGuire, 1968), the research providing some evidence that low self-esteem, and a feeling of social inadequacy and depression, is positively correlated with the persuasability of a person (Hovland *et al.*, 1953).

The studies of persuasive communication carried out in the 1950s and 1960s were focused on the effectiveness of persuasion in terms of the source, message and recipient, and clearly ignored the reciprocal nature of human communication. Persuasive communication was explored as a one-way flow, from the persuader to the recipient, with the recipient being treated as an object of manipulation, passively yielding to the force of the persuader. While in ordinary interpersonal communication the role of the participants is symmetrical and they mutually regulate each other's contribution, research into persuasive communication was based on the assumption that there is an

active speaker (persuader) and relatively *passive audience* (persuadees); . . . for even after one pays the customary, contemporary homage to the importance of audience feedback, there still remains no doubt about the locus of major activity, involvement and energy. . . . In the traditional rhetorical (persuasive) paradigm, the persuader *acts*, while the persuadee is *acted upon* (Miller and Burgoon, 1973, p. 12).

This point of view fits in with the basic aim of persuasion, which is to make others feel, think, and do what the persuader wants them to feel, think and do, rather than what is in the interest of the persuadee (Weinstein, 1969; Miller and Burgoon, 1973). The persuadee was treated, at least to some degree, as a non-agent. In the 1970s and 1980s persuasive communication has lost its popularity as a major research topic in social psychology. Those studies that have continued to study persuasion have concentrated on the study of taxonomies and the identification of persuasive strategies (e.g. Falbo, 1977; Falbo and Peplau, 1980; Johnson, 1975; Tedeschi *et al.*, 1972; Rule *et al.*, 1985). In accord with the previous work, the taxonomical studies also focus on persuaders' strategies for making a target person do something without considering the target's interests (Rule *et al.*, 1985).

In ordinary life, as each of us knows too well, persuasion is one of the commonest forms of communication. Children try to persuade parents to provide more pocket money, an employee tries to persuade the employer to increase his or her salary, a salesman attempts to make one buy a particular product, and so on. Persuasion is often mutual: two interactants try to persuade each other about the rightness of their respective positions, negotiating or bargaining their cases (Tedeschi and Rosenfeld, 1981). But, bearing in mind that laboratory study of persuasive communication treats the other person as a non-agent, one must seriously ask why a social psychologist should study *the effectiveness of persuasive communication*. Why should it be important to know how to control the other person better, and how to manipulate the other person's thoughts and feelings? Answers to these questions must be left to the historian of social psychology. Perhaps future generations of social psychologists will endeavour to identify the individual and societal conditions for the *occurrence* of persuasive communication, rather than study its effectiveness.

There certainly are issues where it is important to change people's thoughts, feelings and behaviour, either for the well-being of the individual or for society. Thus, health education, education in the prevention of disease, cruelty and pollution, and in other societal issues have become part of present-day life. Education based on the presentation of relevant information and rational arguments aims to raise self- and other-awareness, and treats people as agents: to educate enables people to make their own decisions and judgements on the basis of available information.

Machiavellianism

If the persuader does not take into consideration the interests and point of view of the persuadee, the machiavellian does so even less. Machiavellianism is a manipulation of situations, emotions, information and anything else available to mould the other person in the manner required by the manipulator. The machiavellian will lie, cheat, deceive, and use his or her power status, position or emotional relationship with the other person in order to obtain the latter's recognition or any other goal he or she may have (Christie and Geis, 1970). The greater one's ability to understand the feelings, thoughts, desires and intentions of the other person, the more one can use the other person in a machiavellian way to reach one's own goals. In this sense the ability to empathize, and in general to be aware of the other person, can be abused by the machiavellian.

The notion of 'machiavellianism' comes from the name of Niccolo Machiavelli, a sixteenth-century politician and writer. In his book *The Prince*, Machiavelli (1513b) expressed his views, not very flattering, of human nature, and of the way people should be managed by the ruler. Machiavelli argued that the ruler must assume that people are egoistic, he should trust nobody and should not rely on people obeying the moral code. Having no illusions about people, Machiavelli advised the ruler how to use power over people in order to keep them under his control. Power is an art and skill that has to be learned and used efficiently. It is wiser for the ruler to keep people in fear than to be loved by them, because fear of punishment will make them obey, while love can always be withdrawn. However, if cruelty and force are used, they must be justified. Tyranny, just like its opposite, idealism, should be avoided.

Social psychological interest in machiavellianism stems from studies by Christie, Geis and their colleagues (Christie and Geis, 1970). In order to discover which kind of person would be most effective in controlling others, Christie (1970) interviewed people and found the following characteristics:

1 *A relative lack of affect in interpersonal relationship:* Success in getting others to do what one wishes is increased by viewing them as objects to be manipulated rather than as individuals with whom one empathizes. The greater one's emotional involvement with others the greater is the likelihood that one might identify with their point of view and so fail to manipulate them.

2 *A lack of concern with conventional morality:* Although 'conventional morality' is difficult to define, Christie (1970) was concerned with the fact that lying and various forms of deceit, although commonly used by people, are not approved by them as acceptable forms of behaviour. The machiavellian, however, takes a utilitarian view of life and therefore holds that deceit is acceptable if one can justify it to oneself.

3 *A lack of psychopathology:* The success of the machiavellian in manipulating others depends largely on his or her ability to accurately evaluate the needs, capacities and potentialities of others. Psychotic and neurotic personalities, presumably, would have difficulties in manipulating people, being unable to make the accurate perceptions of them and situations necessary for the machiavellian instrumentalist approach to others.

4 *Low ideological commitment:* The essence of successful manipulation is getting things done rather than having long-range ideological goals. The manipulator has to be flexible in the choice of tactics, using all available means to attain his or her immediate ends.

The main interest of Christie and Geis (1970) was to conceive of machiavellianism as a personality trait and to develop a scale to measure machiavellianism, the ability to manipulate others. The authors first carried out a number of interviews with people of different social backgrounds and, using statements from Machiavelli's *The Prince* (1513b) and *The Discourse* (1513a), developed several scales of machiavellianism. Originally, seventy-one items were believed to be congruent with statements from Machiavelli's two books. Examples of such statements are the following:

1   a white lie is often a good thing;
2   there is no point in keeping a promise if it is to your advantage
    to break it.

Experimental subjects were required to indicate the level of
their agreement with such statements on a 5-point scale ranging
from strong disagreement to strong agreement. The final scale,
consisting of twenty items, has been extensively used to
measure machiavellianism as a personality trait (for a review
of studies see Vleeming, 1979). For example, machiavellianism
has been explored in relation to lying (Wardle and Gloss, 1982;
Geis and Moon, 1981), to communication styles
(Hermanowicz, 1982), and to professional roles (Hunt and
Chonko, 1984; Hollon, 1983).

Machiavellianism, just like persuasion, covers a broad spec-
trum of mutually overlapping activities that differ with respect
to the *severity* of the manipulation, i.e. the quality and quantity
of the treatment of the other person as a physical object, the
awareness the manipulator has of his or her actions, and the
reasons for the manipulation. As with persuasive communication, potential researchers in this area should seriously question the ethics of such work and the contribution it can make
to knowledge.

Summary

The capacity for self- and other-awareness enables people not
only to enhance their interpersonal interaction and to
communicate more effectively, but also to manipulate each
other. Two types of manipulating strategies have been
discussed in this chapter: those associated with the search for
social recognition, and those used to advance the individual's
other self-interests.

Just as the self confirms others as agents and reflexive beings,
so he or she desires to be confirmed in this way. In order to
accomplish this aim, the self can use two kinds of strategies for
social recognition: Me-strategies and I-strategies. Using Me-
strategies, one acknowledges that the other person is a self-
aware agent, and pays heed to the other's evaluation of oneself.
Being aware that one is the object of other people's perception
and awareness, one disguises one's private thoughts and feelings
when one expresses oneself in public, and thus creates a gulf
between reality and appearance. Although pre-school children

have some awareness of what is real and what only appears to be real, the ability to employ such a distinction deliberately develops in pre-adolescent age. Self-presentation has been studied extensively both in interpersonal and in group interaction. The chief form of self-presentation in interpersonal interaction is ingratiation. Group self-presentation has been investigated principally in terms of public compliance and public individuation. Sometimes self-presentation does not come off, and the individual may experience various forms of social anxiety, such as embarrassment or shame.

In the case of I-strategies, the self focuses on its own agency. It imposes its own power upon others in order to achieve their recognition of its agency. Examples of I-strategies discussed in this chapter are verbal and physical aggression. It is most important for our understanding of human awareness that the I- and Me-strategies for social recognition should be conceived as mutually interdependent, and the individual as using a combination of I- and Me-strategies in his or her search for social recognition. In addition to the strategies for social recognition one may use other manipulative strategies, such as persuasion and machiavellianism, in one's attempt to improve one's social position.

7 Human awareness in its societal context

So far, we have discussed awareness of *the self* and *the other* at the interpersonal level. We have, however, implicitly assumed and often explicitly stated that *the other*, in relationship to *the self*, is not to be conceived just in terms of a *single individual other*, but also in terms of a *collective other*, i.e. in terms of groups and societal institutions. In the final chapter of this book we shall explicitly explore awareness as a relationship between *the self* and the *collective other*.

Just as the relationship between the self and the individual other is dynamic and constantly changing, so is the relationship between the self and the collective other: the self's awareness is continuously shaped by the collective other and the collective other is affected by the individual selves. As a result of this mutual effect, both the individual selves and the collective other undergo change and development. There are, however, important differences between the relationship of the self and the individual other, and the relationship of the self and the collective other. While in the relationship between the self and individual other both participants can, in principle, exert an equal effect on each other, the effect of the self on the collective other is usually small, or even negligible, in comparison to the effect of the collective other on the self. Indeed, the implicit and explicit pressures that the collective other exerts upon the self in terms of social norms, prescriptions, conventions, shared knowledge and otherwise, can be so dramatic that the self may have a sense of utter helplessness in face of these pressures. Being subdued to societal forces, one may even perceive oneself as a passive instrument manipulated by powerful agencies. Societal pressures, however, also play a positive role in the life of the individual who, born into a culture with traditions, customs, and a language, adopts the established societal values and routines. These established values and routines provide the self with a feeling of security and certainty with respect to existing social reality. Individuals adopt the values of the collective other and accumulate social customs and traditions, transmitting them from generation to generation. At the same time, however, it is *conceptually essential* to maintain that every individual contributes towards change of the collective other even if his or her contribution to such change is relatively very small: every human being is a self-aware agent and must be conceptualized as such rather than as a passive object moulded by external forces. Just how important it is, in the context of societal change, that the individual should be conceptualized in terms of agency, will become apparent in our discussion. This will be based on the now familiar *three step developmental model* (cf. Chapter 5). We shall first consider the influence of the collective other upon the self; second, we shall discuss the self's effect upon the collective other; and finally, we shall draw attention to the mutual interaction of the human agent and the collective other in the initiation and maintenance of the evolutionary social process.

The effect of the collective other upon the self

The idea that one's awareness of oneself and of others is dependent on societal or 'collective thought' comes from German social philosophers of the eighteenth and nineteenth centuries, such as Herder, Humboldt, Fichte, and Hegel. Following these, Wundt devoted the ten volumes of his *Folkpsychology* to the study of religion, myths, magic, language, and other collective mental phenomena (see Farr, 1983, for a most valuable analysis of Wundt's contribution to social psychology). Wundt argued, as did the earlier German philosophers, that individual consciousness cannot be explained through the functioning of individual mental processes. Instead, in order to understand individual consciousness, one must study the history of human thought in its cultural and societal context (Wundt, 1916). In a similar vein the sociologist Durkheim became involved in the study of *collective consciousness* and its influence upon *individual consciousness*. Durkheim (1915) argued that the force of collective consciousness revealed itself in human history particularly through religion, which he saw as the basis of such collective mental processes as science, art and myth. Collective consciousness, renamed later by Durkheim as collective representations, was for him the spiritual social pressure exerted by the group upon the individual mind. He maintained that societal power penetrates and organizes itself through individual thought, and in this sense every society lives through individual self-awareness.

In social psychology, the effect of the collective other upon the self has been explored most commonly in terms of the generalized other (Mead, 1934), social norms (Asch, 1956; Sherif, 1936; Newcomb, 1950; Festinger *et al.*, 1950; Rommetveit, 1954), the effect of majorities upon minorities (Moscovici, 1976), morality (Piaget, 1932), conventions (Turiel, 1983), and social representations (Moscovici, 1961, 1981; Farr and Moscovici, 1984). The purpose of this chapter is not to provide a review of these approaches to the effect of the collective other upon the self, but rather to draw attention to two major kinds of societal pressures upon the self: *the implicit* and *the explicit*. These two kinds of pressure of the collective other have different implications for the self's awareness and, consequently, for the *agent's action*. While making this distinction between implicit and explicit pressure, we must be aware that they are transient, and that they operate at several levels and merge one into the other in actual social situations.

The *implicit effect* of the collective other on the self is subtle and difficult to specify. People are born into a particular social world in which the collective other exists in the form of various groups, societal institutions, language, shared knowledge, values and conventions. The self adopts these forms of the collective other mostly unaware of their influence. Indeed, the less aware the self is of their influence, the greater their influence will be (Moscovici, 1984). Accordingly, for non-adherence to the implicit forms of the collective other the self is punished *implicitly*. The self may stand out as deviant, but this deviance may never be spelled out by others and the individual concerned may never realize the reasons for his or her punishment. In one case of this kind, a woman wanted to work as a counsellor in a particular community where people had rather traditional expectations as to how a social worker or other member of a caring profession should be dressed. The counsellor was a sensitive person responding well to the needs of the community. However, the rather artistic fashion of her dresses made the community untrustful, and she never succeeded in the area. She never knew why, and nobody ever told her.

The *explicit effect* of the collective other on the self, in contrast, is clearly defined. It is either formalized, as in legal and moral rules, or is explicitly stated, as in conventions, norms or rules of etiquette. For non-compliance with such explicit rules and norms the self is punished *explicitly*. Therefore, the self is made explicitly aware of such rules in the process of socialization. They are taught by the family, peer and other groups, and by societal institutions at school, in church, and so on. In addition to being punished explicitly for non-compliance, the individual's sense of duty may emerge to pressurize him or her into resolving the conflict with the collective other. The more the individual is aware of, and is concerned with, such conflict, and the more he or she takes responsibility for any consequences of his or her actions, the greater the pressure towards the resolution of conflict with the collective other that he or she experiences. In the remainder of this section we shall discuss some examples of the implicit and the explicit pressure of the collective other exerted upon the self. Our examples of implicit pressures will be *social representations* and *language;* explicit pressures will be discussed in terms of *norms, conventions* and *morality*.

Implicit pressure: social representations

Human beings are born into the social world of categories and objects, and of concepts, ideas, and beliefs. For instance, the child of the 1980s lives in a world of computers, television, the threat of nuclear disaster, and political strife. The *meanings* of such events, objects and concepts, for the individual, are determined by the ways in which existing society parcels out the world into these particular events, objects and concepts. The individual adopts the world, parcelled out in this manner, as the existing *social reality*, and, indeed, takes this particular kind of parcelling out for granted. Such pre-established determination of one's world to a considerable degree guides one's attitudes towards people and things, one's values and beliefs, and even whom and what one regards as worth looking at and thinking about. In other words, one's social world is determined by collectively developed and collectively maintained ideas, images and thoughts. These collectively formed and collectively maintained ideas, images and thoughts that penetrate one's eyes, ears, and minds (Moscovici, 1984) have a powerful effect on the individual. Their effect is due to the fact that since they form the individual's social psychological environment, the individual adopts them *unreflectively, being unaware* of their effect.

Although all one's concepts are learned through a particular kind of parcelling out of the social world, there are important differences between the ways different concepts are acquired by the individual. Some concepts are learned through the individual's own actions and interactions, applying his or her reasoning ability and judgements based upon the evidence of the senses and personal experience. Thus, a child acquires the concept of, say, a *spoon* during activites such as eating with a spoon, feeding a dolly with a spoon, throwing a spoon on the floor, playing with it, and so on; a person acquires the concept of *friendship* by having a friend, being loyal to the friend, playing with the friend, being betrayed by the friend, and so on. When a child learns scientific concepts, here again he or she is provided with the facts, must follow the teacher's argument, make his or her own experiments related to the event in question, and so on.

However, other social and physical phenomena are too complex or too unfamiliar to be treated in the above manner, and concepts referring to such phenomena cannot be acquired by personal involvement with them, or by reasoning. In such cases, Moscovici (1961, 1984) maintains, the individual is dependent on the existing *social representations* of the phenomena in question. Moscovici defines social representations as sets of concepts, statements and explanations with their *own logic and language;* and as systems of values, ideas and practices. Such social representations have two basic functions. First, their purpose is to establish some order in which individuals can orientate themselves in the complex social world so that they think they can control and predict it, at least to some degree. Second, social representations make it possible for individuals to communicate unambiguously among themselves about various aspects of their social world, and their personal and group history (Moscovici, 1973, p. xiii). Take, for example, the possibility of conceptualizing such a complex and unfamiliar event as that of a nuclear disaster. How does a layperson grasp the concept of such a complex and unfamiliar event? In order to clarify this problem, one can consider Humphrey's (1983) essay 'Four minutes to midnight' in his book *Consciousness Regained*. The title of Humphrey's essay is taken from the front cover of the *Bulletin of the Atomic Scientists*, showing the doomsday clock set on four minutes to twelve. The doomsday clock represents the threat of the nuclear arms race which might lead to a catastrophe beyond any comparison in human history. The threat itself, as Humphrey says, is incomprehensible to many. It appears impossible, he argues, for a human being to picture the 140,000 dead bodies of Hiroshima, and to feel sympathy for each single individual whose life was so tragically wasted. Yet that bomb weighed only 25 pounds. How much more incomprehensible, therefore, is an event caused by a bomb whose capacity for destruction has been magnified several thousand times since Hiroshima?

Moscovici has raised the question as to how one forms concepts of phenomena that are too complex (e.g. scientific concepts, for the layperson), too unfamiliar (e.g. people of different cultures), or too threatening (e.g. a nuclear catastrophe) for normal modes of understanding. Moscovici's answer to this question is that one copes with complex, unfamiliar and threatening phenomena by *conventionalizing* them and so forming their social representations. To conventionalize an idea means to make it simpler, familiar and non-threatening. There are two basic ways, according to Moscovici, of conventionalizing ideas and generating social representation: *anchoring* and *objectification*.

Anchoring is the process of categorizing and naming phenomena. One copes with the complexity of the world by classifying people or phenomena into groups and treating them as similar or equivalent so that one can understand, explain and interpret them. Categorization gives phenomena definite forms and values and one responds to such phenomena on the basis of the attributed forms and values.

Take once again the event of a nuclear disaster. In order to make sense of such an unfamiliar phenomenon, it can be *anchored* to something people already know and understand, such as a conventional war. In a conventional war, many people are killed but many survive; civilians try to protect themselves by hiding in shelters. In this vein, Humphrey (1983) points out that the magazine of the nuclear shelter industry, *Protect and Survive Monthly*, encourages the building of nuclear shelters. In the spirit of the magazine, Humphrey maintains, survivors of a nuclear world war, somewhere in England, are described as leading 'heroically self-sufficient lives off the thin of the land, smiling and whistling and shooting their way out of all difficulties' (Humphrey, 1983, p. 207). In other words, since the event of a nuclear disaster itself is unthinkable and incomprehensible, it can be made more familiar by likening it to something people can imagine and understand, i.e. to a conventional war.

Another example of the formation of social representations by means of anchoring can be taken from Sontag's (1979) essay *Illness as Metaphor*. Sontag illuminates the vicissitudes of the public and medical images of fatal diseases, such as tuberculosis and cancer, from a historical perspective. Before such diseases become de-mystified through scientific understanding, even the names of these diseases have a magic power over people:

In Stendhal's *Armance* (1827), the hero's mother refuses to say 'tuberculosis', for fear that pronouncing the word will hasten the course of her son's malady. And Karl Menninger has observed (in *The Vital Balance*) that 'the very word "cancer" is said to kill some patients who would not have succumbed (so quickly) to the malignancy from which they suffer' (Sontag, 1979, p. 10).

In a similar vein, Kafka wrote to a friend two months before he died: 'in discussing tuberculosis . . . everybody drops into a shy, evasive, glassy-eyed manner of speech' (quoted by Sontag, 1979, p. 11).

Before the tubercle bacillus was discovered, tuberculosis fully understood and a simple cure for it found, the disease was surrounded in the eighteenth and nineteenth centuries by fantasies and metaphors. The medical profession and ordinary people both tried to understand the disease, and social representations of it were formed by *anchoring* tuberculosis to familiar phenomena using metaphors drawn from economics and the expansion of early capitalism. Thus, tuberculosis was described as a disease of low energy, consumption, of the wasting and squandering of vitality. In contrast, present-day social representations of cancer are anchored to warfare: cancer cells are described as *invasive*, they *colonize* remote parts of the body, and the body's *defences* are rarely sufficient to cope with the *destructive* cells. Treatment, too, uses warfare metaphors, starting with *scanning* the body, followed by *radical* surgical interventions and chemotherapy using *poisons*. The anchoring of diseases to warfare in present-day medical and public images is not restricted to cancer, but, as Sontag points out, has become quite common since the identification of bacteria as causes of diseases at the end of the nineteenth century, when bacteria were described as invading or infiltrating an organism.

Moreover, before the tubercle bacillus was discoverd by Koch in 1881, tuberculosis was believed to have a variety of causes. According to standard medical textbooks the causes of tuberculosis involved anything from hereditary disposition, unfavourable climate, sedentary indoor life, defective ventilation, and deficiency of light, to depressing emotions (Sontag, 1978, p. 58). Public representations of the causes of tuberculosis were even more varied. In the romantic period of the eighteenth and nineteenth centuries tuberculosis was associated with the excess passion that afflicted oversensual and reckless individuals, or with a bohemian style of life, and with particular psychological characteristics such as melancholy, oversensitivity, and passivity. Similarly, cancer today is believed to be caused by a variety of conditions, such as cancer causing substances in industrial environments, artefacts and chemicals in food, genetic factors, stress, cancer personality, and so on. The public and the mass media form social representations of the disease by anchoring cancer to a variety of psychological characteristics:

A study by Dr Caroline Bedell Thomas of the Johns Hopkins University School of Medicine was thus summarized in one recent newspaper article ('Can Your Personality Kill You?'): 'In brief, cancer victims are low-gear persons, seldom prey to outbursts of emotion. They have feelings of isolation from their parents dating back to childhood.' Drs Claus and Marjorie Bahnson at the Eastern Pennsylvania Psychiatric Institute have 'charted a personality pattern of denial of hostility, depression and of memory of emotional deprivation in childhood' and 'difficulty in maintaining close relationships.' Dr O Carl Simonton, a radiologist in Fort Worth, Texas, who gives patients both radiation and psychotherapy, describes the cancer personality as someone with 'a great tendency for self-pity and a markedly impaired ability to make and maintain meaningful relationships.' Lawrence LeShan, a New York psychologist and psychotherapist (*You can Fight for Your Life: Emotional Factors in the Causation of Cancer* (1977)), claims that 'there is a general type of personality configuration among the majority of cancer patients' and a world-view that cancer patients share and 'which pre-dates the development of cancer.' He divides 'the basic emotional pattern of the cancer patient' into three parts: 'a childhood or adolescence marked by feelings of isolation', the loss of the 'meaningful relationship' found in adulthood, and a subsequent 'conviction that life holds no more hope.' 'The cancer patient,' LeShan writes, 'almost invariably is contemptuous of himself, and of his abilities and possibilities.' Cancer patients are 'empty of feeling and devoid of self' (Sontag, 1979, p. 55).

In general, anchoring a disease to phenomena that can be understood provides the public with a feeling of control. Inventing potential causes of fatal diseases makes these diseases less fearful: one thinks one can avoid coming into contact with particular invented causes of diseases, and one thinks one can avoid developing and maintaining particular psychological characteristics, making one less likely to contract such diseases. Such social representations disappear once the vital missing factors are discovered.

The other process of generating social representations, according to Moscovici, is *objectification*. To objectify an idea means to transform an idea that was originally treated as purely hypothetical into something real. For example, the idea of evolution, when originally formulated by Darwin, was conceived by the general public and societal institutions as totally incredible, evil and a matter of contempt. Immediately after the *Descent of Man* was published in 1871, cartoons picturing Darwin's head with an ape's body appeared (Gruber, 1974), innoculating the public against the 'nonsense of evolution'. However, for subsequent generations the idea of evolution became a *social reality*, something to be taken for granted and no longer questioned. Another example of objectification of an idea was the public adoption of the concept of *psychoanalysis*, in particular in France (Moscovici, 1961). Psychoanalysis was originally a scientific hypothesis proposed by Sigmund Freud. However, through objectification a social representation of this hypothesis was formed that became a public explanation for numerous psychological problems used in popular magazines, the mass media, literature, and so on. Thus, a slip of the tongue became a Freudian slip, a person's dislike for a parent became an Oedipus complex, and various psychological problems took the form of other complexes. Social representations of psychoanalysis provided a ready-made explanation for all sorts of different problems. As Moscovici puts it, 'objectification saturates the idea of unfamiliarity with reality, turns it into the very essence of reality' (Moscovici, 1984, p. 38). While in the first stage of the process of objectification the idea must become familiar to the public, in the second stage people actually perceive phenomena in terms of the idea. In other words, in the first stage of objectification, the idea in question, e.g.

psychoanalysis or biological evolution, is mediated to the lay-person through the experts in psychology or biology. In the next stage, when it has become a social representation and therefore a part of social reality, the lay individual has a direct grasp of the idea. He or she then actually perceives the other person as hating his or her parent because of an Oedipus complex, or actually perceives in nature the evidence of biological evolution.

In conclusion, social representations, once created, can be said to live relatively independent lives of their own, circulating among people, merging and repelling each other, creating new representations while old ones cease to exist (Moscovici, 1984). They form an essential part of our everyday psychological environment, and, as such, they exert an invisible and often undetectable pressure upon individuals, predisposing them to think, feel and act in a predetermined way. The less one is aware of socially transmitted values, experience, knowledge and emotions, the greater the power of such social representations.

Implicit pressure: language

Just as individuals are born into the world of social representations so they are born into the world of language, a collective product of people passed on from generation to generation. Language, the collective means of expressing collective ideas and social representations, can also be said in a certain sense to live an independent life of its own. Referring to Hegel's ideas on language, Wallace expressed this view nearly a hundred years ago:

By means of words, intelligence turns its ideas or representations into quasi-realities: it creates a sort of superior sense-world, the world of language, where ideas live a potential, which is also an actual, life (Wallace, 1894, p. clxxiv).

The claim that social representations and language live an independent life of their own must not be misunderstood. Every human activity, when fully learned, becomes automatized and one can carry it out without constant mental monitoring. Examples of such activities are driving a car, making coffee or even washing and dressing oneself. The activity becomes so automatic that if one's actions are suddenly interrupted one finds it difficult to remember which gear the car is in or whether sugar was put in the coffee. It is in this sense that it can be said that a human activity lives a life of its own, with a self-aware human being interfering only when the stream of activity is for some reason interrupted. In similar vein, once one acquires particular kinds of social representations and particular namings of people and of events, one is no longer aware of the actual meaning of what one says. One often uses words unreflectively, quite unaware of the damage one can inflict in this way, in particular on those who have been labelled and stigmatized. In relation to this issue let us remind ourselves again of Goffman's (1968) analysis of stigma with reference to language:

We use specific stigma terms such as 'cripple', 'bastard', 'moron' in our daily discourse as a source of metaphor and imagery, typically without giving thought to the original meaning (Goffman, 1968, p. 15).

In his study of the effect of labelling, Rosenhan (1973) found that the label 'schizophrenia' was so powerful that once a person was labelled in this way he or she was stuck with it. When a person was discharged from hospital, the label went with him or her 'in remission': once someone is insane, he or she can never be sane again but only be in remission. Moreover, in Rosenhan's study a label was also shown to have an effect on the staff's perception and interpretation of the past history and present behaviour of a person. The normal behaviour of a person was overlooked while any signs of abnormality were emphasized, and the same behaviour in a person so labelled and in a person believed to be normal were interpreted differently. As Rosenhan puts it

A psychiatric label has a life and an influence of its own. Once the impression has been formed that the patient is schizophrenic, the expectation is that he will continue to be schizophrenic (Rosenhan, 1973, p. 253).

Examples of the ways in which language, as a collective product, influences individuals are innumerable: the advertising business tries to predispose people into buying particular products by loading words with images of beauty and natural resources, calling things 'Sunsilk' or 'Natural Wonder'; reporters may call an event a riot or a demonstration or a street battle depending on their political stance and the ways in which they wish to influence readers; words define people in terms of their positions in society and public evaluations. Thus, words are laden with our collective implicit theories about people and events. Consider the following example of the effect of theory laden language upon individuals, in the use of sexist language. Male dominance is built not only into the family, political, legal and other societal systems, but also manifests itself in the meanings of words (Lakoff, 1975; Thorne and Henley, 1975). These authors point out that in the meanings of words the male is usually associated with the universal and general while the female is associated with the particular or with the trivial; female words are more often negative and convey weaknesses and immaturity. Schulz (1975) refers to derogatory sexual connotations with respect to stereotyping and prejudice against women that are apparent from an analysis of the meanings of words carried out from the historical perspective. She considers, for example, some matched pairs of words designating males and females. The connotations of *bachelor* and *spinster* or *old maid* are different, with 'bachelor' more positive than the female counterparts. Thus, while one can call a woman a bachelor without implying abuse, calling a man a spinster or an old maid is associated with nervousness and fretting over unimportant details. Schulz also demonstrates that while terms referring to the female such as 'queen', 'princess', 'wife', 'daughter', 'niece', 'mother', 'sister' and many others have undergone changes with respect to pejoration and sexual abuse, the male counterparts have not.

A change in the use of a particular word and a substitution of that word by another may signify a change in our implicit theories and in social representations. For example, an attempt to change the positions of minority groups and the social representations related to minority groups, such as the mentally handicapped, women, the sick, is also accompanied by effort to change the corresponding words. Moscovici (1984, p. 11) draws attention to the attempt of the American Psychiatric Association to discard the terms 'neurosis' and 'neurotic' that define specific disorders and to substitute these terms by the more general word 'disorder'. He points out, in this context, that a change in the use of a term has consequences 'far beyond its mere significance in a sentence or in psychiatry'. Rather, it signifies a change in our personal interrelations and in our social representations and, necessarily, also a change in our awareness of ourselves and of other selves. Bearing on the same issue, in her analysis of androcentrism, i.e. male dominance, in language, Bodine (1975) focuses on the history of the use of 'he' and 'she' in English. She points out that for about two centuries there have been discussions concerning the use of these two pronouns with the current attack of the feminist movement starting about 1970. Bodine discusses the history of arguments by grammarians according to whom, 'at least in grammar', 'male' should be more important than 'female', and the pronoun 'he' should be used whenever both sexes are implicated. An Act of Parliament in 1850 legally replaced the use of 'they' and 'he or she' with 'he' (Bodine, 1975, p. 136). The act stated that for the purpose of shortening the language, in future, words implying the masculine gender will also 'be deemed and taken to include females'. Another interesting document is White's (1886) discussion concerning the use of various words, among others the word *marry*. Discussing the forms in which marriage announcements were written at the time, White said that it was incorrect to announce that John Smith was married to Mary Jones; it was also incorrect to make announcements using forms such as 'Married, John Smith with Mary Jones, or John Smith and Mary Jones'. He concluded, instead, that the woman was married to the man:

It is her name that is lost in his, not his in hers; she becomes a member of his family, not he of hers; it is her life that is merged, or supposed to be merged, in his, not his in hers; she follows his fortunes, and takes his station, not he hers. And thus, manifestly, she has been attached to him by a legal bond, not he to her; except, indeed, as all attachment is necessarily mutual. But, nevertheless, we do not speak of tying a ship to a boat, but a boat to a ship. And so long, at least, as man is the larger, the stronger, the more individually important, as long as woman generally lives in her husband's house and bears his name, . . . it is the woman who is married to the man (White, 1886, pp. 139–40, quoted by Bodine, 1975, p. 137).

In conclusion, the examples in this section show that words do not simply stand for objects and events; rather, they diagnose, evaluate, and provide judgements on the basis of which objects and events are given their places in the social order. Once the diagnosis, evaluation, or judgement has been pronounced, considerable effort is required if it is to be altered. The overwhelming pressure of language, just like that of social representations, consists in the fact that, overtly, the self may not experience any pressure at all. Knowing their language so well, to a large extent people use it automatically, unaware of the consequences, whether positive or negative, that the meanings of the words and messages they utter have on others.

Explicit pressure: social rules, conventions, and morality

Explicit pressure of the collective other expresses itself in terms of the individual's awareness of the rules, prescriptions and obligations exerted upon him or her. Moreover, the individual is also aware of the potential sanctions for his or her non-compliance. The reader is reminded, though, that any attempt to classify the pressures of the collective other categorically as *either* implicit *or* explicit would be grossly to oversimplify the issue.

Explicit pressure is one of the basic characteristics of the child's socialization in the family and peer groups, but the child's awareness of the pressure differs from one stage of the socialization process to another, and from one situation to another. For example, in the earliest phase a whole set of parental norms may exist with respect to a child's behaviour of which the child may be only partly aware. He or she may learn a rule habitually, e.g. to offer a seat to an older person, without having had such a rule clearly spelled out. At the other extreme of explicit pressure is over-awareness of social norms, or, as Rommetveit (1954) calls it, *over-socialization*. The individual may experience so much social pressure from others that he or she may feel obligations and anticipate sanctions even if none are imposed by the others. While such situations may be experienced by everybody occasionally, such over-awareness may become neurotic if it occurs habitually. In addition, misinterpretation of obligations and sanctions may characterize the interactions of entire groups, with everybody having false expectations of everybody else, and everybody developing false stereotypes and beliefs (Rommetveit, 1954).

The individual's awareness of the explicit pressure of the collective other has already been partly discussed in Chapter 6 with respect to conformity and public compliance. Being aware of possible sanctions, the individual develops various kinds of Me-strategies to present him- or herself favourably to others, thus perpetuating the existing social rules. We shall now supplement this discussion by raising some issues with respect to explicit pressure, in the context of child socialization.

Both Piaget (1932) and Mead (1934) made important contributions to the study of the child's awareness of explicit pressure in their concern with the child's understanding of social rules. Piaget, in accordance with his theory of cognitive development, sought to identify stages in a child's moral development during which the child undergoes qualitative changes in his or her awareness of social rules. According to Piaget, up to about 6–8 years of age children are aware of a social rule as an independently existing social reality that has a constant power of its own. When children reach the operational stage they no longer take rules as permanent entities, but become aware of them as relative, with respect to persons, circumstances and situations. Moreover, children become aware of their own ability to impose rules during organized activities such as games and interpersonal interactions, during which various social contracts are established and breached. As Piaget (1932) pointed out, children become aware of what is just and unjust in their personal *opposition to* the adult, rather than acquiring the concepts of justice and injustice *from* the adult. It is through the child's own feeling of injustice, whether real or imaginary, that he or she starts developing the concept of justice.

Mead (1934) explored the child's awareness and understanding of rules in the context of *play* and *games* (cf. Chapter 4). In *playing* at something the child becomes aware of the obligations and expectations attached to the roles he or she plays, and comes to know the established conventions and connections between particular actions, and their causal relationships: for example, one has to be ill in order to be attended by a nurse; one has to commit a crime in order to be put into prison. *A game*, on the other hand, is formalized and the child must now be prepared to take on any roles required by the game and not just those he or she likes. The game has rules that have been created for the specific purpose of that particular game. They constitute a force coming from the collective other.

Recent research on children's understanding of social rules has focused on the child's distinction between *conventions* and *moral principles*. Conventions are arbitrarily established behavioural uniformities that co-ordinate stable interactions of individuals within a particular social system. Examples of conventions are modes of greeting, rules of etiquette, and forms of address (Turiel, 1983). Moral principles, on the other hand, are obligatory requirements for action concerning the most important interests of other people (Gewirth, 1978). For a prescription to become a moral principle, it is not enough for it to obtain public agreement, it must be justified with respect to the welfare of the members of the particular social group or of humankind in general. As people's views about welfare, rights and obligations change, so, too, do moral principles.

The research of Damon (1977), Selman (1976), Turiel (1978, 1983), and Shantz (1982), has shown that a preschool child does not make distinctions between the seriousness of breaches of conventions, on the one hand, and of moral principles, on the other. Rather, for preschool children, all regularities introduced by adults are unbreachable. Only at between 6 and 8 years of age do children start making distinctions between breaches of conventions and breaches of moral principles. Thus, Shantz (1982) in her research with children in their first and second year at school found significant differences between their judgements of violations of conventions and of moral principles. While the children did not distinguish between the seriousness of different kinds of violations of moral principles such as stealing, hitting the other person or not sharing something with another, their judgement of the seriousness of breaches of conventions was highly idiosyncratic. For example, not combing one's hair was judged as more serious than sex role violations such as boys playing with dolls. Understandably, conventions are much more flexible and changeable than moral rules because their relationship with people's welfare is not direct. In particular, conventions concerning sex roles are currently undergoing considerable changes. It is not, therefore, surprising that children's reasonings about, and interpretations of, the social world are influenced by such changes.

The effect of the self on the collective other

The effect of minorities on majorities

Moscovici and his co-workers (e.g. Faucheux and Moscovici, 1967; Moscovici et al., 1969; Moscovici, 1976) modified the Asch (1956) experiment on conformity (see Chapter 6) in an important way. In the Asch experiment the majority of the people involved in the investigations were the experimenter's confederates, presenting a unified point of view to the pressure of which the naive minority yielded. In contrast, Moscovici and his co-workers reversed the situation and instructed the minority to express a firm and consistent point of view. In the Faucheux and Moscovici (1967) experiment, people involved in the study were presented with geometrical shapes varying in size, colour, and other dimensions. They were asked to indicate their opinion as to which dimension would be most easily discriminated in air navigation. A confederate in a minority of one was instructed to make the same response at every trial, selecting colour as the best dimension. The results of the experiment showed that a proportion of the naive majority were swayed by the firm opinion of the minority and also chose colour as the best dimension. Among the numerous experiments that were designed to explore the effect of a minority upon a majority, the experiment by Moscovici, Lage and Naffrechoux (1969) has become a classic. People, involved in the study in groups of six, were asked to express their judgements of the colour of thirty-six projected slides. All the slides were blue but they differed in their brightness. The confederates in a minority of two were instructed to judge slides *consistently* as green. This consistent minority influenced the opinions of naive subjects in about 8 per cent of all trials, and 32 per cent of naive subjects 'perceived' a 'green' slide on at least one occasion. In a variation of this experiment the minority was not consistent in expressing their view that the slides were green. In this case their influence on the majority was insignificant. The theoretical aspects of minority influence were developed by Moscovici (1976), focusing on the behavioural styles of minorities, and in particular on the consistency of their behaviour. Consistency, based on firmness, coherence, repetition and personal involvement, appears to be crucial for a minority's success in influencing a majority. By being consistent in expressing their point of view minorities create social instability and generate a social conflict. Mugny (1982) refers to two aspects by which a minority's consistent point of view destabilizes the existing state of affairs. First, it upsets the existing rules of the game according to which the minority is expected to conform to the majority. Second, it focuses attention on the minority and points towards the possibility of a social change. In this sense it functions as a catalyst or a dynamic releaser of a social development. Mugny (1982) makes it clear, however, that consistency, although necessary, is not sufficient to account for a minority's influence. If a minority expresses a rigid and dogmatic point of view without *negotiating* the conflict in question with the majority, its chances of influencing the population are slim.

Research evidence (cf. Nemeth, 1986) has demonstrated that the influence of majorities is based on different kinds of processes than that of minorities. First, the influence of majorities seems to be based on *informational* and *normative* effects. With respect to the informational effect, the general assumption is that the majority is more likely to be correct than the minority; with respect to the normative effect, since it is the majority that determines norms, acceptance of the norms means acceptance of the majority's point of view. In contrast, and as already pointed out, the influence of a minority stems from its behavioural style, the most important aspect of which is consistency. Second, the majority's influence is usually direct, in the sense that people tend to accept overtly the majority's position, although they do not necessarily accept it internally. The effect of a minority, on the other hand, is usually indirect. At first its position is likely to be considered incorrect, although consistent behaviour on its part will induce a social conflict. In this way it has a latent effect upon the others which later on may become manifest. Third, and as Nemeth (1986) argues, majorities and minorities seem to stimulate different kinds of thought and different kinds of decision-making. Thus, according to her, majorities facilitate convergent thought, focus attention on the position they propose to defend, and increase the probability of acceptance of the strongest and most dominant response; at the same time they decrease the likelihood of acceptance of the competing alternatives. Those exposed to majority influence focus their attention on the proposed position, neglecting possible alternatives, i.e. they think convergently. On the other hand, minorities facilitate divergent thought. They focus attention on novel solutions, propose alternatives to the existing point of view, and attend to various aspects of the situation. Divergent thought stimulates creative problem-solving in novel situations, and it directs attention to alternative conclusions. In sum, Nemeth argues that the differences between minorities and majorities are based on cognitive differences in the ways the two parties exercise their influence.

Bearing in mind that human beings are self-aware agents, one can view the effect of majorities and minorities from yet another point of view, i.e. that of *the search for social recognition.*

A minority, *trying to change* an existing situation with respect to norms or accepted ways of thinking, manifests itself as the I, constructing and creating its environment, posing new problems for itself and others. Human agents become more aware of themselves in the process of moulding their environment, shaping objects with their hands and using their own ideas. Violation of the existing social norms of the collective other is one example of the attempt to mould one's social environment according to one's own ideas and to gain social recognition as an agent. The influence of a minority is one of an agent, and by definition an agent's influence is based on presenting a point of view that encourages original thought, persuasion and commitment to consistent action.

In contrast, a minority *conforming* to norms or accepted ways of thinking, manifests itself as the Me, searching for recognition by others by presenting itself favourably in order to be accepted. Such presentation of the self may, or may not, be genuine. Indeed, Moscovici and his co-workers, too, observed that the manifest influence of majorities may invoke only the individual's *public compliance* but not his or her *private acceptance* of the norm.

Whether one stimulates *divergent* thought in others or adopts *convergent* thought oneself depends on whether one acts as *the I* or as *the Me*. Whether one applies a consistent behavioural style to influence others, or whether one accepts a normative influence depends, too, on how one sees oneself with respect to the particular situation, as a subject, the I, or as an object, the Me. If one follows this line of thought, the effects of majorities and minorities represent forms of the expression of human awareness in general, and a search for social recognition in particular. Consequently, it is essential that these forms of human awareness are not reduced, in social psychological research, to cognitive processes or behavioural styles.

The effect of creative individuals on the collective other

In a sense every human being is in a minority of one in opposition to the majority of the collective other (Farr, 1984). From the very beginning of their lives children learn to test their personal forces against the environment, whether in learning language and creating new words, or in coping with the restrictions of adults. Piaget has shown that the child's cognitive growth is a continuous active construction and reconstruction of the world he or she experiences. Moreover, such reconstruction is not limited just to processes in the child's mind but also involves practical activities and changing his or her psychological environment by making things, destroying objects, and interacting with people. Gruber (1973) likened the creative activity of children to that of creative individuals in science. Just as children are born into an already existing world, so creative scientists find themselves in a world of existing social, scientific and semi-scientific beliefs, and in order to develop their own ideas, such individuals must depart from those commonly accepted by their culture. More generally, a scientist who breaks new grounds in the development of a discipline is a more pronounced case of an individual expressing himself or herself as a *self-aware agent*.

Gruber (1974) has made an important contribution to the study of the creative process in science by showing that human creativity must be explored in relation to the environment in which the creative individual lives. Scientific creativity is not just a one-off act but a long process that manifests itself through the individual's life at different levels: first, in a private form in the thoughts of the researcher; second, in a semi-private form as the new ideas appear in discussions among the scientists's close friends and in private letters; and finally, at the public level as it appears in scientific journals, research meetings and in books. One would also want to add the level of social representations, discussed earlier, at which a scientific idea transforms itself into publicly shared social knowledge and becomes common sense to laypersons. Gruber's particular interest is to follow up the path of a creative scientist, in his case of Charles Darwin, from his private thoughts on evolution to the public expression of the evolutionary theory in Darwin's published work. To emphasize his interest in *the creative process* itself, Gruber points out that studies in the history of ideas usually tend to concentrate themselves on the successful and final version of the idea, while the creative process itself and its different levels of manifestation tend to be forgotten. Providing evidence of the actual transformation of Darwin's ideas of evolution, Gruber demonstrates the interdependence between this transformation and the various societal and personal events in Darwin's life. Among these, the fear of persecution, or, one could say, Darwin's awareness of the possible sanctions for violating the majority's point of view, played an important role in shaping his ideas and in delaying his publications. At that time, it was becoming more and more difficult to reconcile the growing geological knowledge with the view that Creation was completed in six days and that the subsequent history of human beings had lasted only a few thousand years. However, some scientists, such as the geologist Lyell who was one of the most important of Darwin's teachers, understood that it was important to present his views in a way that would minimize possible attacks by the establishment. Thus, in his *Principles of Geology*, while convinced that the earth was millions of years old, he carefully talked about 'twenty thousand years or more' (Gruber, 1974, p. 87). As a young man, Darwin was well aware of the explosion to which his ideas on evolution might lead, and of the persecution that he himself might suffer. He was acquainted with the persecution of the chemist Joseph Priestley, who was well known to the Darwin family before Charles himself was born. When the famous Birmingham riot broke out, Priestley's house was burnt down, and his books, papers and laboratory were totally destroyed. Another example, pointing to the possibility of persecution of which Charles Darwin was aware, was the publication of the *Vestiges of the Natural History of Creation*, anonymously, in London in 1844. In this book, evidence for evolution of the solar system, of the earth, of organisms, of human beings and their civiliz-ation, was presented. The book was severely criticized and widely discussed, but the identity of the author, Robert Cham-bers, was revealed only after his death, in the twelfth edition of the book (Gruber, 1974, p. 45).

In addition to the explicit societal pressures of which fear of persecution is but one instance, other, more implicit, societal factors inhibit the development of creative ideas. Scientific observation itself is laden with existing theories (Hanson, 1958) which prevent the scientist from seeing things that are not part of the accepted theoretical system. Concerning inhibiting factors of a personal nature, Gruber refers to the fact that as the scientist departs from the accepted conceptual framework, he or she enters the area of theoretical and empirical darkness with ill-defined problems and no available methods to solve them. Moreover, in entering such an area, the scientist increases his or her intellectual distance from others by not being able to communicate the novel ideas and concepts to others. Not only is it difficult to communicate such ill-defined and undeveloped ideas, but the scientific majority, working within a different conceptual framework, simply do not understand things that are not part of their frame of reference. All these factors, both societal and personal, inhibit changes in the creative process and the scientist must struggle against them.

In the early stages of the creative process, a novel idea may be only an implicit part of the individual's system of thought, while later it may become explicitly recognized and formulated by him or her. By becoming aware of the idea explicitly, the individual can develop it actively and purposefully, reflect upon it, and see its potential explanatory value (Gruber, 1974, p. 174). The transformation of Darwin's evolutionary thought from implicit to explicit expression can be seen in the following scheme of Gruber's:

A. 1832 and before: The Creator has made an organic world (O) and a physical world (P); O is perfectly adapted to P.

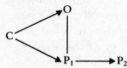

B. 1832–1834: The physical world undergoes continuous change, governed by natural laws as summarized in Lyell's Principles of Geology. In other respects, B resembles A.

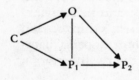

C. 1835: The activities of living organisms contribute to the evolution of the physical world, as exemplified by the action of the coral organism in making coral reefs. In other respects, C resembles B.

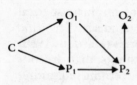

D. 1836–1837: Changes in the physical world imply changes in the organic world, if adaptation is to be maintained; the direct action of the physical milieu induces the appropriate biological adaptations. In other respects, D resembles C.

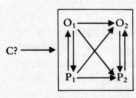

E. 1838 and after: The physical and organic worlds are both continuously evolving and interacting with each other. The Creator, if one exists, may have set the natural system in being, but He does not interfere with its operation, standing outside the system (Gruber, 1974, p. 127).

In conclusion, we have tried to show that a creative self-aware agent, unlike a minority group in a social psychological experiment, is faced with a very complex task. The creative individual not only attempts to influence the normative majority, but must first of all develop his or her own point of view against the background of problems, such as the fear of non-recognition, must struggle against the system of established ways of thinking and seeing things, and be able to communicate to others one's views and perhaps still rather underdeveloped ideas. Problems of this kind, and, in general, problems involved in the creative process of self-aware agents, still await exploration by social and developmental psychologists.

Interaction between the collective other and the self-aware agent in producing social change

Gruber (1974) maintains that there are two major theories explaining the appearance of creative individuals. First is the theory that attributes the emergence of a creative individual entirely to the *Zeitgeist*, i.e. to objective conditions that have developed in society. The appearance of a creative individual is simply a reflection of such conditions. For example, if the creative individual named Charles Darwin had not existed, surely someone else would have appeared and formulated the theory, because the Zeitgeist, i.e. the spirit of the time, was ready for the discovery of the evolutionary theory. According to this point of view, 'the person is a vehicle and not an agent' (Gruber, 1974, p. 246). As Gruber points out, this approach to human creativity totally *depersonalizes* and *externalizes* the creative process. The other approach is quite the opposite, based on *desocializing* and *internalizing* the creative process. According to this approach, the creative individual is a 'sleepwalker' in whom the best of his or her ideas occur in a dreamlike manner or in an actual dream (Koestler, 1959). The conscious effort of the creative individual is undervalued and the emphasis is on non-rational mental activity. Support for this approach is sought in verbal accounts by the creative scientists of the activities and situations in which their great insights emerged. Indeed, some creative individuals, such as the mathematician Poincaré, and the chemist Kekulé, both claimed that their discoveries occurred to them in dreams. Gruber argues against both such approaches, the one ignoring human agency, and the other ignoring the societal aspect of creativity. For him, a creative process is a process of growth of ideas in which the human creative agent constructs and faces problems in a particular social context, perseveres against personal and societal obstacles, and uses all available resources, personal and societal, to solve such problems. Great insights do not just *happen* to a person, but a human agent, through his or her 'active search and inquiry', makes insights possible. A human agent is not simply a vehicle of the Zeitgeist. Although one operates within a particular Zeitgeist, one can choose to do things, and make decisions about things. Human freedom is an expression of such possibilities as to choose and decide.

The history of ideas provides a great many examples demonstrating that for actual *social change* to take place the two opposite factors, the individual and the societal, must interact with each other. To clarify this claim, consider the following examples of such interaction. In his study of scientific revolutions Kuhn (1962) demonstrated that preconceived systems of ideas, or 'paradigms', are so influential that they determine the kinds of theories scientists postulate, and consequently the kinds of objects people actually see. New discoveries are not always made when relevant knowledge is accumulated and relevant techniques become available: scientists may be unable to make a discovery if their mind operates within the 'wrong' conceptual framework. Kuhn gives a number of examples from the history of science to illustrate this point. One example is the discovery of the pendulum by Galileo only in the sixteenth century, although all the knowledge necessary for this was available to scientists almost 2000 years before in the Aristotelian era. The Aristotelian scientists, however, could not see a pendulum when looking at a stone swinging on a rope because they focused on the idea of constrained fall; they operated with concepts such as the weight of a stone, the height from which it falls, and the time required for it to achieve rest. Galileo, on the other hand, was concerned with concepts such as angular displacement, the radius of the circle and time per swing. These were relevant concepts for the discovery of a pendulum, and therefore Galileo saw a pendulum while Aristotelian scientists did not. Another example of the same point is the discovery of Uranus in 1781. As Kuhn points out, although since 1690 a number of astronomers had seen stars in positions of Uranus, they were not identified as a single object, a planet. One consequence of seeing several 'stars' as a single planet was that astronomers were able to see many minor planets using the same standard instruments as they used before. After the discovery of Uranus, their minds were prepared for more similar discoveries.

In contrast to these examples that demonstrate that in spite of accumulated knowledge a discovery may not be made, other examples show that a discovery may be made by the individual but remain totally unrecognized if the scientific world is not, so to speak, ready for the discovery. To illustrate this point, there is the well-known case of Gregor Mendel whose far-reaching discovery of the statistical laws of inheritance were totally ignored when originally presented in 1865 to the Natural History Society in Brno and when published one year later. It has often been said that biological science was not prepared for Mendel's discovery because it was dominated by Darwin's evolutionary theory. Mendel's papers were only found in 1900 in a search of the literature for an explanation of some striking discontinuous changes in species which had lately been discovered.

In his *Rediscoveries in Art* Haskell (1976) analyses changes in the appreciation of art in the nineteenth century. Thus, during the eighteenth century the Old Masters were generally admired and criteria for the excellence to be found in their work were clearly defined, whereas in the nineteenth century important external changes appeared to alter the situation, such as the impact of contemporary art, the religious or political loyalties that influenced aesthetic criteria, and so on. One of those who was 'knocked down' was Botticelli, and even at the end of the last century he was labelled as decadent. The interdependence between the artist's painting style and the established pictorial representations of the world within particular cultural traditions was explored by Gombrich (1960). The essence of his analysis of 'the riddle of style' is the assumption that the artist's achievement is not simply an expression of his or her personal taste and personal vision of the world but of the accepted, collective vision: 'If art were only, or mainly, an expression of personal vision, there could be no history of art' (Gombrich, 1960, p. 3). Moreover, 'it is because art operates with a structured style governed by technique and the schemata of tradition that representation could become the instrument not only of information but also of expression' (ibid., pp. 319–20). Different artistic styles dominate the scene at different times, and one takes it for granted that trees painted by Dutch masters look different from those painted by the Chinese. However, one rarely asks why it is so easy to recognize the style to which such a depicted tree belongs. Gombrich makes it quite clear, just like Kuhn with respect to science, that different pictorial representations of the world determine the different kinds of art dominating in particular historical contexts, and that 'not everything is possible in every period' (ibid., p. 4). Similar analyses, of course, can be carried out on music, literature, and other forms of art.

Further evidence demonstrating a mutual interaction between creative individuals and their environment is once again provided by Gruber (1974) in his analyses of the development of evolutionary theory by Darwin and by Wallace. Both scientists developed their ideas over very long periods of their lives. Both were stimulated to think about evolution through their particular experiences obtained at archipelagos where they had ample opportunity to observe small-scale examples of evolution. Finally, both scientists attributed significant importance in the direction of their thinking to the reading of Malthus, and they both acknowledged that Malthus inspired them to find a solution to the problem of changes in species. Gruber maintains that in both cases the role of external stimuli was effective in shaping the development of the scientist's thought, although such stimuli can be effective 'only in ways that are constrained by the developing thought process itself' (ibid., p. 120). Here again, both the scientist's active search and inquiry, and the environmental conditions play a role in initiating a creative process. To be creative, according to Gruber, is not just to have isolated creative ideas. Many people are able to produce very quickly a whole range of ideas of considerable originality. To be truly creative one must be able to organize such ideas into a coherent and intelligible system of knowledge. Such thought must 'strike effective balance between adaptive stability and adaptive variation' (Gruber, 1974, p. 120). It means that the individual's thought, although it changes and develops in the life process, also retains, in some sense, some recognizable identity. The preservation of balance between stability and variability is a fundamental characteristic of any evolutionary process and therefore, also, of human creativity.

The above examples from the history of science referring to 'paradigms' and from the history of art pointing to 'traditions' all have in common the shaping of the self's perception and understanding of the world by the ways in which the self has been perceptually, cognitively, and aesthetically *socialized*. The self's world, the possibilities and limitations of which the self is totally, partly, or not at all aware, are dependent on the societal representations of the world. These representations constitute constrictions upon the mental and practical operation of the self.

Although this final section has been devoted to a discussion of the interaction between unusually creative individuals and the collective other, one must not forget that every human being is a self-aware creative agent who contributes to social change in his or her own unique way. In this sense, every self-aware agent is an unrepeatable microcosm (Kon, 1978). However, this unrepeatable microcosm is not an isolated monad, but each such microcosm includes in itself universal human values that have developed in the process of social evolution. In addition, each such microcosm directs its creative activities towards others. As Kon says, one's discovery of one's self is nothing but a practical realization of this fact. The awareness of human finiteness and the recognition that a deed started by one human being will be continued by others is the essence of the moral and responsible self for which Kon is striving: it is the evolutionarily acquired *I* that is *We* and *We* that is *I*. Kon finished his book on the *Discovery of the Self* with a quotation from a poetic metaphor by Prishvin (1972), and I shall borrow it too in conclusion of this brief inquiry into human awareness:

Below the window the ice is strong but the sun is getting warmer, icicles dangle from the roof – the time for the thaw has begun. I, I, I – rings every drop of water, dying. It lives but a few seconds. I – the pain of helplessness.

A small hole has appeared in the ice, now it is bigger, the ice melts and is gone and from the roof the glittering droplets continue ringing.

A droplet now falling on a rock says clearly: I. The rock is large and strong, it may lie there another thousand years, and the droplet lives a single moment and that moment is a pain of helplessness. The water droplets keep on falling from the roof, and there is a hole in the rock. Now together they become a great strong river; now they don't just make a hole in the rock but embrace the rock and take it away in their stormy arms.

References

Allport, G. W. (1954). *The Nature of Prejudice*, Reading and Palo Alto: Addison-Wesley

Amsterdam, B. (1972). Mirror self-image reactions before age two, *Developmental Psychobiology*, **5**, 297–305

Anderson, C. (1940). The development of a level of aspiration in young children. Dissertation, University of Iowa, reported by K. Lewin *et al.*, Level of aspiration, in J. McV. Hunt, (ed.), *Personality and the Behavior Disorders*, vol.1, New York: The Ronald Press, 1944

Anderson, J. R. (1984). The development of self-recognition: a review, *Developmental Psychology*, **17**, 35–49

Argyle, M. and Dean, J. (1965). Eye-contact, distance and affiliation, *Sociometry*, **28**, 289–304

Arlitt, A. H. (1930). *Psychology of Infancy and Early Childhood*, New York: McGraw Hill

Armsby, R. E. (1971). A re-examination of the development of moral judgments in children, *Child Development*, **42**, 1241–8

Aronson, E. (1968). Dissononance Theory: progress and problems. In R. P. Abelson, E. Aronson, W. J. McGuire, N. T. Newcomb, M. J. Rosenberg, and P. Tannenbaum (eds.), *Theories of Cognitive Consistency: A Source Book*, Chicago: Rand McNally

Asch, S. E. (1952). *Social Psychology*, New York: Prentice-Hall

Asch, S. E. (1956). Studies of independence and conformity, *Psychological Monographs*, **70** (9, whole no. 416)

Aydin, O. (1976). The description of peers and the perception of intentions by popular and unpopular children, PhD thesis, University of Stirling

Baron, R. and Eggleston, R. (1972). Performance on the 'aggression machine': motivation to help or harm? *Psychonomic Science*, **26**, 321–2

Bateson, M. C. (1975). Mother-infant exchanges: the epigenesis of conversational interaction. In D. Aaronson and R. W.

Rieber (eds.), *Developmental Psycholinguistics and Communication Disorders*, New York: New York Academy of Sciences

Baumeister, R. F. (1982). A self-presentational view of social phenomena, *Psychological Bulletin*, **91**, 3–26

Beattie, G. (1983). *Talk: An Analysis of Speech and Non-Verbal Behaviour in Conversation*, Milton Keynes: Open University Press

Beloff, H. (1985). *Camera Culture*, Oxford: Blackwell

Bem, D. J. (1967). Self-perception: an alternative interpretation of cognitive dissonance phenomena, *Psychological Review*, **74**, 183–200

Bem, D. J. (1972). Self-perception theory. In L. Berkowitz (ed.), *Experimental Social Psychology*, vol.6, New York and London: Academic Press

Beninger, R. J., Kendall, S. B., Vanderwolf, C. H. (1974). The ability of rats to discriminate their own behaviours, *Canadian Journal of Psychology*, **28**, 79–91

Berger, C. R. and Bradac, J. J. (1982). *Language and Social Knowledge*, London: Edward Arnold

Berger, S. M. (1962). Conditioning through vicarious instigation, *Psychological Review*, **29**, 450–66

Berko-Gleason, J. (1973). Code switching in children's language. In T. E. Moore (ed.), *Cognitive Development and the Acquisition of Language*, New York: Academic Press

Berko-Gleason, J. and Weintraub, S. (1978). Input language and the acquisition of communicative competence. In K. Nelson (ed.), *Children's Language*, vol.1, New York: Gardiner Press

Bernstein, B. (1970). Social class, language and socialization. In P. P. Giglioli (ed.) (1972), *Language and Social Context*, Harmondsworth: Penguin

Bernstein, B. (1971). *Class, Codes and Control I: Theoretical Studies Towards a Sociology of Language*, London: Routledge and Kegan Paul

Bernstein, R. M. (1980). The development of the self-system during adolescence, *Journal of Genetic Psychology*, **136**, 231–45

Berthenthal, B. I. and Fischer, K. W. (1978). Development of self-recognition in the infant, *Developmental Psychology*, **14**, 44–50

Bharati, A. (1985). The self in Hindu thought and action. In A. J. Marsella, G. DeVos, and F. L. K. Hsu (eds.), *Culture and Self*, New York and London: Tavistock

Birdwhistell, R. L. (1970). *Kinesics and Context*, Philadelphia: University of Pennsylvania Press

Blumer, H. (1966). Sociological implications of the thought of George Herbert Mead, *American Journal of Sociology*, **71**, 535–44

Bodine, A. (1975). Androcentrism in prescriptive grammar: singular 'they', sex-indefinite 'he', and 'he or she', *Language in Society*, **4**, 129–46

Bohannon III, J. N. and Hirsh-Pasek, K, (1984). Do children say as they're told? A new perspective on motherese. In L. Feagans, C. Garvey, and R. Golinkoff (eds.), *The Origins and Growth of Communication*, Norwood: Ablex

Bohannon, J. and Marquis, A. (1977). Children's control of adult speech, *Child Development*, **48**, 1002–8

Bohannon, J. and Warren-Leubecker, A. (1982). Speech to foreigness: effects of expectation and feedback, *Journal of Psycholinguistic Research*, **11**, 207–15

Boorman, S. A. and Levitt, P. R. (1980). *The Genetics of Altruism*, New York and London: Academic Press

Borke, H. (1971). Interpersonal perception of young children: egocentrism or empathy, *Developmental Psychology*, **5**, 263–9

Borke, H. (1973). The development of empathy in Chinese and American children between three and six years of age: a cross-cultural study, *Developmental Psychology*, **9**, 102–8

Borke, H. (1975). Piaget's mountains revisited: changes in the egocentric landscape, *Developmental Psychology*, **11**, 240–3

Boyle, J. (1977). *A Sense of Freedom*, London: Pan

Braunwald, S. R. (1978). Context, word and meaning toward a communicational analysis of lexical acquisition. In A. Lock (ed.), *Action, Gesture and Symbol: The Emergence of Language*, London: Academic Press

Brazelton, T. B., Koslowski, B., and Main, M. (1974). The origins of reciprocity: the early mother-infant interaction. In M. Lewis and L. A. Rosenblum (eds.), *The Effect of the Infant on its Caregiver*, London and New York: Wiley

Breakwell, G. M. (1986). *Coping with Threatened Identities*, London: Methuen

Bridges, K. M. B. (1931). *The Social and Emotional Development of the Pre-school Child*, London: Kegan Paul

Bronson, G. W. (1972). Infants' reactions to unfamiliar persons and novel objects, *Monographs of the Society for Research in Child Development*, **47**, (3, serial no. 148)

Brooks, J. and Lewis, M. (1976). Infants' responses to strangers: midgets, adult and child, *Child Development*, **45**, 243–7

Brooks-Gunn, J. and Lewis, M. (1979). 'Why mamma and papa?'. The development of social labels. *Child Development*, **50**, 1203–6

Broughton, J. (1978). Development of concepts of self, mind, reality and knowledge, *New Directions for Child Development*, **24**, 13–32

Brown, J. A. C. (1963). *Techniques of Persuasion*, Harmondsworth: Penguin

Bruner, J. S. (1978). From communication to language: a psychological perspective. In I. Markova (ed.), *The Social Context of Language*, Chichester and New York: Wiley

Bryant, B. K. (1982). An index of empathy for children and adolescents, *Child Development*, **53**, 413–25

Buchanan, J. P. and Thompson, S. K. (1973). A quantitative methodology to examine the development of moral judgment, *Child Development*, **44**, 186–9

Buck, R. W., Savin, V. J., Miller, R. E. and McCaul, W. F. (1972). Communication of affect through facial expressions in humans, *Journal of Personality and Social Psychology*, **23**, 362–71

Bühler, C. and Hetzer, H. (1928). Das erste Verstandnis fur Ausdruck in ersten Lebenjahr, *Zeitschrift fur Psychologie*, **107**, 50–61

Buss, A. H. (1980). *Self-consciousness and Social Anxiety*, San Francisco: Freeman

Buss, A. H. (1984), A conception of shyness. In J. A. Daly and J. C. McCroskey (eds.), *Avoiding Communication*, Beverly Hills and London: Sage

Byers, P. (1976). Biological rhythms as information channels in interpersonal communication behavior. In P. P. G. Bateson and P. H. Klopfer (eds.), *Perspectives in Ethology*, vol.2, New York and London: Plenum

Byrne, D. (1971). *The Attraction Paradigm*, New York: Academic Press

Campbell, D. T. (1975). On the conflicts between biological and social evolution and between psychology and moral tradition, *American Psychologist*, **30**, 1103–26

Cappella, J. N. (1979). Talk-silence sequences in informal conversations I. *Human Communication Research*, **6**, 3–17

Cappella, J. N. (1980). Talk-silence sequences in informal conversations II. *Human Communication Research*, **6**, 130–45.

Cazden, C. B. (1976). Play with language and meta-linguistic awareness. In J. S. Bruner, A. Jolly, and K. Sylva (eds.), *Play – Its Role in Development and Evaluation*, Harmondsworth: Penguin Books

Chagnon, N. A. (1968). *Yanomamo: The Fierce People*, New York: Holt, Rinehart, and Winston

Chandler, M. J. and Greenspan, S. (1972). Ersatz egocentricism: a reply to H. Borke, *Developmental Psychology*, **7**, 104–6

Chomsky, N. (1962). Exploratory models in linguistics. In E. Nagel, P. Suppes, and A. Tarski (eds.), *Logic, Methodology and Philosophy of Science*, Stanford, California: Stanford University Press

Christie, R. (1970). Why Machiavelli? In R. Christie and F. L. Geis (eds.), *Studies in Machiavellianism*, New York and London: Academic Press

Christie, R. and Geis, F. L. (1970). *Studies in Machiavellianism*, New York: Academic Press

Chu, G. C. (1985). The changing concept of self in contemporary China. In A. J. Marsella, G. DeVos, and F. K. Hsu (eds.), *Culture and Self*, New York and London: Tavistock

Chukovsky, K. (1963). *From Two to Five*, Berkeley: University of California Press

Church, R. M. (1959). Emotional reactions of rats to the pain of others, *Journal of Comparative and Physiological Psychology*, **52**, 132–4

Cialdini, R. B., Broner, S. L. and Lewis, S. K. (1974). Attributional bias and the easily persuaded other, *Journal of Personality and Social Psychology*, **30**, 631–7

Coberly, L. (1972). An interactional analysis of ten curing ceremonies, M.A. thesis, Columbia University

Collis, G. M. (1977). Visual co-orientation and maternal speech. In H. R. Schaffer (ed.), *Studies in Mother-Infant Interaction*, London and New York: Academic Press

Collis, G. M. and Schaffer, H. R. (1975). Synchronization of visual attention in mother-infant pairs, *Journal of Child Psychology and Psychiatry*, **16**, 315–20

Condon, W. S. (1970). Method of micro-analysis of sound films of behaviour, *Behavioral Research Methods and Instrumentation*, **2**, 51–4

Condon, W. S. (1977). A primary phase in the organization of infant responding. In H. R. Schaffer (ed.), *Studies in Mother-Infant Interaction*, London and New York: Academic Press

Condon, W. S. (1979). Neonatal entrainment and enculturation. In M. Bullowa (ed.), *Before Speech: The Beginning of Interpersonal Communication*, Cambridge and New York: Cambridge University Press

Condon, W. S. and Brosin, H. W. (1971). Micro linguistic-kinesic events in schizophrenic behavior. In D. V. Sankar (ed.), *Schizophrenia: Current Concepts and Research*, Hicksville, NY: PJD Publications

Condon, W. S. and Ogston, W. D. (1966). Sound film analysis of normal and pathological behavior patterns, *Journal of Nervous and Mental Disease*, **143**, 338–47

Condon, W. S., and Ogston, W. D. (1971). Speech and body motion synchrony of the speaker hearer. In D. L. Harton and J. J. Jenkins (eds.), *Perception of Language*. Proceedings of a symposium at Pittsburgh University January 1968, Columbus, Ohio: Merrill

Condon, W. S. and Sander, L. W. (1974a). Neonate movement is synchronized with adult speech: interactional participation and language acquisition, *Science*, **183**, 99–101

Condon, W. S., and Sander, L. W. (1974b). Synchrony demonstrated between movements of the neonate and adult speech, *Child Development*, **45**, 456–62

Cook, T. D. and Insko, C. A. (1968). Persistence of attitude change as a function of conclusion re-exposure: a laboratory – field experiment, *Journal of Personality and Social Psychology*, **9**, 322–8

Coser, R. L. (1959). Some social functions of laughter, *Human Relations*, **27**, 171–82

Coser, R. L. (1960). Laughter among colleagues, *Psychiatry*, **23**, 81–95

Cottrell, L. S. (1950). Some neglected problems in social psychology, *American Sociological Review*, **15**, 705–12

Craig, R. T. and Tracy, K. (1983). *Conversational Coherence*, Beverly Hills and London: Sage

Crook, J. H. (1980). *The Evolution of Human Consciousness*, Oxford: Clarendon Press

Cross, T. G. (1978). Mothers' speech and its association with rate of linguistic development in young children. In N. Waterson and C. Snow (eds.), *The Development of Communication*, Chichester and New York: Wiley

Damon, W. (1977). *The Social World of the Child*, San Francisco: Jossey-Bass

Damon, W. and Hart, D. (1982). The development of self-understanding from infancy through adolescence, *Child Development*, **53**, 841–64

Darley, J. M. and Darley, S. A. (1976). Conformity and deviation. In J. Thibaut, J. Spence, and R. Carson (eds.), *Contemporary Topics in Social Psychology*, Morristown: General Learning Press

Darwin, C. (1871). *The Descent of Man*, 2nd edn 1874, London: John Murray

Darwin, C. (1872). *The Expression of the Emotions in Man and Animals*, London: Appleton

Darwin, C. (1877). A biographical sketch of an infant, *Mind*, **2**, 285–94

Dembo, T. (1931). Der Ärger als dynamisches Problem. (Untersuchungen zur Handlungs – and Affektpsychologie X ed. K Lewins, *Psychologische Forschung*, **15**, 1–144

De Paulo, B. M., Jordan, A., Irvine, A. and Laser, P. S. (1982). Age changes in the detection of deception, *Child Development*, **53**, 701–9

Deutsch, F. (1974). Female preschoolers' perceptions of affective responses and interpersonal behavior in videotaped episodes, *Developmental Psychology*, **10**, 733–40

Deutsch, F. and Gerard, H. G. (1955). A study of normative and informational social influence upon individual judgment, *Journal of Abnormal and Social Psychology*, **51**, 629–36

Deutsch, F. and Madle, R. A. (1975). Empathy: historic and current conceptualizations, measurement, and a cognitive theoretical perspective, *Human Development*, **18**, 267–87

DeVos, G. (1985). Dimensions of the self in Japanese culture. In A. J. Marsella, G. DeVos, and F. L. K. Hsu (eds.), *Culture and Self*, New York and London: Tavistock

Dittmar, N. (1984). Descriptive and explanatory power of rules in sociolinguistics. In B. Bain, (ed.), *The Sociogenesis of Language and Human Conduct*, New York and London: Plenum Press

Dowd, J. M. and Tronick, E. Z. (1982). The temporal organisation of infant links movements. Paper presented at the International Conference on Infant Studies, Austin, Texas

Duncan, S. (1972). Some signals and rules for taking speaking turns in conversations, *Journal of Personality and Social Psychology*, **23**, 283–92

Duncan, S. (1974). On the structure of speaker – auditor interaction during speaking turns, *Language in Society*, **2**, 161–80

Duncan, S. Jr (1983). Speaking turns: studies of structure and individual differences. In J. M. Wiemann and R. P. Harrison (eds.), *Nonverbal Interaction*, Beverly Hills and London: Sage

Duncan, S. Jr and Fiske, D. W. (1977). *Face to Face Interaction*, Hillsdale, NJ: Lawrence Erlbaum

Durkheim, E. (1915). *The Elementary Forms of the Religious Life*, trs. J. W. Swain, London: Novello and Company

Duval, S. and Wicklund, R. A. (1972). *A Theory of Objective Self-Awareness*, New York: Academic Press

Dymond, R. (1949). A scale for the measurement of empathic ability, *Journal of Consulting Psychology*, **13**, 127–33

Eisenstein, E. L. (1979). *The Printing Press As an Agent of Change*, Cambridge and New York: Cambridge University Press

Eisenstein, E. L. (1983). *The Printing Revolution in Early Modern Europe*, Cambridge and New York: Cambridge University Press

Ekman, P. (1971). Universals and cultural differences in facial expressions of emotions. In J. K. Cole (ed.), *Nebraska Symposium on Motivation*, **19**, Lincoln: University of Nebraska Press

Elliot, A. J. (1981). *Child Language*, Cambridge: Cambridge University Press

Ellison, R. (1965). *Invisible Man*, Harmondsworth: Penguin Books

Erickson, F. and Shultz, J. (1982). *The Counselor as Gatekeeper*, New York and London: Academic Press

Erikson, E. H. (1959). Identity and the life cycle, *Psychological Issues*, **1**, 1–171

Ervin-Tripp, S. (1979). Children's verbal turn-taking. In E. Ochs, and B. B. Schiefflin (eds.), *Developmental Progmatics*, New York and London: Academic Press

Escalona, S. K. (1945). Feeding disturbances in very young children, *American Journal of Orthopsychiatry*, **15**, 76–80

Evans, R. M. (1967). Early aggressive responses in domestic chicks, *Animal Behavior*, **16**, 24–8

Falbo, T. (1977). Multidimensional scaling of power strategies, *Journal of Personality and Social Psychology*, **35**, 537–47

Falbo, T. and Peplau, L. A. (1980). Power strategies in intimate relationships, *Journal of Personality and Social Psychology*, **38**, 618–28

Fales, E. (1937). Genesis of level of aspiration in children from one and one-half to three years of age, reported by K. Lewin *et al.*, Level of aspiration, in J. McV. Hunt (ed.), *Personality and the Behavior Disorders*, vol.1, New York: The Ronald Press, 1944

Human Awareness

Farnill, D. (1974). The effects of social judgment set on children's use of intent information, *Journal of Personality*, **42**, 276–89

Farr, R. M. (1980a). On reading Darwin and discovering social psychology. In R. Gilmour and S. Duck (eds.), *The Development of Social Psychology*, London: Academic Press

Farr, R. M. (1980b). Homo loquens in social psychological perspective. In H. Giles, W. P. Robinson and P. M. Smith (eds.), *Language: Social Psychological Perspectives*, Oxford and New York: Pergamon

Farr, R. M. (1981). On the nature of human nature and the science of behaviour. In P. Heelas and A. Lock (eds.), *Indigenous Psychologies: the Anthropology of the Self*, London: Academic Press

Farr, R. M. (1983). The impact of Wundt on the development of social psychology: A critical reappraisal. In G. Eckardt and L. Spring (eds.), *Advances in the Historiography of Psychology*, Berlin: VEB Deutscher Verlag der Wissenschaften

Farr, R. M. (1984). Social representations: their role in the design and execution of laboratory experiments. In R. M. Farr and S. Moscovici (eds.), *Social Representations*, Cambridge and New York: Cambridge University Press; and Paris: Editions de la Maison des Science de l'Homme

Farr, R. M. and Anderson, A. (1983). Beyond actor/observer differences in perspective: extensions and applications. In M. Hewstone (ed.), *Attribution Theory: Social and Functional Extensions*, Oxford: Blackwell

Farr, R. M. and Moscovici S. (eds.), (1984). *Social Representations*, Cambridge and New York: Cambridge University Press; and Paris: Editions de la Maison des Sciences de l'Homme

Faucheux, C. and Moscovici, S. (1967). Le style de comportement d'une minorite et son influence sur les réponses d'une majorité, *Bulletin du CERP*, **16**, 337–60

Ferguson, C. A. (1977). Baby talk as a simplified register. In C. E. Snow and C. A. Ferguson (eds.), *Talking to Children*, Cambridge: Cambridge University Press

Fernald, A. (1984). The perceptual & affective salience of mothers' speech to infants. In L. Feagans, C. Garvey, and R. Golinkoff (eds.), *The Origins & Growth of Communication*, Norwood, NJ: Ablex

Feshbach, N. D. (1978). Studies of empathic behavior in children. In B. A. Maher (ed.), *Progess in Experimental Personality Research*, vol. 8, New York and London: Academic Press

Feshbach, N. D. and Roe, K. (1968). Empathy in six– and seven-year olds. *Child Development*, **39**, 133–45

Festinger, L. (1942). Wish, expectations, and group standards as factors influencing level of aspiration, *Journal of Abnormal and Social Psychology*, **37**, 184–200

Festinger, L., Schacter, S. and Back, K. (1950). *Social Pressures in Informal Groups*, New York: Harper; London: Tavistock (1959)

Fielding, G. and Fraser, C. (1978). Language and interpersonal relations. In I. Markova (ed.), *The Social Conduct of Language*, Chichester and New York: Wiley

Fillmore, C. J. (1971). Verbs of judging: an exercise in semantic description. In C. J. Fillmore and T. D. Langendoen (eds.), *Studies in Linguistic Semantics*, New York: Holt, Rinehart and Winston

Fincham, F. and Jaspars, J. (1979). Attribution of responsibility to the self and other in children and adults, *Journal of Personality and Social Psychology*, **37**, 1589–1602

Fishman, J. A. (1972). *The Sociology of Language*, Rowley Mass.: Newbury House

Flavell, J. H., Botkin, P. T., Fry, C. L. Jr, Wright, J. W. and Jarvis, P. E. (1968). *The Development of Role-taking and Communication Skills in Children*, New York: Wiley

Flavell, J. H., Flavell, E. R. and Green, F. L. (1983a). Development of the appearance-reality distinction, *Cognitive Psychology*, **15**, 95–120

Flavell, J. H., Zhang, X-D., Zou, H., Qi, S. and Dong, Q. (1983b). A comparison between the development of the appearance-reality distinction in the People's Republic of China and the United States, *Cognitive Psychology*, **15**, 459–66

Fogel, A. (1977). Temporal organization in mother-infant face-to-face interaction. In H. R. Schaffer (ed.), *Studies in Mother-Infant Interaction*, London and New York: Academic Press

Freedman, J. L. and Doob, A. N. (1968). *Deviancy*, New York: Academic Press

Freud, A. (1937). *The Ego and the Mechanisms of Defence*, trs. C. Baines, London: The Hogarth Press

Freud, S. (1905). Jokes and their relation to the unconscious. *The Complete Psychological Works*, Standard Edn, vol. VIII, trs. and ed. J. Strachey, 1960, London: The Hogarth Press

Freud, S. (1921). Group psychology and the analysis of the ego. *The Complete Psychological Works*, Standard Edn, vol. XVIII, trs. and ed. J. Strachey, 1955, London: The Hogarth Press

Freud, S. (1923). The Ego and the Id. *The Complete Psychological Works*, Standard Edn, vol. XIX, trs. and ed. J. Strachey, 1961, London: The Hogarth Press

Frisch, von K. (1967). *The Dance Language and Orientation of Bees*, trs. by L. E. Chadwick, Cambridge, Mass.: The Belknap Press of Harvard University Press; London: Oxford University Press

Frisch, von K. (1974). Decoding the language of the bee, *Science*, **185**, 663–8

From, F. (1971). *Perception of Other People*, New York and London: Columbia University Press

Furrow, D., Nelson, K. and Benedict, H. (1979). Mothers' speech to children and syntactic development: some simple relationships, *Journal of Child Language*, **6**, 423–42

Gallup, G. G. Jr (1970). Chimpanzees: self-recognition, *Science*, **167**, 86–7

Gallup, G. G. Jr (1983). Toward a comparative psychology of mind. In R. L. Mellgren (ed.), *Animal Cognition and Behavior*, Amsterdam: North-Holland

Gardner, B. T. and Gardner, R. A. (1969). Teaching sign language to a chimpanzee, *Science*, **165**, 664–72

Garnica, O. K. (1978). Non-verbal concomitants of language input to children. In N. Waterson and C. E. Snow (eds.), *The Development of Communication*, Chichester and New York: Wiley

Garvey, C. (1976). Some properties of social play. In J. S. Bruner, A. Jolly and K. Sylva (eds.), *Play – Its Role in Development and Evolution*, Harmondsworth: Penguin Books

Garvey, C. (1977). Play with language. In B. Tizard and D. Harvey (eds.), *Biology of Play*, London: Heinemann

Garvey, C. (1984). *Children's Talk*, Oxford: Fontana

Geis, F. L. and Moon, T. H. (1981). Machiavellianism and deception, *Journal of Personality and Social Psychology*, **41**, 766–75

Gergen, K. J. (1977). The social construction of self-knowledge. In T. Mischel (ed.), *The Self: Psychological and Philosophical Issues*, Oxford: Blackwell

Gergen, K. J. (1984). Theory of the self: impasse and evolution.

In L. Berkowitz (ed.), *Advances in Experimental Social Psychology*, **17**, 49–115

Gergen, K. J. (1987). Toward self as relationship. In K. M. Yardley and T. M. Honess (eds.), *Self and Identity*, Chichester and New York: Wiley

Gewirth, A. (1978). *Reason and Morality*, Chicago: University of Chicago Press

Goffman, E. (1959). *The Presentation of Self in Everyday Life*, Garden City: Doubleday

Goffman, E. (1963). *Behavior in Public Places*, Glencoe: Free Press

Goffman, E. (1967). Embarrassment and social organisation. In E. Goffman, *Interaction Ritual*, Harmondsworth: Penguin

Goffman, E. (1968). *Stigma*, Harmondsworth: Penguin

Gombrich, E. H. (1960). *Art and Illusion*, London: Phaidon

Goodall, J. (1968). The behaviour of free-living chimpanzees in the Gombe Stream Reserve, *Animal Behaviour Monographs*, **1**, 161–311

Gould, R. (1939). An experimental analysis of 'level of aspiration', *Genetic Psychology Monographs*, **21**, 1–116

Griffin, D. R. (1981). *The Question of Animal Awareness*, New York: The Rockfeller University Press

Griffin, D. R. (1984). *Animal Thinking*, Cambridge and London: Harvard University Press

Gruber, H. E. (1973). Courage and cognitive growth in children and scientists. In M. Schwebel and J. Raph (eds.), *Piaget In the Classroom*, Basic Books. Reprinted (1974), London: Routledge and Kegan Paul

Gruber, H. E. (1974). *Darwin On Man*, together with Darwin's early and unpublished notebooks, transcribed and annotated by P. H. Barrett, London: Wildwood

Guardo, C. J. and Bohan, J. B. (1971). Development of a sense of self-identity in children, *Child Development*, **42**, 1909–21

Gumperz, J. J. (1982). *Discourse Strategies*, Cambridge: Cambridge University Press

Gumperz, J. J. and Cook-Gumperz, J. (1982). Introduction: language and the communication of social identity. In J. J. Gumperz (ed.), *Language and Social Identity*, Cambridge: Cambridge University Press

Guralnick, M. J. and Paul-Brown, D. (1977). The nature of verbal interactions among handicapped and non-handicapped preschool children. *Child Development*, **48**, 254–60

Hall, E. T. (1959). *The Silent Language*, Garden City, NY: Doubleday

Hall, E. T. (1966). *The Hidden Dimension*, Garden City, NY: Doubleday

Hamilton, M. L. (1973). Imitative behavior and expressive ability in facial expression of emotion, *Developmental Psychology*, **8**, 138

Hamlyn, D. (1977). Self-knowledge. In T. Mischel (ed.), *The Self: Psychological and Philosophical Issues*, Oxford: Blackwell

Hanson, N. R. (1958). *Patterns of Discovery*, Cambridge: Cambridge University Press

Harkness, S. (1977). Aspects of social environment and first language acquisition in rural Africa. In C. E. Snow and C. A. Ferguson (eds.), *Talking to Children*, Cambridge: Cambridge University Press

Harré, R. (1979). *Social Being*, Oxford: Basil Blackwell

Harré, R. (1983). *Personal Being: A Theory for Individual Psychology*, Oxford: Blackwell

Harris, P. L. (1983). Children's understanding of the link between situation and emotion, *Journal of Experimental Child Psychology*, **36**, 491–509

Harris, P. L., Guz, G. R., Lipian, M. S. and Man-Shu, Z., (1985). Insight into the time course of emotion among Western and Chinese children, *Child Development*, **56**, 972–88

Harris, P. L. Olthof, T. and Meerum Terwogt, M. (1981). Children's knowledge of emotion, *Journal of Child Psychology and Psychiatry*, **22**, 247–61

Harris, P. L. and Olthof, T. (1982). The child's concept of emotion. In G. Butterworth and P. Light (eds.), *The Individual and the Social in Cognitive Development*, Brighton, Sussex: Harvester

Harter, S. (1982). The perceived competence scale for children, *Child Development*, **53**, 87–97

Harth, E. (1982). *Windows on the Mind*, Brighton: Harvester Press

Harvey, J. H. and Weary, G. (1981). *Perspectives on Attributional Processes*, Dubuque: Brown

Haskell, F. (1976). *Rediscoveries in Art*, London: Phaidon

Hegel, G. W. F. (1807). *The Phenomenology of Mind*, trs. J. B. Baillie (1949), London: George Allen and Unwin; New York: Macmillan

Heider, F. (1958). *The Psychology of Interpersonal Relations*, New York and London: Wiley

Heider, F. (1967). On social cognition, *American Psychologist*, **22**, 25–31

Heider, F. and Simmel, M. (1944). An experimental study of apparent behavior, *American Journal of Psychology*, **57**, 243–59

Herder, J. G. (1771). *On the Origin of Language*. In J. G. Herder, *Sämtliche Werke*, ed. B. Suphon, reprinted 1967, Hildesheim: George Olins

Hermanowicz, V. (1982). Effect of 'authenticity' and machiavellian attitudes on communication styles, *Polish Psychological Bulletin*, **13**, 45–51

Hoffman, M. L. (1975). Developmental synthesis of affect and cognition and its implications for altruistic motivation, *Developmental Psychology*, **11**, 607–22

Hoffman, M. L. (1976). Empathy, role-taking, guilt, and development of altruistic motives. In T. Lickona (ed.), *Moral Development and Behavior: Theory, Research and Social Issues*, New York: Holt, Rinehart & Winston

Hoffman, M. L. (1978a). Toward a theory of empathic arousal and development. In M. Lewis and L. A. Rosenblum (eds.), *The Development of Affect*, New York and London: Plenum

Hoffman, M. L. (1978b). Empathy, its development and prosocial implications. In C. B. Keasey (ed.), *Nebraska Symposium on Motivation 1977: Social Cognitive Development*, Lincoln and London: University of Nebraska Press

Hollon, C. J. (1983). Machiavellianism and managerial work attitudes and perceptions, *Psychological Reports*, **52**, 432–4

Hovland, C. I., Janis, I. L. and Kelley, H. H. (1953). *Communication and Persuasion*, New Haven and London: Yale University Press

Hovland, C. I. and Mandell, W. (1952). An experimental comparison of conclusion-drawing by the communicator and by the audience, *Journal of Abnormal and Social Psychology*, **47**, 581–8

Hovland, C. I. and Weiss, W. (1951). The influence of source credibility on communication effectiveness, *Public Opinion Quarterly*, **15**, 635–50

Humboldt, W. von (1836). *Linguistic Variability and Intellectual Development*, trs. E. C. Buck and F. A. Raven, Coral Gables: University of Miami Press (1971)

Humphrey, G. (1922). The conditioned reflex and the elementary social reaction, *Journal of Abnormal and Social Psychology*, **17**, 113–19

Humphrey, N. (1979). Nature's psychologists. In B. Josephson and B. S. Ramachandra (eds.), *Consciousness and the Physical World*. New York: Pergamon Press

Humphrey, N. (1983). *Consciousness Regained*, Oxford and New York: Oxford University Press

Hunt, S. D. and Chonko, L. B. (1984). Marketing and machiavellianism, *Journal of Marketing*, **48**, 30–42

Ianotti, R. J. (1985). Naturalistic and structured assessments of prosocial behavior in preschool children: the influence of empathy and perspective taking, *Developmental Psychology*, **21**, 46–55

Ichheiser, G. (1949). Misunderstanding in human relations: a study in false social perception, *American Journal of Sociology*, supplement to September issue, 1–72

Inhelder, B. and Piaget, J. (1958). *The Growth of Logical Thinking from Childhood to Adolescence*, New York: Basic Books

Isaacs, S. (1933). *Social Development in Young Children*, New York: Harcourt Brace

Jaffe, J. and Feldstein, S. (1970). *Rhythms of Dialogue*, New York: Academic Press

Jahoda, M. (1977). *Freud and the Dilemmas of Psychology*, London: The Hogarth Press

Jakobson, R. (1941–68). *Child Language, Aphasia and Phonological Universals*, The Hague: Mouton

James, W. (1890). *Principles of Psychology*, vol. 1, New York: Holt

Janis, I. L. and Feshbach, S. (1953). Effect of fear-arousing communications, *Journal of Abnormal and Social Psychology*, **48**, 78–92

Jaynes, J. (1976). *The Origin of Consciousness in the Breakdown of the Bicameral Mind*, London: Allen Lane

Jocić, M. (1978). Adaptation in adult speech during communication with children. In N. Waterson and C. Snow (eds.), *The Development of Communication*, Chichester and New York: Wiley

Johnson, D. B. (1982). Altruistic behavior and the development of the self in infants, *Merrill-Palmer Quarterly*, **28**, 379–88

Johnson, P. (1975). Woman and power: toward a theory of effectiveness, *Journal of Social Issues*, **39**, 99–110

Jones, E. E. (1964). *Ingratiation: A Social Psychological Analysis*, New York: Appleton-Century-Crofts

Jones, E. E. and Davis, K. E. (1965). From acts to dispositions: The attribution process in person perception. In L. Berkowitz (ed.), *Advances in Experimental Social Psychology*, New York: Academic Press

Jones, E. E. and Nisbett, R. E. (1972). The actor and the observer: divergent perceptions of the causes of behavior. In E. E. Jones, D. E. Kanouse, H. H. Kelley, R. E. Nisbett, S. Valins and B. Weiner (eds.), *Attribution: Perceiving the Causes of Behavior*, Morristown: General Learning Press

Jones, E. E. and Pittman, T. S. (1982). Toward a general theory of strategic self-presentation. In J. M. Suls (ed.), *Psychological Perspectives on the Self*, Hillsdale: Lawrence Erlbaum Associates

Jones, E. E. and Wortman, C. (1973). *Ingratiation: An Attributional Approach*, Morristown: General Learning Press

Jucknat, M. (1937). Leistung, Anschpruchsniveau and Selbstbewusstsein, *Psychologische Forschung*, **22**, 89–179

Karniol, R. (1978). Children's use of intention cues in evaluating behavior, *Psychological Bulletin*, **85**, 76–85

Kaye, K. (1977). Toward the origin of dialogue. In H. R. Schaffer (ed.), *Studies in Mother-Infant Interaction*, London and New York: Academic Press

Kaye, K. (1982). *The Mental & Social Life of Babies: How Parents Create Persons*, Brighton: Harvester Press

Kaye, K. and Wells, A. (1980). Mothers' jiggling and the burst-pause pattern in neonatal sucking, *Impact Behavior and Development*, **3**, 29–46

Keller, A., Ford, L. H. Jr, and Meacham, J. A. (1978). Dimensions of self-concept in preschool children, *Developmental Psychology*, **14**, 483–9

Kelley, H. H. (1967). Attribution theory in social psychology. In D. Levine (ed.), *Nebraska Symposium on Motivation*, **15**, 192–238

Kelley, H. H. and Michela, J. L. (1980). Attribution theory and research. In *Annual Review of Psychology*, **31**, 457–501

Kelman, H. C. and Hovland, C. I. (1953). 'Reinstatement' of the communicator in delayed measurement of opinion change, *Journal of Abnormal and Social Psychology*, **48**, 327–35

Kempton, W. (1980). The rhythmic basis of interactional micro-synchrony. In M. R. Key (ed.), *The Relationship of Verbal and Nonverbal Communication*, The Hague: Mouton

Kendon, A. (1972). Some relationships between body motion and speech. An analysis of an example. In A. W. Siegman and B. Pope (eds.), *Studies in Dyadic Communication*, New York: Pergamon

Key, M. R. (1980). Language and nonverbal behavior as organizers of social systems. In M. R. Key (ed.), *The Relationship of Verbal and Nonverbal Communication*, The Hague: Mouton

King, M. (1971). The development of some intention concepts in young children, *Child Development*, **42**, 1145–52

Klein, R. (1971). Some factors influencing empathy in six and seven year old children varying in ethnic background (Doctoral dissertn, University of California, Los Angeles, School of Education, 1970). *Dissertation Abstracts Interactional*, 1971, **31**, 396a (University Microfilms no. 71–3862)

Kline, P. (1984). *Psychology and Freudian Theory*, London and New York: Methuen

Koestler, A. (1959). *The Sleepwalkers*, London: Hutchinson

Kohlberg, L. (1969). Stage and sequence: the cognitive-developmental approach to socialisation. In D. A. Goslin (ed.), *Handbook of Socialisation Theory and Research*, Chicago: Rand McNally

Köhler, W. (1927). *The Mentality of Apes*, trs. from the 2nd revsd edn of 1925 by E. Winter, London: Kegan Paul, Trench, Trubner

Kon, I. S. (1978). *Otkritye Ja* (*Discovery of the Self*), Moscow: Politzdat

Krauss, R. and Glucksberg, S. (1969). The development of communication competence as a function of age, *Child Development*, **40**, 255–66

Krebs, D. (1975). Empathy and altruism, *Journal of Personality and Social Psychology*, **32**, 1124–46

Kreckel, M. (1981). *Communicative Acts and Shared Knowledge in Natural Discourse*, London and New York: Academic Press

Kuhn, M. H. and McPartland, S. (1954). An empirical investigation of self attitudes, *American Sociological Review*, **19**, 68–76

Kuhn, T. S. (1962). *The Structure of Scientific Revolutions*, Chicago: Chicago University Press

Labov, W. (1969). The logic of non-standard English, *Georgetown Monographs on Language and Linguistics*, **22**, 1–31

Labov, W. and Fanshel, D. (1977). *Therapeutic Discourse: Psychotherapy as Conversation*, New York: Academic Press

Laing, R. D. (1961). *Self and Others*, London: Tavistock

Lakoff, R. (1975). *Language and Woman's Place*, New York: Harper and Row

Leary, M. R. and Schlenker, B. R. (1981). The social psychology of shyness: a self-presentation model. In J. T. Tedeschi (ed.), *Impression Management Theory and Social Psychological Research*, New York and London: Academic Press

Ledbetter, D. H. and Basen, J. A. (1982). Failure to demonstrate self-recognition in gorillas, *American Journal of Primatology*, **2**, 307–10

Leonard-Dolan, C. (1980). A method for film analysis of ethnic communication style. In M. R. Key, *The Relationship of Verbal and Nonverbal Communication*, The Hague: Mouton

Lewin, K. (1935). *A Dynamic Theory of Personality*, New York and London: McGraw-Hill

Lewin, K., Dembo, T., Festinger, L. and Sears, P. S. (1944). Level of aspiration. In J. McV. Hunt (ed.), *Personality and the Behavior Disorders*, vol. 1, New York: Ronald

Lewis, M. and Brooks, J. (1974). Self, other, and fear: infants' reactions to people. In M. Lewis and L. Rosenblum (eds.), *The Origin of Fear: The Origins of Behavior*, vol. II, New York: Wiley

Lewis M. and Brooks-Gunn, J. (1979). *Social Cognition and the Acquisition of Self*, New York and London: Plenum Press

Lewis, M. and Freedle, R. (1973). Mother-infant dyad: the cradle of meaning. In P. Pliner, L. Krames and T. Alloway (eds.), *Communication and Affect: Language and Thought*, New York: Academic Press

Light, P. (1979). *The Development of Social Sensitivity: Role-taking in Young Children*, Cambridge: Cambridge University Press

Lindauer, M. (1971). *Communication Among Social Bees*, 2nd edn, Cambridge, Mass.: Harvard University Press

Lipps, T. (1926). *Psychological Studies*, Baltimore: Williams and Wilkins

Lipps, T. (1935). Empathy, inner imitation of sense feelings. In Radar, *A Modern Book of Esthetics*, New York: Holt

Livesley, W. J. and Bromley, D. B. (1973). *Person Perception in Childhood and Adolescence*, London: Wiley

Lumsdaine, A. A. and Janis, I. L. (1953). Resistance to 'counterpropaganda' produced by one-sided and two–sided 'propaganda' presentations, *Public Opinions Quarterly*, **17**, 311–18

Luria, A. R. (1976). *Cognitive Development: Its Cultural and*

Social Foundations, trs. M. Lopez-Morillas and L. Solotaroff, Cambridge, Mass. and London: Harvard University Press

Lyons, J. O. (1978). *The Invention of the Self*, Carbondale and Edwardsville: Southern Illinois University Press

Maass, A. and Clark, R. D. III (1984). The hidden impact of minorities: Fourteen years of minority influence research, *Psychological Bulletin*, **95**, 428–50

McDowall, J. J. (1978). Interactional synchrony: a reappraisal, *Journal of Personality and Social Psychology*, **36**, 963–75

McGuire, W. J. (1968). Personality and susceptibility to social influence. In E. F. Borgatta and W. W. Lambert (eds.), *Handbook of Personality Theory and Research*, Chicago: Rand McNally

Machiavelli, N. (1513a). *Discourses on the First Ten Books of Titus Livius*, trs. A. Gilbert, in *Chief Works and Others*, Durham: Duke University Press (1965)

Machiavelli, N. (1513b). *The Prince*, trs. A. Gilbert, in *Chief Works and Others*, Durham: Duke University Press (1965)

MacLean, P. D. (1967). The brain in relation to empathy and medical education, *Journal of Nervous Mental Disease*, **144**, 374–82

MacLean, P. D. (1973). *A Triune Concept of the Brain and Behavior*, Toronto: University of Toronto Press

Maher, B. (1972). The language of schizophrenia: a review and interpretation, *British Journal of Psychiatry*, **120**, 3–17

Marcus, R. F., Telleen, S. and Roke, E. J. (1979). Relation between cooperation and empathy in young children, *Developmental Psychology*, **15**, 346–7

Markova, I. (1978a). Attributions, meaning of verbs and reasoning. In I. Markova (ed.), *The Social Context of Language*, Chichester and New York: Wiley

Markova, I. (1978b). Verbs of judging and acts of judging. In R. Campbell and P. T. Smith (eds.), *Recent Advances in the Psychology of Language*, Series III, New York and London: Plenum Press

Markova, I. (1982). *Paradigms, Thought, and Language*, Chichester and New York: Wiley

Markova, I. (1983). The origin of the social psychology of language in German expressivism, *British Journal of Social Psychology*, **22**, 315–25

Markova, I. (1987). Knowledge of the self through interaction. In K. M. Yardley and T. M. Honess (eds.), *Self and Identity*, Chichester and New York: Wiley

Markova, I. (in press). On the interaction of opposites in psychological processes, *Journal for the Theory of Social Behaviour*.

Markova, I., Lockyer, R. and Forbes, C. (1980a). Self-perception of employed and unemployed haemophiliacs, *Psychological Medicine*, **10**, 559–65

Markova, I., Macdonald, K, and Forbes, C. (1980b). Impact of haemophilia on child learning and parental co-operation, *Journal of Child Psychology and Psychiatry*, **21**, 153–62

Marriott, M. (1976). Hindu transactions: diversity without dualism. In B. Kapherer (ed.), *Transaction and Meaning. Directions in the Anthropology of Exchange and Symbolic Behavior*, Philadelphia: Institute for the Study of Human Issues

Martin, J. G. (1972). Rhythmic (hierarchical) versus serial structure in speech and other behavior, *Psychological Review*, **79**, 487–509

Maslach, C., Stapp, J. and Santee, R. T. (1985). Individuation: conceptual analysis and assessment, *Journal of Personality and Social Psychology*, **49**, 729–38

Maslow, A. H. (1962). *Toward a Psychology of Being*, New York: Van Nostrand

Mason, W. A. (1976). Windows on the mind, *Science*, **194**, 930–1

Mead, G. H. (1925). The genesis of self and social control, *International Journal of Ethics*, **35**, 251–73

Mead, G. H. (1934). *Mind, Self and Society*, Chicago: Chicago University Press

Mead, G. H. (1936). *Movements of Thought in the Nineteenth Century*, Chicago and London: University of Chicago Press

Mehrabian, A. and Epstein, N. (1972). A measure of emotional empathy, *Journal of Personality*, **40**, 525–43

Meltzer, B. N. (1964). Mead's social psychology. In J. G. Manis and B. N. Meltzer (eds., 1972), *Symbolic Interaction*, 2nd edn, Boston: Allyn and Bacon

Menzel, E. W. Jr (1975). Natural language of young chimpanzees, *New Scientist*, **65**, 127–30

Milgram, S. (1977). The image freezing machine. In S. Milgram (ed.), *The Individual in a Social World: Essays and Experiments*, Reading, Mass.: Addison-Wesley

Miller, C. L. and Byrne, J. M. (1984). The role of temporal clues in the development of language and communication. In L. Feagans, C. Garvey and R. Golinkoff (eds.), *The Origins & Growth of Communication*, Norwood, NJ: Ablex

Miller, D. L. (1973). *George Herbert Mead: Self, Language and the World*, Austin and London: University of Texas Press

Miller, G. R. and Burgoon, M. (1973). *New Techniques of Persuasion*, New York and London: Harper and Row

Miller, G. R. and Steinberg, M. (1975). *Between People: A New Analysis of Interpersonal Communication*, Chicago: Science Research Associates

Miller, R. E. (1967). Experimental approaches to the physiological and behavioral concomitants of affective communication in rhesus monkeys. In S. A. Altman (ed.), *Social Communication Among Primates*, Chicago: University of Chicago Press

Miller, R. E., Banks, J. H. Jr and Kuwahara, H. (1966). The communication of affects in monkeys: Co-operative reward conditioning, *Journal of Genetic Psychology*, **108**, 121–34

Miller, R. E., Banks, J. H. Jr and Ogawa, N. (1963). Role of facial expression in 'cooperative-avoidance conditioning' in monkeys, *Journal of Abnormal and Social Psychology*, **67**, 24–30

Mills, J. and Jellison, J. M. (1968). Effect on opinion change of similarity between the communicator and the audience he addressed, *Journal of Personality and Social Psychology*, **9**, 43–56

Mood, D. W., Johnson, J. E. and Shantz, C. U. (1974). Affection and cognitive components of empathy in young children. Mimeo, Department of Oncology, Wayne State University School of Medicine, Detroit, Michigan

Morishima, M. (1982). *Why Has Japan 'Succeeded'?*, Cambridge and New York: Cambridge University Press

Morris, C. (1972). *The Discovery of the Individual*, New York: Harper and Row

Moscovici, S. (1961–76). *La Psychanalyse: Son Image Et Son Public*, Paris: Presses Universitaires De France

Moscovici, S. (1973). Foreword to C. Herzlich, *Health and Illness: A Social Psychological Analysis*, London: Academic Press

Moscovici, S. (1976). *Social Influence and Social Change*, London and New York: Academic Press

Moscovici, S. (1981). On social representations. In J. P. Forgas (ed.), *Social Cognition: Perspectives on Everyday Understanding*, London and New York: Academic Press

Moscovici, S. (1984). The phenomenon of social representations. In R. M. Farr and S. Moscovici, *Social Represen-*

tations, Cambridge and New York: Cambridge University Press; and Paris: Editions de la Maison des Sciences de l'Homme

Moscovici, S., Lage, E. and Naffrechoux, M. (1969). Influence of a consistent minority on the responses of a majority in a color perception task, *Sociometry*, **32**, 365–79

Moscovici, S. and Plon, M. (1966), Les situations colloques, *Bulletin de Psychologie*, **19**, 702–22

Mugny, G. (1982). *The Power of Minorities*, London and New York: Academic Press

Neisser, U. (1976). *Cognition and Reality*, San Francisco: Freeman

Nelson, K. (1973). *Structure and Strategy in Learning to Talk*, Monographs of the Society for Research in Child Development, serial no. 149, vol. 38

Nemeth, C. J. (1986). Differential contributions of majority and minority influence, *Psychological Review*, **93**, 23–32

Newcomb, T. M. (1950). *Social Psychology*, New York: Dryden

Newport, E. L., Gleitman, H. and Gleitman, L. R. (1977). Mother, I'd rather do it myself: some effects and non-effects of maternal speech style. In C. E. Snow and C. A. Ferguson (eds.), *Talking to Children*, Cambridge: Cambridge University Press

Nisbett, R. E. and Schachter, S. (1966). Cognitive manipulation of pain, *Journal of Experimental Social Psychology*, **2**, 227–46

Novak, D. W. (1974). Children's reactions to emotional disturbance in imaginary peers, *Journal of Consulting and Clinical Psychology*, **42**, 462

Olson, D. R. (1985). Introduction, in D. R. Olson, N. Torrance, and A. Hildyard (eds.), *Literacy, Language, and Learning*, Cambridge and New York: Cambridge University Press

Osgood, C. E., Suci, G. J. and Tannenbaum, P. H. (1957). *The Measurement of Meaning*, Urbana and London: The University of Illinois Press

Osser, H. (1984). Language as the instrument of school socialisation: an examination of Bernstein's thesis. In B. Bain (ed.), *The Socio-genesis of Language and Human Conduct*, New York and London: Plenum Press

Papoušek, H. and Papoušek, M. (1974). Mirror-image and self-recognition in young human infants: I. A new method of experimental analysis, *Developmental Psychology*, **7**, 149–57

Paranjpe, A. C. (1987). Beyond cognition, action, pain and pleasure: an Eastern view of self and identity. In K. Yardley and T. Honess (eds.), *Self and Identity*, Chichester and New York: Wiley

Patterson, M. L. (1985). The evolution of a functional model of non-verbal exchange: a personal perspective. In R. L. Street Jr and J. N. Cappella (eds.), *Sequence and Pattern in Communicative Behaviour*, London: Edward Arnold

Peevers, B. H. (1984). The self as observer of the self: a developmental analysis of the subjective self. Read at the International Conference on Self and Identity, Cardiff, 9–13 July 1984

Peevers, B. H. and Secord, P. F. (1973). Developmental changes in attribution of descriptive concepts to persons, *Journal of Personality and Social Psychology*, **27**, 120–8

Phares, E. J. (1976). *Locus of Control in Personality*, Morristown: General Learning Press

Piaget, J. (1926). *The Language and Thought of the Child*, London: Routledge and Kegan Paul

Piaget, J. (1932/65). *The Moral Judgement of the Child*, New York: The Free Press

Piaget, J. (1965). Foreword to T. G. Décarie, *Intelligence and Affectivity in Early Childhood*, trs. by E. P. Brandt and L. W. Brandt, New York: International Universities Press

Piaget, J. (1967). *Six Psychological Studies*, New York: Random House

Piaget, J. and Inhelder, B. (1956). *The Child's Conception of Space*, London: Routledge and Kegan Paul

Pope, A. (1734). Moral essays: epistle to Cobham. In *The Poems of Alexander Pope* ed. by J. Butt (1965), London: Methuen

Premack, D. (1976). *Intelligence in Apes and Man*, Hillsdale, NJ: Lawrence Erlbaum Associates

Premack, D. and Woodruff, G. (1978). Does the chimpanzee have a theory of mind?, *The Behavioral and Brain Sciences*, **4**, 515–26

President's Commission on Civil Disorders (1968), *Report of the National Advisory Commission on Civil Disorders*, New York: Bantam Books and E. P. Dutton

Preyer, W. (1893). *Mind of the Child*, vol. 2, New York: Appleton

Prishvin, M. M. (1972). *Izbrannyje Proizvedenija*, I, Moscow: chudozestvennaja literatura

Reik, R. (1962). *Jewish Wit*, New York: Gamut Press

Retherford, K., Schwartz, B. and Chapman, R. (1981). Semantic roles and residual grammatical categories in mother and child speech: who tunes to whom?, *Journal of Child Language*, **8**, 583–608

Riesman, D. (1950). *The Lonely Crowd*, New Haven and London: Yale University Press

Rogers, C. (1951). *Client-centered Therapy: Its Current Practice, Implications and Theory*, Boston: Houghton Mifflin

Rogers, C. (1961). *On Becoming a Person*, Boston: Houghton Mifflin

Rommetveit, R. (1954). *Social Norms and Roles*, Oslo: Universitetsforlaget

Rommetveit, R. (1968). *Words, Meanings, and Messages*, New York and London: Academic Press; Oslo: Universitetsforlaget

Rommetveit, R. (1974). *On Message Structure*, New York and London: Wiley

Rosenfeld, H. M. (1981). Whither interactional synchrony?. In K. Bloom (ed.), *Prospective Issues in Infancy Research*, Hillsdale, NJ: Lawrence Erlbaum Associates

Rosenhan, D. (1973). On being sane in insane places, *Science*, **179**, 250–8

Ross, L. (1977). The intuitive psychologist and his shortcomings: distortions in the attribution process. In L. Berkowitz (ed.), *Advances in Experimental Social Psychology*, vol. 10, New York and London: Academic Press

Rothenberg, B. B. (1970). Children's social sensitivity and the relationship to interpersonal competence, intrapersonal comfort, and intellectual level, *Developmental Psychology*, **2**, 335–50

Rule, B. G., Bisanz, G. L. and Kohn, M. (1985). Anatomy of a persuasion schema: targets, goals, and strategies, *Journal of Personality and Social Psychology*, **48**, 1127–40

Rushton, J. P. and Sorrentino, R. M. (1981). *Altruism and Helping Behavior: Social, Personality, and Developmental Perspectives*, Hillsdale: Lawrence Erlbaum

Saarni, C. (1979). Children's understanding of display rules for expressive behavior, *Developmental Psychology*, **15**, 424–9

Saarni, C. (1982). Social and affective functions of non-verbal behavior: developmental concerns. In R. Feldman (ed.), *Development of Nonverbal Behavior in Children*, New York: Springer-Verlag, pp. 123–47

Saarni, C. (1984). An observational study of children's attempts to monitor their expressive behavior, *Child Development*, **56**, 1504–13

Sacks, H., Schegloff, E. and Jefferson, G. (1974). A simplest systematics for the organisation of turn-taking in conversation, *Language*, **50**, 696–735

Sagi, A. and Hoffman, M. L. (1976). Empathic distress in newborns. *Developmental Psychology*, **12**, 175–6

Santee, R. T. and Maslach, C. (1982). To agree or not to agree: personal dissent amid social pressure to conform, *Journal of Personality and Social Psychology*, **42**, 690–700

Sarbin, T. R. (1954). Role theory. In A. Lindzey and E. Aronson (eds.), *Handbook of Social Psychology*, vol. 2, Cambridge, Mass.: Addison-Wesley

Scaife, M. and Bruner, J. S. (1975). The capacity for joint visual attention in the infant, *Nature*, **253**, 265–6

Schachter, S. (1959). *The Psychology of Affiliation*, London: Tavistock

Schachter, S. (1964). The interaction of cognitive and physiological determinants of emotional state. In L. Berkowitz (ed.), *Advances in Experimental Social Psychology*, vol. 1, New York and London: Academic Press

Schachter, S. and Singer, J. E. (1962). Cognitive, social and physiological determinants of emotional state, *Psychological Review*, **69**, 379–99

Schaffer, H. R. (1977). *Mothering*, London: Open Books; New York: Harvard University Press

Schaffer, H. R. (1979). Acquiring the concept of the dialogue. In M. H. Bornstein and W. Kessen (eds.), *Psychological Development From Infancy*, Hillsdale, NJ: Lawrence Erlbaum Associates

Schaffer, H. R., Collis, G. M. and Parsons, G. (1977). Vocal interchange and visual regard in verbal and pre-verbal children. In H. R. Schaffer (ed.), *Studies in Mother-Infant Interaction*, London and New York: Academic Press

Scheflen, A. E. (1968). Human communication: behavioral programs and their integration in interaction, *Behavioral Science*, **13**, 44–55

Schegloff, E. A. and Sacks, H. (1973). Opening up closings, *Semiotica*, **8**, 289–327

Scherer, K. R. and Giles, H. (eds.) (1979), *Social Markers in Speech*, Cambridge: Cambridge University Press

Schjelderup-Ebbe, T. (1935). Social behavior in birds. In

Murchison's *Handbook of Social Psychology*, Worcester: Clark University Press

Schlenker, B. R. and Leary, M. R. (1982). Social anxiety and self-presentation: a conceptualization and model, *Psychological Bulletin*, **92**, 641–69

Schulman, A. H. and Kaplanowitz, C. (1977). Mirror-image response during the first two years of life, *Developmental Psychobiology*, **10**, 133–42

Schulz, M. R. (1975). The semantic derogation of woman. In B. Thorne and N. Henley (eds.), *Language and Sex: Difference and Dominance*, Rowley, Mass.: Newbury House

Searle, J. R. (1969). *Speech Acts*, London: Cambridge University Press

Sears, P. S. (1940). Levels of aspiration in academically successful and unsuccessful children, *Journal of Abnormal and Social Psychology*, **35**, 498–536

Sedlak, A. J. (1979), Developmental differences in understanding plans and evaluating actors, *Child Development*, **50**, 536–60

Selman, R. L. (1976). Social cognitive understanding: a guide to educational and clinical practice. In T. Lickona (ed.), *Moral Development and Behavior: Theory, Research and Social Issues*, New York: Holt, Rinehart and Winston

Selman, R. L. (1980). *The Growth of Interpersonal Understanding*, New York: Academic Press

Selman, R. L. and Jaquette, D. (1977). Stability and oscillation in interpersonal awareness: a clinical developmental approach. In C. B. Keasy (ed.), *Twenty-Fifth Nebraska Symposium on Motivation*, Lincoln: University of Nebraska Press

Shakespeare, R. (1975). *The Psychology of Handicap*, London: Methuen

Shantz, C. U. (1975). The development of social cognition. In E. M. Hetherington (ed.), *Review of Child Development Research*, vol. 5, Chicago: University of Chicago Press

Shantz, C. U. (1982). Children's understanding of social rules and the social context. In F. C. Serafica (ed.), *Social-cognitive Development in Context*, New York: Guilford Press; London: Methuen

Shatz, M. and Gelman, R. (1973). The development of communication skills: modifications in the speech of young children as a function of listener, *Monographs of the Society for Research in Child Development*, **38**, 1–37 (series no. 152)

Shaw, M. E., Briscoe, M. E. and Garcia-Estéve, J. (1968). A cross-cultural study of attribution of responsibility, *International Journal of Psychology*, **3**, 51–60

Shaw, M. E. and Iwawaki, S. (1972). Attribution of responsibility by Japanese and Americans as a function of age, *Journal of Cross-Cultural Psychology*, **3**, 71–81

Shaw, M. E. and Schneider, P. W. (1969). Negro-white differences in attribution of responsibility as a function of age, *Psychonomic Science*, **6**, 289–91

Shaw, M. E. and Sulzer, J. L. (1964). An empirical test of Heider's levels in attribution of responsibility, *Journal of Abnormal and Social Psychology*, **69**, 39–46

Shaw, S. (1979). Attribution of responsibility: effects of severity of outcome and similarity of subject to perpetrator or victim. Final year undergraduate project, University of Stirling

Sherif, M. (1936). *The Psychology of Social Norms*, New York: Harper

Siann, G. (1985). *Accounting for Aggression: Perspectives on Aggression and Violence*, Boston: Allen and Unwin

Simner, M. L. (1971). Newborn's response to the cry of another infant, *Developmental Psychology*, **5**, 136–50

Simons, H. W., Berkowitz, N. M. and Moyer, R. J. (1970). Similarity, credibility, and attitude change, *Psychological Bulletin*, **73**, 1–16

Snow, C. (1972). Mothers' speech to children learning language, *Child Development*, **43**, 549–65

Snow, C. (1977). The development of conversation between mothers and babies, *Journal of Child Language*, **4**, 1–22

Snyder, C. R. and Fromkin, H. L. (1980). *Uniqueness*, New York: Plenum

Sontag, S. (1979). *Illness as Metaphor*, London: Allen Lane (page references to Penguin edition, 1983)

Sroufe, A. L. (1979). Socioemotional development. In J. D. Osofsky (ed.), *Handbook of Infant Development*, New York: Wiley

Staub, E. (1978). *Positive Social Behavior and Morality*, vol. 1, New York and London: Academic Press

Stone, L. (1977). *The Family, Sex, and Marriage in England 1500–1800*, London: Weidenfeld and Nicolson

Stotland, E. (1969). Exploratory investigations of empathy. In L. Berkowitz (ed.), *Advances in Experimental Social Psychology*, New York: Academic Press

Stotland, E., Sherman, S. E. and Shaver, K. G. (1971). Empathy and birth order, *Nebraska Symposium on Motivation*, Lincoln: University of Nebraska Press

Street, R. L. and Cappella, J. N. (1985). *Sequence and Pattern in Communicative Behaviour*, London: Edward Arnold

Suarez, S. D. and Gallup, G. G. Jr (1981). Self-recognition in chimpanzees and orangutans, but not gorillas, *Journal of Human Evolution*, **10**, 175–88

Sullivan, H. S. (1953). *The Interpersonal Theory of Psychiatry*, New York: Norton

Swanson, G. E. (1961). Mead and Freud: their relevance for social psychology, *Sociometry*, **24**, 319–39

Taylor, M. and Flavell, J. H. (1984). Seeing and believing: children's understanding of the distinction between appearance and reality, *Child Development*, **55**, 1710–20

Taylor, S. E., Crocker, J., Fiske, S. T., Sprinzen, M. and Winkler, J. D. (1979). The generalisability of salience effects, *Journal of Personality and Social Psychology*, **37**, 357–68

Tedeschi, J. T. and Rosenfeld, P. (1981). Impression management theory and the forced compliance situation. In J. T. Tedeschi (ed.), *Impression Management Theory and Social Psychological Research*, New York: Academic Press

Tedeschi, J. T., Schlenker, B. R., and Lindskold, S. (1972). The exercise of power and influence: the source of influence processes. In J. T. Tedeschi (ed.), *Social Influence Processes*, Chicago: Aldine

Teleki, G. (1973). Group response to the accidental death of a chimpanzee in Gombe National Park, Tanzania, *Folia Primatologica*, **20**, 81–94

Tetlock, P. E. and Manstead, A. S. R. (1985). Impression management versus intrapsychic explanations in social psychology: a useful dichotomy? *Psychological Review*, **92**, 59–77

Thomas, W. I. and Znaniecki, F. (1918–20). *The Polish Peasant in Europe and America*, 5 volumes, Boston: Badger

Thorne, B. and Henley, N. (1975). Difference and dominance: an overview of language, gender, and society. In B. Thorne and N. Henley (eds.), *Language and Sex: Difference and Dominance*, Rowley, Mass.: Newbury House

Thornton, T. J. (1964). Terror as a weapon of political agitation. In H. Eckstein (ed.), *Internal War*, New York: The Free Press; London: Collier-Macmillan

Toch, H. (1969). *Violent Men*, Chicago: Aldine

Toulmin, S. E. (1977). Self-knowledge and knowledge of the 'self'. In T. Mischel (ed.), *The Self: Psychological and Philosophical Issues*, Oxford: Blackwell

Tracy, K. (1985). Conversational coherence: a cognitively grounded rules approach. In R. L. Street and J. N. Cappella (eds.), *Sequence and Pattern in Communicative Behaviour*, London: Edward Arnold

Trivers, R. (1985). *Social Evolution*, Menlo Park: Benjamin/Cummings

Turiel, E. (1978). The development of concepts of social structure: social convention. In J. Glick and A. Clarke-Stewart (eds.), *The Development of Social Understanding*, New York: Gardner Press

Turiel, E. (1983). *The Development of Social Knowledge*, Cambridge and London: Cambridge University Press

Turner, R. H. (1971). The self-conception in social interaction. In C. Gordon and K. J. Gergen (eds.), *The Self in Social Interaction*, vol. 1, New York and London: Wiley

Turner, V. (1967). *The Forest of Symbols: Aspects of Ndembu Ritual*, Ithaca: Cornell University Press

Tyler, L. E. (1965). *The Psychology of Human Differences*, New York: Appleton-Century-Crofts

Umiker-Sebeok, D. J. (1980). Silence is golden? The changing role of non-talk in preschool conversations. In M. R. Key (ed.), *The Relationship of Verbal and Nonverbal Communication*, The Hague, Paris and New York: Mouton

Valins, S. and Nisbett, R. E. (1972). Attribution processes in the development and treatment of emotional disorders. In E. E. Jones, D. E. Kanouse, H. H. Kelley, R. E. Nisbett, S. Valins and B. Weiner (eds.), *Attribution: Perceiving the Causes of Behavior*, Morristown, NJ: General Learning Press

Vleeming, R. G. (1979). Machiavellianism: a preliminary review, *Psychological Reports*, **44**, 295–310

Vygotsky, L. S. (1962). *Thought and Language*, New York: Wiley

Vygotsky, L. S. (1978). *Mind in Society: The Development of Higher Psychological Processes*. Ed. M. Cole, V. John-Steiner, S. Scribner, and E. Souberman, Cambridge, Mass., and London: Harvard University Press

Wagatsuma, H. and DeVos, G. (1978). A Koan of sincerity: Osama Dazai, *Hartford Studies in Literature*, **10**, 156–81

Wallace, W. (1894). Psycho-genesis. In *Hegel's Philosophy of Mind*, trs. W. Wallace, Oxford: Clarendon Press

Walton, M. D. (1985). Negotiations of responsibility: judgments of blameworthiness in a natural setting, *Developmental Psychology*, **21**, 725–36

Wardle, M. G. and Gloss, D. S. (1982). Effects of lying and conformity on decision-making behavior, *Psychological Reports*, **51**, 871–7

Watzlawick, P., Bearin, J. H. and Jackson, D. D. (1967). *Pragmatics of Human Communication*, New York: Norton

Wei-ming, T. (1985). Selfhood and otherness in Confucian thought. In A. J. Marsella, G. DeVos, and F. L. K. Hsu (eds.), *Culture and Self*, New York and London: Tavistock

Weiner, B. (1985). An attributional theory of achievement motivation and emotion, *Psychological Review*, **92**, 548–73

Weinstein, E. A. (1969). The development of interpersonal competence. In D. A. Goslin (ed.), *Handbook of Socialisation Theory and Research*, Chicago: Rand McNally

Weiss, W. (1953). A sleeper effect in opinion change, *Journal of Abnormal and Social Psychology*, **48**, 173–80

Wells, P. H. and Wenner, A. M. (1975). Do honey bees have a language?, *Nature*, **241**, 171–5

Werner, H. and Kaplan, B. (1963). *Symbol Formation*, New York: Wiley

White, R. G. (1886). *Words and Their Uses*, Boston: Houghton Mifflin

White, R. K. and Lippitt, H. R. (1960). *Autocracy and Democracy*, Westport: Greenwood

Wicklund, R. A. (1982). How society uses self-awareness. In J. M. Suls (ed.), *Psychological Perspectives on the Self*, vol. 1, Hillsdale: Lawrence Erlbaum

Wiemann, J. M. (1985). Interpersonal control and regulation in conversation. In R. L. Street Jr and J. N. Capella (eds.), *Sequence and Patterns in Communicative Behaviour*, London: Edward Arnold

Wilson, C. P. (1979). *Jokes: Form, Content, Use and Function*, London and New York: Academic Press

Wilson, E. O. (1971). *The Insect Societies*, Cambridge, Mass.: Harvard University Press

Wilson, T. P., Wiemann, J. M. and Zimmerman, D. H. (1984). Models of turn takings in conversational interaction, *Journal of Language and Social Psychology*, **3**, 159–83

Winchester, I. (1985). Atlantans, Centaurians, and the litron bomb: some personal and social implications of literacy. In D. R. Olson, N. Torrance, and A. Hildyard (eds.), *Literacy,*

Language, and Learning, Cambridge and New York: Cambridge University Press

Woodruff, G. and Premack, D. (1979). Intentional communication in the chimpanzee: the development of deception, *Cognition*, **7**, 333–62

Wundt, W. (1916). *Elements of Folk Psychology*, trans. E. L. Schaub, London: George Allen and Unwin; and New York: The Macmillan Company

Wylie, R. C. (1979). *The Self-Concept: Theory and Research on Selected Topics* (rev edn), vol. 2, Lincoln: University of Nebraska Press

Zajonc, R. B., Wilson, W. R. and Rajecki, D. W. (1975). Affiliation and social discrimination produced by brief exposure in day-old domestic chicks, *Animal Behavior*, **23**, 131–8

Zeigernik, B. (1927). Das Berhalten erledigter und unerledigter Handlungen (on the retention of completed and uncompleted activities), *Psychologische Forschungen*, **9**, 1–85

Zimbardo, P. G. (1977). *Shyness: What It Is And What To Do About It*, New York: Jove

Zipf, G. K. (1935). *The Psycho-biology of Language*, Boston: Houghton Mifflin

Zuckerman, M., DeFrank, R., Hall, J. and Rosenthal, R. (1976). Encoding and decoding of spontaneous and posed facial expressions, *Journal of Personality and Social Psychology*, **34**, 966–77

Name index

Allport, G. W.   185, 232
Amsterdam, B.   114, 232
Anderson, A.   89–91, 240
Anderson, C.   96, 232
Anderson, J. R.   113–14, 119, 232
Argyle, M.   162, 232
Aristotle   228
Arlitt, A. H.   45, 232
Armsby, R. E.   83, 232
Aronson, E.   132, 232
Asch, S. E.   186–7, 207, 220–1, 232
Aydin, O.   79, 232

Back, K.   241
Bahnson, C. and M.   212
Banks, J. H., Jr.   252
Basen, J. A.   21, 249
Bateson, M. C.   143, 232
Baumeister, R. F.   183, 233
Bearin, J. H.   261
Beattie, G.   158, 233
Beloff, H.   117–18, 233
Bem, D. J.   108–9, 233
Benedict, H.   233
Beninger, R. J.   22, 233
Berger, C. R.   173, 233
Berger, S. M.   56, 233
Berko-Gleason, J.   156–7, 233
Berkowitz, N. M.   258
Bernstein, B.   165–7, 233
Bernstein, R. M.   127, 233
Berthenthal, B. I.   114, 233
Bharati, A.   39–40, 233
Birdwhistell, R. L.   139, 146–7, 159–60, 234
Bisanz, G. L.   255
Blumer, H.   85, 234
Bodine, A.   217, 234
Bohan, J. B.   127, 243

Bohannon, J.   156, 234
Bohannon III, J. N.   155, 234
Boorman, S. A.   16, 234
Borke, H.   48–9, 51, 55, 234
Botkin, P. T.   229, 241
Boyle, J.   196, 234
Bradac, J. J.   173, 233
Braunwald, S. R.   163–4, 234
Brazelton, T. B.   143–4, 234
Breakwell, G. M.   113, 234
Bridges, K. M. B.   46–7, 234
Briscoe, M. E.   82, 258
Bromley, D. B.   78–9, 127, 249
Broner, S. L.   236
Bronson, G. W.   234
Brooks, J.   115, 234, 249
Brooks-Gunn, J.   108, 113–16, 235, 249
Brosin, H. W.   139, 237
Broughton, J.   127, 131, 235
Brown, J. A. C.   198, 235
Bruner, J. S.   143, 163–4, 235, 256
Bryant, B. K.   56, 64, 235
Buchanan, J. P.   83, 235
Buck, R. W.   56, 235
Bühler, C.   45, 235
Burgoon, M.   198, 200, 252
Buss, A. H.   189–91, 235
Byers, P.   141–2, 235
Byrne, D.   187, 235
Byrne, J. M.   141, 251

Campbell, D. T.   16, 235
Cappella, J. N.   153, 158, 235, 259
Cazden, C. B.   99, 236
Chagnon, N. A.   142, 236
Chambers, R.   225
Chandler, M. J.   55, 236
Chapman, R.   156, 255
Chomsky, N.   141, 236

Name index

Chonko, L. B. 203, 246
Christie, R. 201–3, 236
Chu, G. C. 40–1, 236
Chukovsky, K. 99, 236
Church, R. M. 22, 236
Cialdini, R. B. 187–8, 236
Clark, R. D., III 250
Coberly, L. 142, 236
Collis, G. M. 142–3, 236, 256
Condon, W. S. 139–41, 236–7
Confucius 40–1
Cook, T. D. 199, 237
Cook-Gumperz, J. 158–9, 243
Coser, R. L. 185, 237
Cottrell, L. S. 44, 237
Craig, R. T. 158, 237
Crocker, J. 259
Crook, J. H. 16, 20, 237
Cross, T. G. 155–6, 237

Damon, W. 108, 110, 113, 128, 130, 220, 237
Darley, J. M. and S. A. 187, 238
Darwin, C. 16, 19–20, 113–14, 188–9, 213, 224–7, 229–30, 238
Davis, K. E. 77, 247
Dean, J. 162, 232
Dembo, T. 96, 238, 249
De Paulo, B. M. 182, 238
Deutsch, F. 51, 55–6, 187, 238
DeVos, G. 40–1, 238, 260
Dittmar, N. 158, 238
Dong, Q. 241
Doob, A. N. 187, 241
Dowd, J. M. 141, 238
Duncan, S. 153, 158, 238
Duncan, S. Jr 153, 238, 239
Durkheim, E. 206–7, 239
Duval, S. 107–8, 239
Dymond, R. 55–6, 239

Eisenstein, E. L. 33–4, 239
Ekman, P. 60, 180, 239
Elliot, A. J. 154–5, 166–7, 239
Ellison, R. 69
Epstein, N. 56, 251
Erickson, F. 144–5, 171, 239
Erikson, E. H. 188, 239
Ervin-Tripp, S. 151–2, 239
Escalona, S. K. 45–6, 55, 239

Evans, R. M. 26, 239

Falbo, T. 200, 239
Fales, E. 96, 239
Fanshel, D. 168–9, 248
Farnill, D. 83, 240
Farr, R. M. 19, 31, 89–91, 145, 206–7, 223, 240
Faucheux, C. 220–1, 240
Feldstein, S. 153, 246
Ferguson, C. A. 155, 240
Fernald, A. 155, 240
Feshbach, N. D. 49–57, 62, 64–6, 199, 240–1
Feshbach, S. 246
Festinger, L. 110–11, 207, 241, 249
Fielding, G. 156, 241
Fillmore, C. J. 93, 241
Fincham, F. 83–4, 241
Fischer, K. W. 114, 233
Fishman, J. A. 160–1, 241
Fiske, D. W. 153, 239
Fiske, S. T. 259
Flavell, E. R. 179, 241
Flavell, J. H. 49, 179, 241, 258
Fogel, A. 142, 241
Forbes, C. 250
Ford, L. H., Jr 247
Fraser, C. 156, 241
Freedle, R. 143, 249
Freedman, J. L. 187, 241
Freud, A. 63, 241
Freud, S. 55, 59, 104–6, 185–6, 194, 213, 242
Frisch, von K. 25, 242
From, F. 71–2, 242
Fromkin, H. L. 188, 258
Fry, C. L. 241
Furrow, D. 155, 287

Galileo 228
Gallup, G. G. Jr. 21, 114, 119, 242, 259
Garcia-Estéve, J. 82, 258
Gardner, B. T. and R. A. 22, 242
Garnica, O. K. 155, 242
Garvey, C. 99, 150, 159, 242
Geis, F. L. 201–3, 236, 242
Gelman, R. 157, 257
Gerard, H. G. 187, 238

Gergen, K. J.   108, 242–3
Gewirth, A.   220, 243
Giles, H.   156, 256
Gleitman, H. and L. R.   253
Gloss, D. S.   203, 261
Glucksberg, S.   48, 248
Goethe   39
Goffman, E.   69, 112, 183, 190–1, 215, 243
Gombrich, E. H.   229–30, 243
Goodall, J.   24, 243
Gould, R.   111, 243
Green, F. L.   241
Greenspan, S.   55, 236
Griffin, D. R.   16, 21–2, 24–5, 27–8, 243
Gruber, H. E.   213, 224–8, 230, 243
Guardo, C. J.   127, 243
Gumperz, J. J.   158–9, 243
Guralnick, M. J.   158, 243
Guz, G. R.   244

Hall, E. T.   146–7, 160–2, 244
Hall, J.   262
Hamilton, M. L.   56, 244
Hamlyn, D.   108, 129, 244
Hanson, N. R.   225, 244
Harkness, S.   155, 244
Harré, R.   108, 244
Harris, P. L.   181–2, 244
Hart, D.   108, 110, 113, 128, 130, 237
Harter, S.   130, 244
Harth, E.   19, 244
Harvey, J. H.   90, 244
Haskell, F.   229, 244
Hawkins, P.   166
Hegel, G. W. F.   38–9, 206, 214, 244
Heider, F.   68–9, 72–7, 80–4, 89, 92, 178, 245
Henley, N.   216, 259
Herder, J. G.   31, 44, 206, 245
Hermanowicz, V.   203, 245
Hetzer, H.   45, 235
Hirsh-Pasek, K.   155, 234
Hoffman, M. L.   9–10, 45–8, 51, 58, 63, 65–6, 245, 256
Hollon, C. J.   203, 245
Hovland, C. I.   198–9, 245, 247

Humboldt, W. von   31, 206, 245
Humphrey, G.   45, 245
Humphrey, N.   10, 16–17, 209–11, 246
Hunt, S. D.   203, 246

Ianotti, R. J.   54, 246
Ichheiser, G.   63, 88, 135, 183, 246
Inhelder, B.   49, 56, 246
Insko, C. A.   199, 237
Irvine, A.   238
Isaacs, S.   145, 246
Iwawaki, S.   82, 258

Jackson, D. D.   261
Jaffe, J.   153, 246
Jahoda, M.   105, 246
Jakobson, R.   141, 246
James, W.   39, 68, 95, 107, 128–9, 246
Janis, I. L.   199, 249
Jaquette, D.   118–19, 126, 257
Jarvis, P. E.   241
Jaspars, J.   83–4, 241
Jaynes, J.   29–32, 246
Jefferson, G.   158, 256
Jellison, J. M.   199, 252
Jocić, M.   155, 246
Johnson, D. B.   114, 246
Johnson, J. E.   252
Johnson, P.   200, 246
Jones, E. E.   77, 87–9, 92, 183–5, 247
Jordan, A.   238
Jucknat, M.   96, 247

Kafka   211
Kant   39
Kaplan, B.   164, 261
Kaplanowitz, C.   114, 257
Karniol, R.   81, 83, 247
Kaye, K.   142, 247
Kekulé, A.   227
Keller, A.   127, 247
Kelley, H. H.   77, 89, 245, 247
Kelman, H. C.   199, 247
Kempton, W.   140–1, 247
Kendall, S. B.   233
Kendon, A.   139, 248
Key, M. R.   144, 248
King, M.   83, 248

Name index

Klein, R.   65, 248
Kline, P.   105, 248
Koch, R.   212
Koestler, A.   227, 248
Kohlberg, L.   119, 248
Köhler, W.   24, 44, 248
Kohn, M.   255
Kon, I. S.   231, 248
Koslowski, B.   144, 234
Krauss, R.   48, 248
Krebs, D.   56, 65, 248
Kreckel, M.   171–2, 248
Kropotkin   196–7
Kuhn, M. H.   110, 248
Kuhn, T. S.   228–30, 248
Kuwahara, H.   252

Labov, W.   166–9, 248
Lage, E.   221, 253
Laing, R. D.   70–1, 248
Lakoff, R.   216, 249
Laser, P. S.   238
Leary, M. R.   189–90, 249, 257
Ledbetter, D. H.   21, 249
Leonard-Dolan, C.   144, 249
Levitt, P. R.   16, 234
Lewin, K.   96–7, 106, 110–11, 118, 192, 249
Lewis, M.   108, 113–16, 143, 234–5, 249
Lewis, S. K.   236
Light, P.   49, 249
Lindauer, M.   27, 249
Lindskold, S.   259
Lipian, M. S.   244
Lippitt, H. R.   118, 261
Lipps, T.   44, 249
Livesley, W. J.   78–9, 127, 249
Lockyer, R.   250
Lumsdaine, A. A.   199, 249
Luria, A. R.   35–6, 249
Lyell, C.   225–6
Lyons, J. O.   32, 250

Maass, A.   250
McCaul, W. F.   235
Macdonald, K.   251
McDowell, J. J.   140, 250
McGuire, W. J.   199, 250
Machiavelli, N.   201–3, 250
MacLean, P. D.   17–19, 250

McPartland, S.   110, 248
Madle, R. A.   51, 56, 238
Maher, B.   91–2, 250
Main, M.   144, 234
Mandell, W.   199, 245
Man-Shu, Z.   244
Manstead, A. S. R.   183, 259
Marcus, R. F.   64, 250
Markova, I.   31, 91, 93, 98, 106, 154, 250–1
Marquis, A.   156, 234
Marriott, M.   40, 251
Martin, J. G.   140, 251
Maslach, C.   187–8, 251, 256
Maslow, A. H.   188, 251
Mason, W. A.   20, 251
Meacham, J. A.   247
Mead, G. H.   28, 31, 38–9, 56, 62, 95–6, 99–108, 128–9, 135–8, 145, 163, 188–9, 207, 219, 251
Meerum Terwogt, M.   244
Mehrabian, A.   56, 251
Meltzer, B. N.   85, 251
Mendel, G.   229
Menninger, K.   211
Menzel, E. W. Jr   24, 251
Michela, J. L.   77, 89, 247
Milgram, S.   117–18, 251
Miller, C. L.   141, 251
Miller, D. L.   105, 252
Miller, G. R.   173, 198, 200, 252
Miller, R. E.   23, 235, 252
Mills, J.   199, 252
Mood, D. W.   55, 252
Moon, T. H.   203, 242
Morishima, M.   41–2, 252
Morris, C.   32, 252
Moscovici, S.   69, 169–71, 207–14, 216–17, 220–3, 240, 252–3
Moyer, R. J.   258
Mugny, G.   221–2, 253

Naffrechoux, M.   221, 253
Neisser, U.   59, 253
Nelson, K.   156, 163–4, 242, 253
Nemeth, C. J.   222, 253
Newcomb, T. M.   207, 253
Newport, E. L.   155, 253
Nisbett, R. E.   77, 87–9, 92, 112, 253, 260
Novak, D. W.   56, 253

Ogawa, N. 252
Ogston, W. D. 139–40, 237
Olsen 22
Olson, D. R. 35, 253
Olthof, T. 182, 244
Osgood, C. E. 193–4, 253
Osser, H. 166–7, 253

Papousek, H. and M. 114, 116, 253
Paranjpe, A. C. 40, 254
Parsons, G. 256
Patterson, M. L. 162–3, 254
Paul-Brown, D. 158, 243
Peevers, B. H. 79, 127, 130–1, 254
Peplau, L. A. 200, 239
Phares, E. J. 132, 254
Piaget, J. 29, 48–9, 56, 80–1, 83–5, 94, 118–20, 207, 219, 224, 246, 254
Pittman, T. S. 183–5, 247
Plon, M. 169–71, 253
Poincaré, H. 227
Pope, A. 183, 254
Premack, D. 21, 23, 25–6, 254, 262
Preyer, W. 113–14, 254
Priestley, J. 225
Prishvin, M. M. 231, 254

Qi, S. 241

Rajecki, D. W. 262
Reik, R. 186, 254
Retherford, K. 156, 255
Riesman, D. 33, 38, 255
Roe, K. 49–55, 62, 64–6, 241
Rogers, C. 59–60, 109, 255
Roke, E. J. 250
Rommetveit, R. 92–3, 135, 164, 167–8, 170–1, 173, 207, 218, 255
Rosenfeld, H. M. 140–1, 255
Rosenfeld, P. 200, 259
Rosenhan, D. 215, 255
Rosenthal, R. 262
Ross, L. 90, 255
Rothenberg, B. B. 55, 255
Rule, B. G. 200, 255
Rushton, J. P. 16, 255

Saarni, C. 180–1, 255

Sacks, H. 147–8, 153–4, 158, 256
Sagi, A. 45, 246
Sander, L. W. 139–40, 237
Santee, R. T. 187, 251, 256
Sarbin, T. R. 55, 256
Savin, V. J. 235
Scaife, M. 143, 256
Schachter, S. 111–12, 241, 253, 256
Schaffer, H. R. 142–3, 236, 256
Scheflen, A. E. 139, 256
Schegloff, E. 158, 256
Scherer, K. R. 156, 256
Schjelderup-Ebbe, T. 26, 256
Schlenker, B. R. 189–90, 249, 257, 259
Schneider, P. W. 82, 258
Schulman, A. H. 114, 257
Schulz, M. R. 216, 257
Schwartz, B. 156, 255
Searle, J. R. 158, 257
Sears, P. S. 111, 249, 257
Second, P. F. 79, 127, 254
Sedlak, A. J. 84, 257
Selman, R. L. 118–27, 131, 180, 220, 257
Shakespeare, R. 64, 257
Shantz, C. U. 51, 80, 83, 220, 252, 257
Shatz, M. 157, 257
Shaver, K. G. 259
Shaw, M. E. 82–4
Shaw, S. 65, 258
Sherif, M. 207, 258
Sherman, S. E. 259
Shultz, J. 144–5, 171, 239
Siann, G. 196, 258
Simmel, M. 72–4, 92, 245
Simner, M. L. 45, 258
Simons, H. W. 187, 258
Simonton, O. C. 212
Singer, J. E. 112, 256
Snow, C. 148–51, 156, 258
Snyder, C. R. 188, 258
Sontag, S. 211–13, 258
Sorrentino, R. M. 16, 255
Sprinzen, M. 259
Sroufe, A. L. 46–7, 258
Stapp, J. 251
Staub, E. 57, 258
Steinberg, M. 173, 252

Name index

Stendahl 211
Stone, L. 32–3, 36–8, 258
Stotland, E. 55–6, 259
Street, R. L. 158, 259
Suarez, S. D. 21, 259
Suci, G. J. 193–4, 253
Sullivan, H. S. 55, 259
Sulzer, J. L. 82–4, 258
Swanson, G. E. 105, 259

Tannenbaum, P. H. 193–4, 253
Taylor, M. 179, 259
Taylor, S. E. 188, 259
Tedeschi, J. T. 200, 259
Teleki, G. 23, 259
Telleen, S. 250
Tetlock, P. E. 183, 259
Thomas, C. B. 212
Thomas, W. I. 33, 259
Thompson, S. K. 83, 235
Thorne, B. 216, 259
Thornton, T. J. 197, 259
Toch, H. 194–6, 259
Tolstoy 173
Toulmin, S. E. 108, 260
Tracy, K. 158, 237, 260
Trivers, R. 16, 260
Tronick, E. Z. 141, 238
Turiel, E. 207, 220, 260
Turner, R. H. 112, 260
Turner, V. 11, 260
Tyler, L. E. 188, 260

Umiker-Sebeok, D. J. 152, 260

Valins, S. 112, 260
Vanderwolf, C. H. 233
Vleeming, R. G. 203, 260
Vygotsky, L. S. 163–4, 173, 260

Wagatsuma, H. 41, 260

Wallace, W. 214, 230, 260
Walton, M. D. 84–7, 91–2, 261
Wardle, M. G. 203, 261
Warren-Leubecker, A. 156, 234
Watzlawick, P. 69–70, 261
Weary, G. 90, 244
Wei-ming, T. 40, 261
Weiner, B. 132, 261
Weinstein, E. A. 200, 261
Weintraub, S. 156, 233
Weiss, W. 199, 245, 261
Wells, A. 142, 247
Wells, P. H. 25, 261
Wenner, A. M. 25, 261
Werner, H. 164, 261
White, R. G. 217, 261
White, R. K. 118, 261
Wicklund, R. A. 107–8, 128, 239, 261
Wiemann, J. M. 152, 261
Wilson, C. P. 185–6, 194, 261
Wilson, E. O. 27, 261
Wilson, T. P. 152–4, 261
Wilson, W. R. 262
Winchester, I. 34, 261
Winkler, J. D. 259
Woodruff, G. 23, 25–6, 262
Wortman, C. 182, 247
Wright, J. W. 241
Wundt, W. 135, 145, 206, 262
Wylie, R. C. 110, 129–30, 132, 262

Zajonc, R. B. 26, 262
Zeigernik, B. 97, 262
Zhang, X.-D. 241
Zimbardo, P. G. 191, 262
Zimmerman, D. H. 262
Zipf, G. K. 173, 262
Znaniecki, F. 33, 259
Zou, H. 241
Zuckerman, M. 56, 262

Subject index

acts: communicative   134–5;
   social   134–5; violent   194–7
action: effective environmental
   force   76; effective personal
   force   76; evaluation of   92–3;
   Heider's analysis   74–7;
   perception of environmental
   factors in   80ff.; perception of
   personal factors in   80ff.
agency   38–9, 67, 70–1, 90ff.,
   95–6, 176, 196–7;
   acknowledgement of   195–7;
   awareness of   71, 90–1, 96;
   perception of   67–8, 71–4
aggression and violence   192–7;
   physical aggression   194–7;
   verbal aggression   193–4
anchoring   210–13
animal awareness   14ff.; ability to
   infer intentions of others   23–6;
   awareness of mental states of
   others   23–4; awareness of
   objects   21; awareness of
   others   22–4, 27; awareness of
   self   20–2; intentionality in   21,
   24–6; mirror self-recognition
   21; recognition of individuality
   26–8; sign language
   21–2
appearance and reality   11, 100,
   178–82
as if behaviour   55–6
aspiration, levels of   96, 106,
   110–11
attributional processes   80–3;
   attributional research   81–7

bicameral mind   29–30
biological evaluation   10, 16–17
blushing   19–20, 188–9

body language see kinesics

cognition and affect   44–5, 54–6,
   56–8; independence of   57–61;
   inseparability of   56–8
collective other   205ff.; explicit
   pressure of   186ff., 207, 218ff.;
   implicit pressure of   206ff.; role
   in social change   227ff.
collective representations   206–7
communication   134–5; as a mutual
   adjustment   135–8; as a social
   act   135–6; as a three-step
   process   137–8; break-down
   of   147–8; interpersonal   135,
   147, 175; mother and infant
   148; non-verbal   134–5, 145–7;
   persuasive   186, 198ff.;
   reflexive   137–8; verbal   134–5
communicative competence   50,
   53; communicative
   intentions   155–6, 163
compliance, public   186–7,
   218–19, 223
confirmation of self by others
   68–71; search for   68
conformity   177–8, 184, 187–8,
   220–3
conscience   41, 104–5, 177
consciousness   29–30, 123, 142;
   collective   206–7;
   individual   206
contextualization: conventions
   in   158–9; cues   159;
   decontextualization   164, 167
contextualized language   164–7,
   170–1, 172–3; decontextualized
   language   164–7, 170–1, 172–3
conventions   86, 99, 132, 134,
   158ff., 174, 181–2, 205, 207–8,

210ff., 219; breaches of 220;
child's awareness of 86, 180–1;
knowledge of 100–1
conversation 144–5, 147–8, 151,
202–3; conversation of
gestures 136, 145; conversation
as process 154; mother–
infant 148–51; structure
of 152–4
creative actions 98; creative
activity 224; creative
individuals 224ff., 227–8, 231;
creative play with language
98–9
creative process, stages in 226–7
creativity 98–9; influence of social
and personal factors on 224ff.
cultures 147, 160; ancient 29–32;
different rules in proxemics 160;
non-western 39–42; relativity of
values and norms 38; western
29–32, 59, 188

decontextualization 164, 166–8
decontextualized language 164–6,
170–1, 173
development: historical and
cultural 29–32; of attribution of
responsibility 80ff.; of
awareness of action 77ff.; of
empathy 45ff., 57–8; of self-
awareness 30–1, 113ff.; of self-
and other-awareness 14–16,
32–6, 127–33; social 10, 16, 27,
30–8, 138, 205–7; socio-cultural 35
developmental psychology:
developmental and clinical
psychology 119;
developmental levels in self- and
other-awareness 119ff.;
developmental stages in self- and
other-awareness 118ff.;
integration with social
psychology 11–13, 118ff.
dialogue: as a developmental
process 147; preverbal 143,
145; regulation through turn-
taking 145ff.; therapeutic 58
disconfirmation or non-recognition
of self by others 68–71, 189
display rules 60, 64, 180–2

dispositional properties 74–5,
78–80, 87–8, 92, 94

ecological validity 53–4, 84
egocentrism 29, 48–9, 56, 120, 165
elaborated speech codes 165–7
embarrassment 190–1
emotion 17ff.; biological basis
of 17–19; blushing 19–20,
188–9; concealment or masking
of 60, 121–2, 180–3;
conceptualization of 59, 61;
control of 58, 60, 181–2;
embarrassment 68–9, 190–1;
guilt 191; shame 19, 191;
shown (displayed) 180–2;
shyness 19, 189; suppression
of 58, 60
empathy 17, 44ff., 56;
conceptualization 57–8;
development of 45ff, 57–8; in
children 64–5; in early
childhood 45–54, 57–8;
modifiers of 64–6; prerequisites
for 57; stages of 46–8
expression 134, 183

generalized other 101–5, 113, 124,
138, 177, 207
gestures 135–6; conversation
of 136, 145; for the other 163;
for the self 163; non-significant
136–7; non-verbal 163; pointing
163; significant 136–7
guilt 104–5, 191

human awareness 26, 28–9, 32ff.,
134; as a developmental and
cultural phenomenon 14, 29ff.;
as a developmental and social
process 11–12, 32–8; definition
10; its socio-biological nature
16–20

I see self
identification 55, 59–60, 62–3, 102
identity: personal 112–13;
social 112–13
impression 135, 183
individual, role in social
change 227ff.

individuation 186–8
influence: of majorities 220ff.; of minorities 220ff.
ingratiation 184, 186
intentions 67, 76, 92–4, 97, 136; awareness of 71, 80ff.; in animals 24–6; perception of 67, 80ff., 93
interaction 68ff., 116, 123, 135ff., 142ff., 170–1; individual and societal 205, 228ff.; interpersonal 69–71, 116, 134, 139, 141ff., 147, 159, 175, 184ff., 189–90, 192; macro-synchrony in 142–5; micro-synchrony in 139–42; non-verbal regulation, theories of 162–3; regulation of 151ff.; symmetry and asymmetry in 144–5; timing in the process 171
interactional synchrony 138–42

kinesics 159–60
knowledge: common 172; private 172–3; shared 171–3

labelling, effect of 215
language 99, 134, 139–42, 155–6, 158, 164–7, 170, 208, 214–18; context-dependent 163–4; contextualized 164–7, 170–3; conventional aspects 156, 158–9; decontextualized 164–7, 170–2; sexist 216–17
language and awareness of action 92–3
literacy 33ff.

Machiavellianism 188, 201–3
majorities 206–8, 220–3
Me see self
metaphorical switch 161
minorities 220–3
moral code 119
moral judgement 48, 80ff.; criticisms of research into 83–4, 86–7
moral principles 208, 219–20; breaches of 220
moral sense 16, 80, 92;

conscience 105; development of 219; guilt 105, 191
morality 118–19, 207–8, 218ff.; conventional 202
Mote-beam mechanism 63
motherese 154ff.

objectification 213–14
other-awareness 22–9, 40–3, 44ff., 47–8, 64, 70, 75, 115–17, 128
other, the 47, 62–3, 176–8, 205–6; collective 206ff., 218–19, 223ff.; generalized 101–5, 113, 124, 177, 207

perceiver and perceived 67–9, 87, 178; as relational terms 89–90; divergent perspectives of 87–92; interdependence of 89–91
perceiver ignored 68–9
perception: interpersonal 68ff.; manipulated 178; of intentions 80ff.; of physical objects and agents 67–8; person 78–80; social 71
person and environment 74–7; child's awareness of 80–3
perspective taking 120ff.
privacy 36–7; breaches of 191; invasion of 68
projection 47, 62–3, 105–6
proxemics 160
psychological environment 96–7, 192, 214

reality and appearance 11, 97, 100, 178–80
recognition of other-images 115–16
recognition of self-images 113–17; by animals 21
recognition, social 68–9, 176; non-recognition 69–71, 196; search for 68, 176ff., 194–7, 205, 222–3; strategies for 177ff., 187–8, 191ff., 204
reflexion 19, 35, 59, 103, 106–8, 122, 124, 126ff., 134, 137–8, 176, 188, 197
rejection of self by others 69–71, 189

representations: collective 206–7; social 208ff., 212–14, 216–18, 224

research, criticisms of: child empathy 51ff.; children's cognition of intentions 83–4; experimental stories 83–4; levels of responsibility 84; moral judgement 83–4

responsibility 76–7; levels of 76–7, 81–2; objective and subjective 78, 84–5; perception of in a natural setting 84–7; research, criticisms of 83–4

restricted speech codes 165–7

rhythm in speech and communication 141–2, 144–5, 159–60

role-play 100ff., 179ff.

role-taking 44, 57, 62, 65, 100, 157, 179, 190

romanticism 38–9, 88, 212

rules: as a force 101, 219; constitutive 158, 160; display 60, 64, 180–2; in games 101, 219; in play 100–1, 219; knowledge of 100–1; moral 207–8, 219–20; regulative 158; social 101–2, 218–20

science, paradigms of 230–1

self: acknowledgement by others as a human being 68–70; affective aspects 109–12, 129–30; and collective other 205ff.; 220ff.; and environment 95–7; as agent or subject (the I) 39, 90, 95ff., 128–33, 138, 191–2; as object (the Me) 39, 90, 95, 99ff., 103, 117, 128–33, 138; cognitive aspects 108–9; confirmation of 68–70; differentiation from other 47; ego, id, superego 104–6; evaluative aspects 109–12, 129–30; I and Me as relational concepts 102–3; I-strategies for recognition 191ff.; Me-strategies for recognition 178ff.

self- and other-awareness 10ff., 14ff., 20ff., 32–3, 57–8, 173–6,

178, 185; capacity for 10–11, 203; cultural aspects 15–16, 38–9, 42–3, 185; development of 14–15, 31ff.; developmental aspects 14–15; developmental levels 11ff., 119ff., 125–6; developmental stages 118ff.

self-awareness 12, 30–1, 34–5, 37–43, 64, 70, 90–1, 95ff., 120ff., 125ff., 131–3, 185–6; growth of 113ff.; related notions 106ff.

self-consciousness 38, 128–9, 188–9

self-control 41, 105, 123, 133

self-criticism, in jokes 185–6

self-deception 121–2, 124–5

self-evaluation 99–100, 109–12, 129–30, 176

self-identity 112ff.; personal 112; social 112–13

self-images 21, 113–18

self-knowledge 38, 106, 108, 115, 129; social construction of 129

self-perception 98, 108–9

self-presentation 182ff.; spoilt 188–91; strategies of 184ff.

self-recognition 21, 30–1, 38, 113–16

shame 19, 191

shyness 19, 189–90

situational shifts 161

social acts 135–8

social anxiety 187–90

social change 32ff., 227–8

social comparison processes 110–11

social comprehension 49–54, 57

social construction of self-knowledge 129

social desirability 53

social development 10, 16, 27, 30–8, 138, 205–7

social identity 112–13

social norms 205, 207–8, 222

social perception 68, 71, 93, 116–17; as interaction 68; bias in 88

social representations 208ff., 213–14, 216–17, 224

socialization   37, 65, 104, 106, 127, 165–7, 208, 218, 230–1; over-socialization   218
societal pressure   101, 177ff., 186ff., 205ff., 218; explicit   207–8, 218ff., 225; implicit   207–8, 214ff.
speech: adult to children   154–6; children to children   157–8; its embeddedness in social context   167–73
speech codes: elaborated   165–7; restricted   165–7
stability and variability   75, 77; child's awareness of   78–80
stigma   69, 176, 215
symbolic interactionism   85
sympathy   62

synchrony: in interaction   138–45; in mutual gazing   142–3

three-step process in communication   137–8, 206
triune brain   17–19
turn-taking: in dialogue   145ff.; in interaction   143, 145ff.; mother–infant   148–52; theories of   152–4

unconscious becomes conscious   105
unconscious motives   124–5

values: relation of awareness to   29
violence and aggression   192–7; physical aggression   194–7; verbal aggression   193–4